LOS ANGELES
Two Hundred

Vaqueros found sport in lassoing a grizzly bear, then matching it against a bull in a fight to the death.

By David Lavender

Los Angeles Two Hundred

a pictorial and entertaining commentary on the growth and development of Los Angeles, California

by David Lavender

Publishers:
Larry P. Silvey
Douglas S. Drown

Editor:
Ellen Sue Blakey

Associate Editor:
Peggi Ridgway

Art Director:
Rusty Johnson

Assistant Art Director:
James Michael Martin

Historical Photo Editor/Historical
    Consultant:
Carolyn Wagner

Current Photographer:
Einar Moos

Project Director:
Douglass Hoyt

Library of Congress Catalogue Card
Number: 80-66342

ISBN: -0932986-08-0

Los Angeles Two Hundred is sponsored by
The Los Angeles Area
Chamber of Commerce,
404 South Bixel Street,
Los Angeles, California 90017.

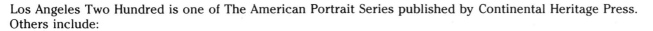

A southern California homesteader receiving the patent to her land.

Los Angeles Two Hundred is one of The American Portrait Series published by Continental Heritage Press. Others include:

Los Angeles is an unlikely place. Neither its beginnings nor its geographic location can account for so enormous a metropolis in so isolated a corner of the Southwest.

Consider its first two-thirds of a century. For 67 years (1781-1848) while Spain and then Mexico ruled, the town's non-Indian population rose from 44 to 1,600. At that point the Americans took over, and shortly thereafter James Marshall discovered gold 400 miles to the north. In the south, the people roused themselves enough to send such easily transportable items as cattle, wine and oranges to the hungry miners. No great promises lay there, however. In 1880, Los Angeles' population was still only 11,000. San Francisco's was 234,000.

Despite such small beginnings, there was determination. Through nimble maneuvering, the basin achieved two competing rail connections with the outside by the 1880s. Tourists flooded in, and although the real estate frenzy they engendered soon faded (temporarily, as matters developed), it

gave local entrepreneurs an entirely new vision of what Los Angeles might be.

It was a crazy dream. But it worked. Those early boosters literally willed a city into being. They reached out hundreds of miles for water. They dredged, redredged and refurbished their harbor again and again. They had neither coal nor wood for energy, but they found oil. They did not invent airplanes, but there in their isolated surroundings, they certainly learned how to build them. For glamor they had the movies. Did anyone in the entire world not know the name Hollywood?

Trouble has come in spasms, as it has to most cities. No matter. Energy and creativity have not diminished. The area's leaders are still insisting — still *willing* — that their unlikely megalopolis — now America's principal gateway to the entire Pacific rim — continue its cultural, social, racial, economic and, more recently, its environmental progress.

It is an improbable tale. But it is a good one.

"Quick, uneasy and restless, prone to attack an unmounted man," the wild descendants of the few hundred head brought north by the first settlers roamed the Los Angeles plains in vast herds throughout the first half of the last century.

5

Sponsors & Benefactors

The following Los Angeles area firms, organizations and individuals, in commemoration of the City's Bicentennial, have invested toward the quality production of this historic book and have thereby expressed their commitment to the future of this great city and to the support of the book's principal sponsor, The Los Angeles Area Chamber of Commerce.

Acco Industries, Inc.
A. R. Adams
Adams, Duque & Hazeltine
Air California Airlines
Air-Sea Forwarders, Inc.
R. H. Alexander Company
Richard H. Alexander
American Fish Co.
American Heart Association, Greater Los Angeles Affiliate
*American Honda Motor Co., Inc.
American Land Program
*American Medical International
American President Lines, Ltd.
Ameritone Paint Corporation
*Ameron.
Arthur Andersen & Co.
John C. Argue
Arrowhead Puritas Waters
Arrowsmith Industries, Inc.
Asbury System
*Atchison, Topeka & Santa Fe Railway Co.
*Atlantic Richfield Company
The Austin Company
Automobile Club of Southern California
N. W. Ayer ABH International

Baiseri Insurance Agency
Banca Serfin, S. A., Los Angeles Agency
Banco do Brasil S. A., Los Angeles Agency
Banco Popular de Puerto Rico
Banco Real S/A.
Bank of America NT & SA
Bank of Boston International Los Angeles
The Bank of California
Bank Hapoalim B.M.
Barger & Wolen, Lawyers
Guy B. Barham Company
Theodore Barry & Associates
Bechtel Power Corporation
*Beckman Instruments, Inc.
*The Bekins Company
Bender Machine, Inc.
*Beneficial Standard Corporation
Benjamin Metals Company
*The Biltmore Hotel
*Bixby Ranch Company
Black & Decker Pacific International
R. F. Black
Blacktop Materials Co.
The Boeing Company
*The Broadway
Brobeck, Phleger and Harrison

M. J. Brock & Sons, Inc.
Brooks Instrument Division
CMC General Contractors
Cal Fed Consultants
Cal Fed Enterprises
Cal Fed Insurance Agency, Inc.
The California Conversion Co.
*California Federal Savings & Loan Association
W. Ross Campbell Co.
The Canadian Indemnity Company
Canteen Food and Vending Service, Division of Canteen Corporation
Carlsberg Corporation
*Carnation Company
Vikki Carr
Carson Industries, Inc., La Verne
Cass and Johansing
Castle Metals
J. N. Ceazan Co.
Century City, Inc.
Chase Bank International — Los Angeles
Chevron U.S.A. Inc.
Chicago Title Insurance Company
Christie Electric Corp.
Citicorp
*Coast Federal Savings and Loan Association

Troy Cobb
*Coca-Cola Bottling Company of Los Angeles
*Collins Foods International, Inc.
Columbia Pictures
Conrock Co.
*Continental Airlines
Coopers & Lybrand
Copper and Brass Sales, Inc.
L. E. Coppersmith, Inc.
Credit-Suisse
Cushman & Wakefield of California, Inc.
John C. Cushman, III
D & B Machine Specialties, Inc.
Daiwa Securities America Inc.
The Honorable Francis L. Dale
Daniel, Mann, Johnson & Mendenhall
Wolfgang D. Daniel
Richard S. Dawson Co.
Dayton & Bakewell
Deloitte Haskins & Sells
Demetriou, Del Guercio & Lovejoy
Development Dimensions International
Die Cast Products, Inc.
Dieterich-Post Company
Dillingham Investments
Dinwiddie Construction Company
*Ducommun Incorporated
Charles Dunn Company
The O.K. Earl Corporation
EPS Associates
Mr. & Mrs. Sven A. Eliason
Environmental Data, Division of Thermo Electron Corp.
*Ernst & Whinney
FEC California Inc.
FNB Financial Company
Far East National Bank
The Fashion Institute

First Commercial Finance
*First Gray Line Corporation
Flewelling & Moody, Architects & Engineers
*Fluor Corporation
Ford Graphics
Forster, Gemmill & Farmer
Fruit Growers Supply Company
John A. Gabriel
The Garrett Corporation
Gateway U.S.A.
General Dynamics Pomona Division
General Telephone
Gibson, Dunn & Crutcher
Robert E. Gibson
Glendale Federal Savings
Golden Pacific Tours, Inc.
*Golden State Mutual Life Insurance Company
*Golden West Broadcasters
Goldman, Sachs & Co.
Thomas P. Gonzalez, Sr.
The Goodglick Company
Government of New South Wales, Australia
Alexander Grant & Company
Clyde G. Grant
Graybar Electric Co., Inc.
Great Lakes Properties, Inc.
Grant L. Hansen
Harmon Associates International Inc.
The Hartford
The Hearst Corporation
Hewlett-Packard Co.
Hill Brothers Chemical Co.
The Hollywood Palladium
Holmes & Narver, Inc.
Hood Corporation
Mr. & Mrs. Joseph K. and William L. Horton
B. D. Howes and Son
Hrachovy & Lyon
*Hughes Aircraft Company

Industrial Indemnity Company
Intercontinental Re, Inc.
International Intelligence, Inc. (INTERTEL)
International Paper Company
Interstate Consolidation Service, Inc.
Japan Line (U.S.A.) Ltd.
Japan Travel Bureau International, Inc.
Jensen & Ritchie Advertising, Inc.
Gilbert E. Johnson, M.D.
*Johnson & Higgins
Johnson & Nielsen Associates
Roger W. Johnson
Jones Brothers Construction Corporation
KLM Royal Dutch Airlines
KMPC
Kaiser Electroprecision
Kaiser-Permanente Medical Care Program
Kaufman and Broad, Inc.
Kearney: Management Consultants
Fred V. Keenan
Peter Keller
Kelsey National Corporation
J. A. Kendall & Co., C.P.A.'s
Keystone Engineering Company
Kirkwood Electric Inc.
*Knudsen Corporation
L. A. Bonaventure Shopping Gallery
L. A. Liquid Handling Systems
LFC Insurance Division of Schiff Terhune
L & L Abrasive Supply Co., Inc.

Ladd-Fab, Inc.
Ray E. Latham
*Lawry's Foods, Inc.
*Lear Siegler, Inc.
Lee, Sperling,
  Hisamune/Accountancy
  Corporation
Lindberg Heat Treating
  Company
Liquid Air Corporation
Litton Industries, Inc.
Lloyd Corporation, Ltd.
Lockheed
Lord-Babcock, Incorporated
*Los Angeles Dodgers, Inc.
The Los Angeles Herald
  Examiner
Los Angeles Junior Chamber
  of Commerce
Los Angeles Magazine
Los Angeles Rubber Co.
Lundberg Survey, Inc.
Arnold Luster
Mail-Well Envelope Company
  of California
Major Properties — Realtors
Jack Malven Corporation
Manufacturers Bank
Henry Marcheschi
Market Basket Supermarkets
Marshall and Swift Publication
  Co.
Adolfo Gompers Mateos
Matlow-Kennedy Corporation
May Company
Mazda Distributors Pacific

Mazda Motors of America
  (Central), Inc.
McCulloch Corporation
McKinsey & Company, Inc.
McMaster Carr Supply Co.
Metromedia, Inc.
Michio Ohiwa
Fred Mills
Mitsui & Co. (USA) Inc.
Mobil Oil Corporation
Mollenhauer, Higashi & Moore,
  Inc.
Montano Securities
  Corporation
Montgomery Ward/American
  Income Properties of
  Chicago
Leonard Moore
Frank S. Morris
Dr. George E. Mueller
MuniciCorp of California
Municipal Motorcycle Officers
  of California
Nabocorp, Ltd. West Africa
National Associates, Inc.
National Medical Enterprises,
  Inc.
Nelson Name Plate Company
New England Mutual Life
  Insurance Company
Newell Color Lab
Nichimen Co., Inc.
The Nippon Credit Bank, Ltd.
Nippon Express U.S.A., Inc.
Paul Norsell & Assoc., Inc.

Northrop Corporation
*Occidental Life Insurance
  Company of California
Michio Ohiwa
Oilwell Division-U.S. Steel
  Corp.
*The Olga Company
Pachmayr Gun Works, Inc.
Pacific Coast Regional Urban
  Small Business
  Development Corporation
*Pacific Mutual Life Insurance
  Company
Pacific Steel Ind., Inc.
Pacific Telephone & Telegraph
  Co.
*Paramount Pictures
  Corporation
Parker, Milliken, Clark &
  O'Hara
The Parsons Corporation
Stephen Patkay & Associates
*Peat, Marwick, Mitchell & Co.
Pertec
J. J. Pinola
Pioneer Theatres, Inc.
Pipe Fabricating & Supply Co.
Plaza Mortgage Company
Ryal R. Poppa
Presto Food Products, Inc.
W. W. Price & Company
Prudential Insurance Company
  of America
Randall/McAnany Company
Dominic P. Renda
Republic Corporation
Douglas Roesch
  Communications, Inc.
Tony A. Rose Accountancy
  Corporation
R. A. Rowan & Co.
*SAFECO Title Insurance
  Company

Sales and Marketing
  Executives Association of
  Los Angeles
*The Salvation Army
Sanitek Products, Inc.
Mr. H. K. Schaefer
Schenkers International
  Forwarders, Inc.
Hans H. Schumacher
Seastrom Manufacturing Co.,
  Inc.
*Security Pacific National Bank
*See's Candy Shops, Inc.
Seidler, Arnett & Spillane
  Incorporated
Seiko Time Corporation
The Shop — The Biltmore
  Hotel
Rocco C. Siciliano
Simpson & Simpson
James B. Skaggs
*Smith International, Inc.
Ludwig T. Smith
Southern California Committee
  For The Olympic Games
Southern California Edison
  Company
Southern California Gas
  Company
Southwest Forest Industries
Standard Cabinet Works, Inc.
*Standard Oil Company of
  California
State Compensation Insurance
  Fund
Stationers Corporation
Kenneth W. Steen
Stewart Smith Haidinger, Inc.
Subaru of America, Inc.
Sunset Magazine, Books &
  Films
Sunset News Company
*Ralph C. Sutro Co.

System Development
  Corporation
Systems Planning Corp.
TRW
Tatung Company of America,
  Inc.
Tesoro Gasoline Marketing
  Company
Thai Farmers Bank, Ltd., Los
  Angeles Agency
Thermal Products Inc.
*Thrifty Corporation
*The Times Mirror Company
Tokai Bank of California
Tooley & Company,
  Investment Builders
*Tosco Corporation
*Touche Ross & Co.
Trane Company
Trans World Airlines
Triumph Adler Inc.
*U.S. Borax & Chemical
  Corporation
U.S. Shopping Centers Inc.
Union Bank
Union Bank of Switzerland —
  Los Angeles Agency
Union Federal Savings & Loan
  Association
Union Oil Company of
  California
United Airlines
United California Bank
United States Aviation
  Underwriters, Inc.
V.I.P. Drugs
Valley Federal Savings
*Van de Kamp's Holland Dutch
  Bakers, Inc.
Vasquez, Quezada & Navarro
Vinnell Corporation
Vons Grocery Co.

Walker Brothers
Walkers Los Angeles Honey
  Company
Wallace Moir Company
Jervis B. Webb Company
Wells Fargo Bank
*Western Airlines
*Western Gear Corporation
Western Oil & Gas Association
Western Tube & Conduit
  Corporation
Westvaco — U.S. Envelope
  Division
Wiggins Connectors Division
  of Transamerica Delaval
  Inc.
Wilbur-Ellis Company
Woodford and Bernard
Kuan-Hsiung Wu
Wyle Laboratories
YWCA of Los Angeles
Mr. & Mrs. Louis Zimmerli

*Corporate Sponsors of *Los
Angeles Two Hundred.* The
histories of these firms and
organizations begin on page
175.

LOS ANGELES
COR. W

SOUTH
LOOKING S

LOS A
CALI

PUBLISHED BY
SEMI-TROPIC HOMESTEAD CO.
STIMSON BLOCK

8

Cupeño wagon train during the Cupa eviction.

11

*Venice during its glory days (below),
the Los Angeles Post Office at the junction
of Main, Spring and Temple Streets at the
turn of the century (facing page inset);
and Los Angeles today.*

A good time was had by all on the beach at Santa Monica.

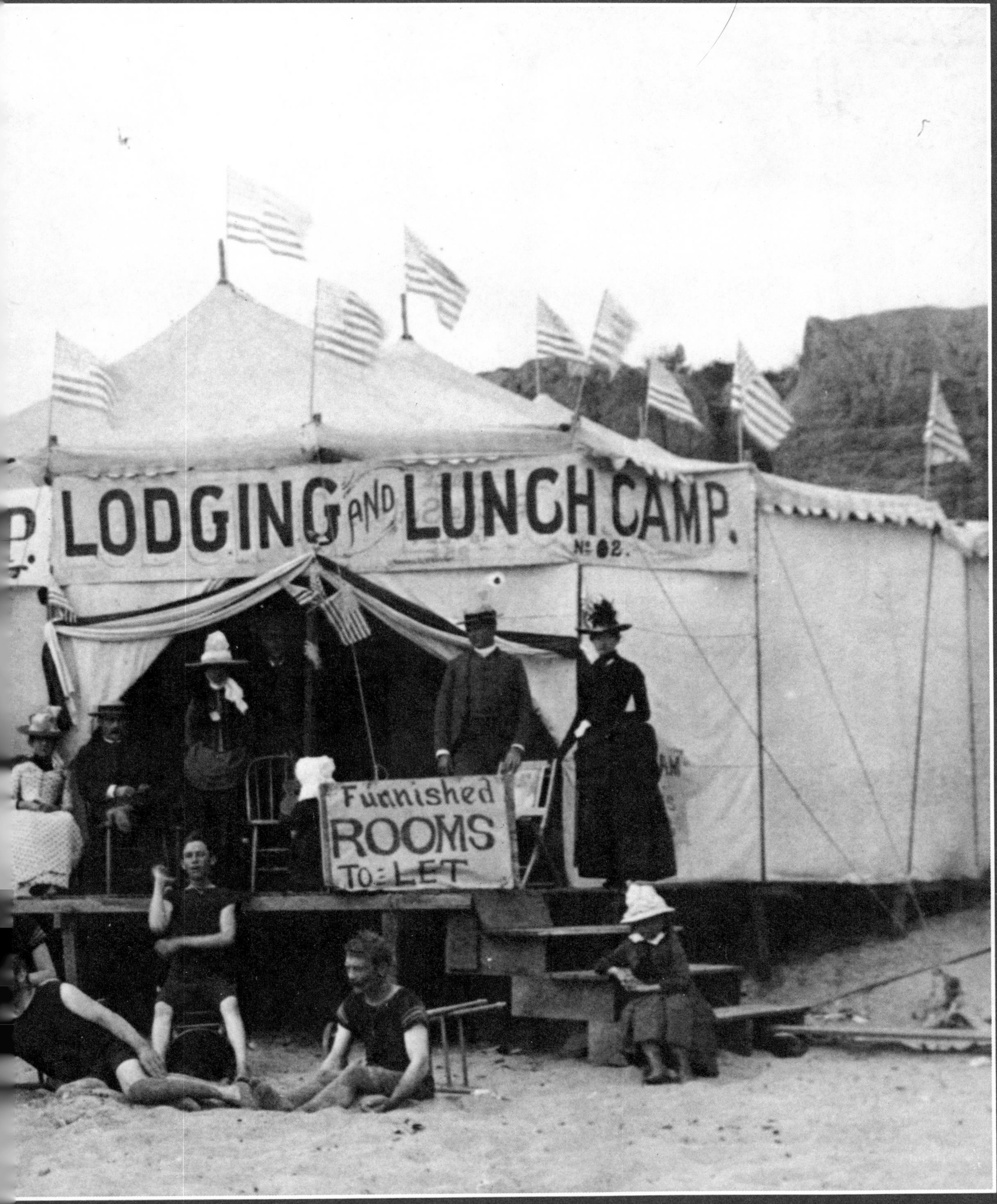
LODGING AND LUNCH CAMP.
No 82.
Furnished
ROOMS
TO LET

Contents

The Los Angeles County Museum of Art.

Shaky beginnings

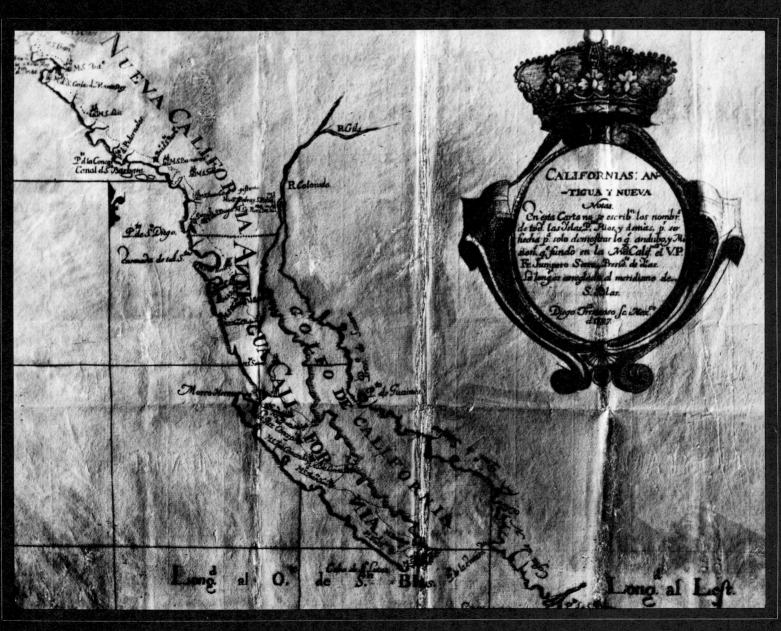

*1787 map of Old (Antigua) and New
(Nueva) California and Camino Real.*

L os Angeles did not get off to a running start. When Colonel Felipe de Neve, military governor of California, first drew up plans for the pueblo (as Spanish towns were called) he asked that between 40 and 60 families be sent him from Mexico. After long delay, 24 were authorized. But recruiting went badly, and there were desertions along the way. Eventually, in 1781, eleven sets of parents and 22 children arrived — hardly one quarter of what Neve would have liked.

Two of the husbands claimed undiluted Spanish blood. One was half Spanish and half Indian, a mestizo. Four were full-blooded Christian Indians. Two of the rest were blacks and two were mulattos. As for the wives, five were Indians, six were mulattos. Not one of the group could read or write. Certainly none of them could have envisioned a metropolis of three million people spreading out from the site that Neve chose for the new town.

The edge of nowhere

The founding was as belated as it was meager. More than two centuries earlier, rumors of great kingdoms far north of Mexico — kingdoms supposedly as rich as the Aztec empire — had stirred intense excitement among Spain's swaggering young *conquistadores*. In 1540 Francisco Vásquez de Coronado had led an ambitious land expedition to investigate what became known as New Mexico. Clumsy little sailing vessels prowled up the Sea of Cortés (today's Gulf of California) and entered the delta of the Colorado River. In the summer of 1542, Mexico's impatient viceroy ordered a navigator named Juan Rodríguez Cabrillo to venture along the continent's far west coast in two undecked, ill-manned, ill-equipped ships scarcely 60 feet long to see what he could find.

In such miserable craft, Cabrillo discovered San Diego Bay. When he was off the shore now bordered by San Pedro and Wilmington, he saw so much smoke hanging in the air — possibly the result of brush fires set by Indians driving rabbits — that he named the area the Bay of Smokes. He probably found Monterey Bay as well and then gave way to roaring, adverse winds and scudded back to San Miguel Island in the Santa Barbara Channel to wait out the winter. There he broke his shoulder, developed blood poisoning and died.

His pilot, Bartolomé Ferrer, continued up the northern coast as far, perhaps, as southern Oregon. No bejeweled, gold-encrusted kingdoms appeared. Nor did they appear to Coronado or to the adventurers in the Sea of Cortés, and Spain lost interest in the north.

Information accumulated, nevertheless. During the 1560s, Spanish navigators established a foothold in the Philippine Islands. Galleons laden with Mexican silver began sailing there to buy Oriental exotics. Their holds stuffed with high-cost luxury goods, the ships then sailed north, picked up the Pacific's westerly trades and ran before them to the vicinity of Cape Mendocino in northern California. From there, coastal winds blowing steadily south hurried them on to the Mexican port of Acapulco.

It was a hellish trip. Since Spain allowed only one galleon to sail from Mexico to the Philippines and back each year, captains skimped on food and water in order to gain space for merchandise. Scurvy killed many a sailor, and there was constant fear of English pirates. When strategists recommended that rest stops be developed on the California coast, a mariner named Sebastian Vizcaíno was given two far better ships than Cabrillo had possessed and told to chart the land. He came back singing the praises of Monterey Bay — to no avail. Even for the sake of their men, galleon captains were unwilling to halt their run so near Acapulco. Faced with their objections, the penny-pinching government let the project drop.

The proposal was remembered, however. During the early 1700s, a famed Jesuit missionary of southern Arizona, Eusebio Francisco Kino, found his way to the lower Colorado River, learned that the coast was within reach across the desert to the west and raised a question. Why not let the Manila galleons unload part of their cargo at Monterey Bay? From there muleskinners could pack it overland to the goods-hungry mine owners of northern Mexico much more quickly than the same articles could be brought all the way up from Acapulco. Reasonable enough — but established merchants in the south complained that they would lose business, and again nothing was done. The idea fell just as flat 30 years later when a tough border captain of northwestern Mexico, Juan Bautista de Anza, offered to open a pack trail to the coast at his own expense.

Among educated Mexicans, the years of inaction became a scandal. In 1757 a propagandist named Andrés Burriel published a scathing book, *Noticia de la California.* Burriel declared that the government would be everlastingly to blame if foreign powers were the first to "erect colonies, forts and presidios on the coast of the Californias." The warning struck home. Explorers in the service of Russia had recently reached Alaska, and in 1763 Great Britain wrenched Canada from France. The activity caused Spanish officials to abruptly develop a fresh interest in the west coast.

It was not the land they wanted. There was nothing except hundreds of miles of sun-warmed mountains and valleys and tens of thousands of Indians. Decadent Spain already had more land and Indians in the New World than the country could manage efficiently. What counted in Madrid were the silver mines of northern Mexico. They had to be protected. And so, in 1768, the king's special representative in Mexico City, the *Visitador-general* José de Gálvez, ordered that Alta (Upper) California — as distinct from the long peninsula of Baja (Lower) California — be occupied as a defensive outpost.

Jose de Galvez was appointed the Vistador-general of New Spain, a special deputy of the king for specific investigations, to increase revenues and replace the then-suspect Jesuits with Franciscans.

Occupation at last

Because California would have to be as nearly self-sustaining as possible, Gálvez decided to place his chief reliance on a handful of Franciscan missionaries under the leadership of Padre Junípero Serra, a physically small but emotionally intense and inspiring leader. The hope was that the Franciscans — scattered at favorable spots along the coast — would be able to draw Indians to their establishments with food and kindness, convert them to Christianity, train them in agriculture and handicrafts and thus form a basis for future settlements. During the early years, the missions would be protected by a few dozen soldiers stationed in *presidios* (small forts) overlooking the two most important bays. San Diego would be occupied first, followed by Monterey which would serve as administrative headquarters of the new province.

Early in 1769, two ships and two land parties launched the advance from a desolate harbor on the inner side of the long peninsula of Baja California. Although several score people were involved, not one was a woman.

In spite of heavy casualties and desertions brought on by hard times on the desert and ocean, San Diego and Monterey took shape as ordered. During the next half-dozen years, Serra's Franciscans — aided by a few Christian Indians sent from Mexico — added three more missions in widely separated valleys between the two originals. San Gabriel Arcángel Mission a few miles south of the rugged line of the Sierra Madre Mountains, separated the southern establishments from those in the north.

Two priests were stationed at each mission. At first their shelters consisted of little more than dome-shaped *jacals* made of upright sticks plastered over with mud. Altars stood outside, shielded from the weather by arbors of boughs. There were corrals for livestock and more huts to house the six or eight soldiers that guarded each unit. The bulk of the military lived in cramped, dirt-floored adobe forts beside the two bays, ready to answer any calls for help or — if needed — to put up a show of

Junipero Serra, Franciscan missionary, founded and supervised nine missions in Alta California. Scattered at favorable spots along the coast, his missions were established largely to attract and convert the Indians.

19

Juan Bautista de Anza headed the development of a land trail over which livestock could be driven from northwestern Mexico to California. In his explorations, he won the friendship of the Yuma Indians who controlled a vital ford across the Colorado River.

Felipe de Neve, the first of California's military governors, was responsible for founding the pueblos of San Jose in 1777 and Los Angeles in 1781, hoping they would be the core of a system to rival the missions and win military dominance over Alta California. His statue stands in the Los Angeles Plaza.

possession against foreign intruders.

Existence was precarious for two reasons. The soldiers were a rough lot, and some would not keep their hands off the Indian women the missionaries were trying to turn into productive Catholic citizens along with the rest of their families. When offended tribesmen struck back, they were crushed by the Spaniards' superior arms. Casualties were never high, but Serra and the military officers fretted continually about a concerted uprising that might shatter the whole program.

Even more pressing was the problem of supplies. It took time to learn the vagaries of the climate and train neophyte Indians to plow, sow and harvest. They were heavily dependent on the two supply ships sent north once a year. It was a thin reed to lean on. Because of persistently contrary winds, the vessels generally arrived late and sometimes could not reach Monterey at all. During emergencies, soldiers occasionally killed enough bears to provide tough steaks — the animals roamed the isolated valleys almost in herds — and converted Indians brought seeds, roots, berries, cactus apples — even grasshoppers — to the Franciscans. But such make-shifts could hardly guarantee permanence.

There had to be a better system of supply and control. So in 1772, Junípero Serra traveled to Mexico City to see the new viceroy, Antonio Bucareli. The priest won most of his points. In the future a majority of the soldiers sent to California would be married men accompanied by their families. Such men, it was hoped, would not bother Indian women. When their terms of enlistment expired, perhaps they would settle down on farms outside the presidios and grow crops for their former comrades.

A notable part of the new program — and one that would eventually have marked effect on Los Angeles — was the working out of a land trail over which large herds of livestock could be driven from northwestern Mexico to California. The pioneer to head the development was Juan Bautista de Anza, grandson of the man who many years before had been denied permission to search for the route even though he had offered to pay the expenses himself.

Young Anza was delighted. During the winter of 1773-74, he conducted his explorations. He won the friendship of the Yuma Indians who controlled a vital ford across the Colorado River, and in 1775 he started west with 40 married soldiers, their wives, 125 children and assorted officers, priests and cowboys for driving 695 horses and 355 cattle. Part of the personnel would found a third presidio and two more missions near San Francisco Bay.

The town maker

Anza's cold, rain-swept march was a success, but farming by soldiers was not. The little presidios they were supposed to serve had naturally been placed on vantage points overlooking the harbors they guarded. But the high ground meant that irrigation water could not be brought to the fields from the deeply gullied streams. The cold sea air and fog checked the growth of food crops. The increasing numbers of converts at the missions left them with nothing to spare.

Dependable supplies of food — the first of California's military governors to come to real grips with this problem was Colonel Felipe de Neve. Neve was an aristocratic Spaniard who sailed to the New World for a short stay but proved so efficient that he was never allowed to return to his family. An exceptional administrator, loyal, meticulous and farsighted, he was trusted implicitly by his superiors. Whatever recommendations he offered were almost certainly followed.

Neve decided to create communities separate from both the missions and presidios. Their sole function would be food production. The idea was not new to colonial Spain, but until Neve's time the government had avoided the plan in California because of its expense.

The program went like this. Farm people were lured to the frontier by grants of land and animals. They were supported by annual subsidies until they were able to stand on their own feet. The surplus commodities they raised were sold at set prices to the nearest presidio. Once the community began to flourish it would attract new immigrants, retiring soldiers and converted Indians. Soon a new pueblo, sturdy enough to take care of itself and even to furnish militia recruits to the frontier army, would be marked on the maps of the world. Or so the theory ran.

How many towns should California have? Where should they be located? The questions traveled with Neve during the winter of 1776-77 as he rode 1,300 miles north from Loreto in Baja California to take over his new job. Two spots (already noticed by earlier observers) struck him. One was a grassy, tree-shaded swale beside the little Porciúncula River, nine miles west of the Mission of San Gabriel Arcángel. Another was on a plain that rolled south from the tip of San Francisco Bay.

He chose first the one beside the bay since the food problem was even more acute in the north than in the south. Neve recruited farmers at the Monterey and San Francisco presidios from among married soldiers whose terms of enlistment were running out. He signed on eleven couples, most of whom had arrived only a year before with Anza. He directed Lieutenant José Moraga to lead them and their 46 children to the site beside the Guadalupe River. There in the fall of 1777, California's first civil colony — San José — was launched.

Founding the pueblo beside the Porciúncula River proved more difficult. There was no pool of married soldiers in the south. Recruiting had to be done in northwestern Mexico among civilians. But most of them thought California (if they had even heard of it) was a savage land somewhere beyond the edges of comprehension. Still the attempt was necessary for the sake of the presidio at San Diego as well as for a new, larger one that Neve and Serra hoped to found — along with additional missions — beside the Santa Barbara Channel.

A logical idea occurred. Why not coordinate the founding of town and fort? Late in 1779, the thankless chore of recruiting personnel and buying livestock for both places was given to a 68-year-old professional soldier, Captain Fernando Rivera y Moncado, who had been in Alta California off and on since its occupation. Rivera left his dreary station at Loreto and crossed the Gulf to the mainland. He devoted most of his own time to searching out 961 young, sound horses and mules. His assistants rounded up volunteers in the provinces of Sinaloa and Sonora. Fifty-nine soldiers finally agreed to move with their families to Alta California. Civilians were more resistant even though poverty was widespread in the area and the government offered generous terms.

Each head of a family would receive the equivalent of $116.44 a year in clothing and supplies the first two years of service and $60 a year for the next three. For three years the entire family would be issued standard army rations. Each household would be loaned two cows, two mares, two female goats, two ewes, two oxen and a mule. (Male breeding animals belonged to the community as a whole.) Repayment would be made gradually from natural increase. Loans of tools would be paid off with produce delivered to either San Diego or Santa Barbara presidio which the pueblo served.

The great boon was land — house lots in the town, farm plots outside and the right to graze livestock on the communal pastures. There were restrictions. Titles would not become firm for five years, during which time the occupant had to build a house, plant fruit trees, ditch his fields for irrigation and make other improvements. He also had to agree not to change his residence for ten years, work as directed on community projects and refrain from mortgaging his holdings.

It was not enough — not in exchange for going to California. Only fourteen of the desired 24 civilians signed on. Of that number, two ran away after drawing the advance extended all recruits for buying equipment.

The founders of Los Angeles.

Los Angeles' original settlers

Eleven families — 44 persons in all — settled Los Angeles in 1781. The group of *pobladores* included two Spaniards, nine Indians, one mestizo, eight mulattos and two blacks. They were:

1. José de Lara, a 50-year-old Spaniard who had an Indian wife and three children.

2. José Antonio Navarro, a 42-year-old mestizo who, with his mulatto wife, had three children.

3. Basilio Rosas, a 67-year-old Indian who, with his mulatto wife, had six children.

4. Antonio Mesa, a 38-year-old black who had a mulatto wife and two children.

5. Antonio Felix Villavicencio, a 30-year-old Spaniard who had an Indian wife and one child.

6. José Vanegas, a 28-year-old Indian who had an Indian wife and one child.

7. Alejandro Rosas, a 19-year-old Indian and his Indian wife.

8. Pablo Rodriguez, a 25-year-old Indian and his Indian wife and child.

9. Manuel Camero, a 30-year-old mulatto and his mulatto wife.

10. Luis Quintero, a 55-year-old black and his mulatto wife and five children.

11. José Moreno, a 22-year-old mulatto and his mulatto wife.

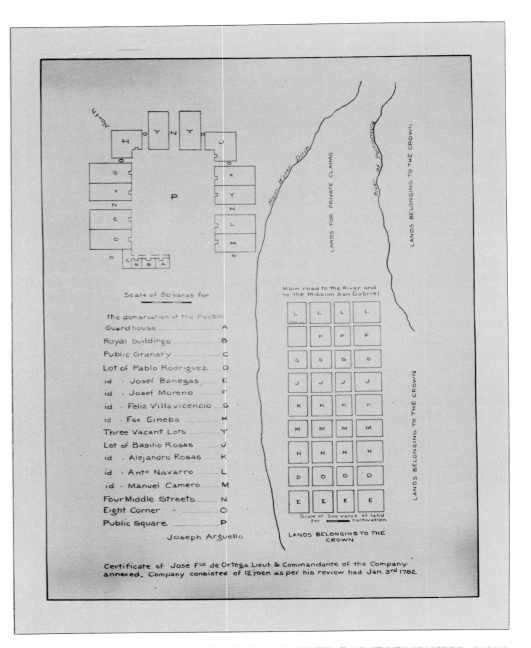

Scale of 50 Varas for

The demarcation of the Pueblo

Guard house	A
Royal buildings	B
Public Granary	C
Lot of Pablo Rodriguez	D
id · Josef Banegas	E
id · Josef Moreno	F
id · Feliz Villavicencio	G
id · Fso Gineba	H
Three Vacant Lots	Y
Lot of Basilio Rosas	J
id · Alejandro Rosas	K
id · Anto Navarro	L
id · Manuel Camero	M
Four Middle Streets	N
Eight Corner "	O
Public Square	P

Joseph Arguello

Main road to the River and to the Mission San Gabriel

Scale of 200 varas of land for cultivation

LANDS BELONGING TO THE CROWN

Certificate of José Fco de Ortega Lieut. & Commandante of the Company annexed. Company consisted of 12 men as per his review had Jan. 3rd 1782.

PUEBLO LIFE: Luiseno Indian women (below right) and Chola Martina of Capistrano (below). Plot of the Pueblo de Los Angeles, November 19, 1781.

On the other hand, three couples married just to be eligible for the trip. The youngest adult was 22; the oldest — an Indian — was 67. One widower with a small daughter was accepted, as was one widow.

To prevent crowding on the trail, the civilians and fifteen soldier families — 133 persons altogether — were sent across the Gulf to Baja California early in February 1781. Smallpox appeared in Loreto, and the frightened party began to break apart. Seventeen families who showed no signs of infection — some soldiers, some colonists — went ahead by ship 350 miles up the Gulf to Bahía de San Luis Gonzago. They spent 40 miserable days bucking winter storms and the strong currents that characterize ebb tides in the Sea of Cortés. When they landed, the emigrants crossed the narrow peninsula to its western shore and followed that to San Diego, where two of the order girls in the party promptly married soldiers stationed at the presidio.

The rest of the California-bound settlers followed several days later — except for the lone widower and his daughter. For some reason (either confusion or perhaps because the child was still too ill to travel), they were left behind in Loreto.

Further fragmentation occurred along the way, and the travelers reached Mission San Gabriel in three groups — one in June, another in July, the third in August. Extensive research by Harry Kelsey of the Los Angeles County Museum of Natural History indicates that as soon as a contingent had been given time to collect its breath, it was sent on across the Pociúncula River to the site of the pueblo. Their first assignment was probably to dam the stream and dig the irrigation ditch that would serve both the town and its adjacent farmlands. While they were at this work, they learned of a disaster that may well have terrified them even more than their long companionship with smallpox.

NATIVE LIFE: A Shoshonean Indian wickiup or hut (above) and California mission Indians, 1899 (below).

The massacre

Two months after the Baja group left Mexico, Rivera and the rest of the military recruits — fortified by an escort of nine soldiers from Sonora — started north along the California trail that Juan Bautista de Anza had worked out six years before. Burdening the travelers was an unruly herd of almost a thousand horses and mules. The summer sun beat like a sledge hammer. When the herd reached the ford over the Colorado River, 252 of the animals were too jaded to continue through the grim deserts beyond. After a few days of perplexity, Rivera decided to send the soundest animals to San Gabriel with the married soldiers and the nine-man Sonora escort. He and a handful of bachelors stayed behind to let the other livestock recuperate.

Rivera may have been motivated by the prospect of pleasant company. A little more than a year before, two settlements, located thirteen miles apart, had appeared on the river's west bank. Part mission, part presidio, part pueblo, they had been built as a first step in turning Anza's trail into a permanent highway. They were staffed by 32 civilians and 21 soldiers, most of whom had their families with them. Two friars were stationed at each settlement.

The Yuma Indians who lived in the neighborhood resented the dictatorial ways of the newcomers. Several clashes had occurred already. More followed when Rivera let his recuperating horses invade the Indians' primitive gardens. Outrage came to a head at dawn on July 17. During the bloody fight, most of the intruding males were slain, Rivera among them. Women, children and the few men who survived were then put to work as slaves.

The soldiers and colonists at San Gabriel and Los Angeles heard of the massacre almost by chance. While traveling homeward from the mission to Mexico, the nine-man escort from Sonora rode into the ruins and was horrified to see the decaying corpses. They lost two of their own number to a surprise attack by the Indians before breaking away from the melancholy scene. They rode back to San Gabriel as fast as they could to report to Neve.

By this time, all the colonists had reached California. On August 26, 1781, Neve himself gathered them together at San Gabriel to show them a map he had drawn of the proposed town which he had named *El Pueblo de La Reyna de Los Angeles* — the "Town of the Queen of the Angels." Its heart was a plaza 200 feet wide by 300 feet long. House lots surrounded it on three sides; the fourth side was to contain public buildings. Diagonally to the south was a large block of farm plots. The two units were placed so that the main irrigation ditch from the Porciúncula (now the Los Angeles) River would run close to the edge of the town before flowing down to the fields. Several lots in both the town and the farming area were to be left unassigned to provide for future increases in population.

Drawings determined the assignments of both house and farm lots. As excitement rose and the people prepared to move onto the homesites they had come so far to obtain, the trail-worn survivors of the Sonora escort arrived with word of the Yuma disaster. Terror replaced anticipation. Would the Yumans' success stir other tribes to revolt? If so, what protection would Los Angeles have?

Neve quieted the fears by promising that the soldiers assigned to Santa Barbara — about 50 were on hand — would be held in readiness nearby until he learned what sort of campaign the government proposed to launch against the Yumans. Meanwhile the settlement of the town would continue as scheduled.

Queen of the angels

On September 4, 1781, 44 people — half of them children — straggled back across the shallow Porciúncula River to the tree-dotted terraces that from now on would be home. With them, to keep order and supervise defenses, were a corporal and three soldiers. These men were destined to stay in Los Angeles so long that they, too, deserve listing as founding fathers. Neve did not go along but appointed Lieutenant José Dario Argüello to act in his stead.

Each family quickly dumped its possessions on its new land. There was much to do, and most of the colonists — aided by local Indians — flew to work with vigor. Three who did not — one Spaniard and two blacks — were expelled from the pueblo and their lands confiscated. (The delinquents were sent to Santa Barbara to work under strict supervision on the presidio.) Within a year the original brush shelters were replaced by adobe houses. The diversion dam in the river was completed, and water flowed through the *zanja madre* — the "mother ditch" from which people, animals and crops all drew life in that dry land where rain seldom falls between April and November.

When the five-year probationary period was over on September 4, 1786, Lieutenant Argüello appeared again to give each surviving colonist — plus a ninth who had wandered in from the interior — a deed to his lands and a pre-shaped, duly registered branding iron with which to mark his livestock. It must have been a satisfying moment.

But did the recipients fully understand the responsibilities placed upon them? Punitive expeditions against the Yuma Indians had failed to subdue the tribe, and the overland trail to Mexico remained closed. It would stay closed for as long as Spain's sovereignty over Mexico lasted. The two undependable twice-yearly supply ships were Alta California's only official link with the outside world. Economic and population expansion, if any, would have to be generated within the province itself. How much Los Angeles could or would contribute remained to be seen.

Rancho San Pedro

The Rancho San Pedro is important in California history as the first of the Spanish land grants. It was established by Juan Jose Dominguez as the recipient of 76,000 acres of land in 1784 for service as a soldier in the Spanish colonial army. Dominguez retired from the army and sought aid in obtaining some land. He sent a petition to the governor and was granted permission to use the land in the area south of the new pueblo of Los Angeles.

No maps existed of the rancho named after the Bay of San Pedro, but it encompassed lands between the curving coastline of the Los Angeles river and a line extending west from what is now Compton. An early abstract defined the northern boundary as a line running through a sycamore tree north of what is now Rosecrans Avenue. The "Eagle Tree" still stands in Compton.

The 120 square miles of Rancho San Pedro now comprises close to a dozen cities including parts of Los Angeles and Long Beach, as well as Compton, Gardena, Torrance, Redondo Beach, Hermosa Beach and Carson, which grew up within the rancho's original boundaries.

The original rancho also included the Palos Verdes Peninsula and what later became Los Angeles Harbor. This section — which comprised about 31,000 acres — was claimed in 1846 by the Sepulveda family after a long dispute over rights.

Manuel Dominguez, great-nephew of Juan, was most instrumental in holding and developing the property. He was also an influential citizen of the area, first mayor of the pueblo of Los Angeles in 1828, then a representative of the State Assembly in 1849.

In 1858 the third Rancho San Pedro grant — a formal patent of title assigning the property to Manuel and the Dominguez family — was signed by President James Buchanan.

The rancho was further reduced in size during southern California's pre-1900 land boom. Individual sales of the land by Manuel's six daughters provided the foundation for the city of Redondo Beach and later development of Terminal Island.

Today the 1826 Dominguez house and seventeen acres are occupied by the Order of Claretian Missionary Fathers. The Dominguez family heirs, however, are still the keepers of a large portion of their vast heritage.

Chapter 2

New flags for old

Los Angeles city hall and jail, 1860, was located directly opposite of today's modern one at 200 North Spring Street. The old facility, established in 1850, was a long, one-story adobe building which served for 30 years as a council chamber, treasurer's office, tax collector's office and a residence for the city's jailer.

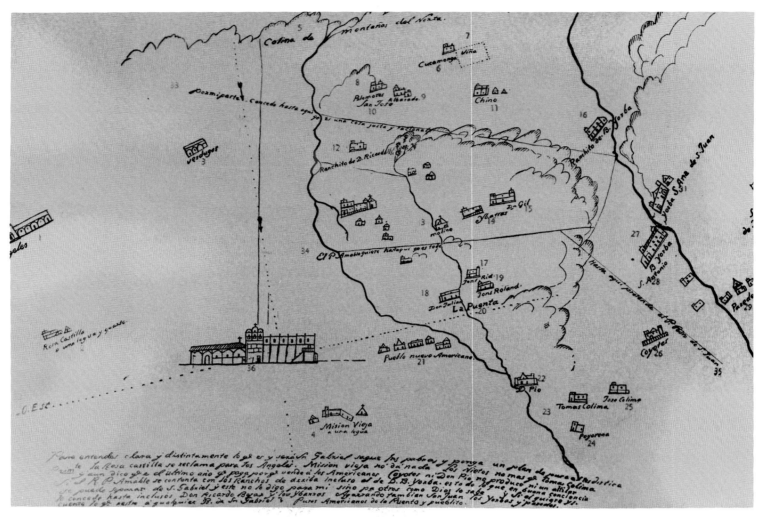

SAN GABRIEL: An early map (top) shows the Mission San Gabriel circuit. There, some of the Indians who lived on the plains around Los Angeles not only worked for food and occasional handouts of rough clothing, but also had to accept religious instruction and attend daily devotions. Jacinta Serrano (above) was a basket maker who lived at San Gabriel in the early days of the mission; she was 90 when the photo was taken.

Early life styles

In a report prepared during the spring of 1796 for the viceroy in Mexico City, Father José Señán tried to explain why the towns that Felipe de Neve founded were not meeting expectations. Unless a man had hope, Señán said, ambition withered. Yet the government left the colonists with small grounds for believing that the future held much meaning for them.

There was only one official market for their produce — the presidios. Payment was made in goods imported once a year on two small ships and marked up to astronomical heights. When a group of husbandmen arrived at the fort after several days on the trail with their laden mule trains and asked for what they and their wives wanted — jackets, satin shoes, chocolate, tea, household utensils, tools — they were often told that nothing was available. The soldiers and their families had first call and had stripped the shelves. The best the colonist could get was a trifle or two and a small credit on the commissary's books.

"Is it any wonder," Señán demanded, "that he feels aversion toward his toil, from which he derives such scant reward?"

There was an escape of sorts. The numerous Indians who lived on the broad plains around Los Angeles were willing to toil in houses and fields for assured daily meals of red beans and mush and occasional handouts of rough clothing — a shapeless gown for the women, homespun trousers and a red sash for the men. If the reward seemed small, the *pobladores* had little more. And many Indians preferred living near the town rather than at Mission San Gabriel nine miles away. There (though Señán did not mention the point) a man or woman not only worked for food but also had

26

to accept religious instruction and attend daily devotions at the tolling of the bells. In addition, unwed young men and women were separated every night lest they yield to what the Fathers regarded as Satan's most insidious temptation. Most of the Indians in the area congregated accordingly near Los Angeles, learning European vices more readily than European virtues.

Another thing that bothered the priest was the growth of ranches, or as he put it, the practice of allowing retired soldiers to "establish themselves separately in remote areas." The custom had begun in 1784 when Governor Pedro Fages gave three of his former soldiers (Juan José Domínguez, Manuel Peréz Nieto and José María Verdugo) separate permits to graze cattle and horses over wide stretches of land near the pueblo — Domínguez south toward San Pedro, Nieto southeast toward what became Whittier, and Verdugo north in the area of present Glendale.

Each applicant promised in his petition "not to harm a living soul, principally the Mission of San Gabriel or even less the Pueblo of the Queen of the Angels." Each was told "to sleep at the pueblo," but the restriction was inconvenient, and no one in authority protested when the grantees or their relatives moved onto the ranches to look after their livestock, again with Indian help.

A bad precedent, said Señán. Proper Spaniards should live in town. For one thing, a rancher's mode of living was too much like that of Indians. Were not the missionaries doing their best to collect the natives into stable communities where they could be taught Christian virtues? To see the ranchers wander at will through deserts and forests upset the Indians. They "conclude that our real purpose is to deprive them of their land. Outlying settlements of this kind must therefore be prohibited."

None of Señán's recommendations were heeded. Each year the decaying Spanish empire proved less able to control its New World colonies. In 1810 restlessness in Mexico crystallized into the opening battles of an eleven-year struggle for independence. Although remote California did not participate in the upheavals, the province was all but paralyzed. Supply ships ceased their visits; presidial soldiers went unpaid; new missionaries were not sent north to relieve the aging Fathers stationed there. The presidios were able to function only by requisitioning Indian-produced food, cloth and artifacts from the missions. Neither the missions nor the Indians were ever paid for this extra work.

Meanwhile the settlers of Los Angeles proved prolific enough that the town's population grew in spite of pinching conditions. In 1822 (the year when news of Mexico's independence from Spain reached the area) the head count stood at 650. Shortly thereafter, Los Angeles replaced the capital Monterey as the most populous spot in the province.

QUEEN OF THE MISSIONS: *Mission San Gabriel, one of the most prosperous in California, as it looked in 1828 (above left) from a painting by Ferdinand Deppe. Its mill, El Molino Viejo (above) is now an office of the California Historical Society. In the bell towers of the mission church (below) hung bells in arches of graduated size; two of the bells were cast as early as 1795.*

The Plaza Church, (below, circa 1885) as it is popularly called, is the oldest place of worship in Los Angeles. Built by Franciscan fathers and Indian neophytes between 1818 and 1822, the Church of Our Lady of the Angels, as it was first known, served worshippers in the pueblo who until then had to travel to Mission San Gabriel. It was not part of the mission system begun by Father Junipero Serra, but functioned as a parish church.

MISSION SAN FERNANDO: On the outskirts of the city of San Fernando and 23 miles from the Plaza in Los Angeles, Mission San Fernando was one of many to fall to rack and ruin with secularization. Sunshine filters in, not through windows but through the roof's skeleton (top) and two lonely date palms (above) stand just north of where the church had been.

Vineyards lined the nearby river and the banks of the irrigation ditches. Wheat, corn, beans and peppers made up the bulk of the other crops. In mid-1822, after years of intermittent work, the town even completed a church building. It was a somewhat quixotic effort since no parish priest was available, and services could be held only if some missionary at San Gabriel could be persuaded to come over for special occasions.

The number of ranches also increased, though with equal slowness. Of the 25 or so grants issued to California residents by Spanish governors between 1784 and 1821, fifteen were on land now embraced by Los Angeles County. Unlike the original grazing permits, these were true grants and conveyed full title to the land. (The grazing permits were soon turned into fee-simple grants.) Ownership brought incentive with it. Ranchers replaced their first huts with sturdier homes, planted gardens, erected corrals and outbuildings. As was true of the pueblo and the missions, the sinew of these huge, many-acred, self-sufficient units was provided by Indians who (in general) were well-treated but remained in the eyes of the *gente de razón* (the rational, ie. civilized, people) socially inferior.

For the pueblo, growth did not necessarily mean civic progress. Los Angeles had no school until 1817. It concerned itself mostly with teaching religious matters and failed after two years. Another followed in 1827, but it too soon died of neglect. Meanwhile the children learned by themselves the skill most admired by the community — horsemanship. Again and again visitors exclaimed in writing over the ability of the tiniest tots to dash across the roughest sort of ground on spirited horses. The education took its toll, however. Scarcely a family in the pueblo or on the ranches had not lost at least one of its children to a riding accident.

The town itself was drab. Dwellings were small dark cubes, their thick adobe walls only occasionally brightened with whitewash. Most had no windows and were lighted with candles made of beef tallow. Floors were of earth packed so hard by use that they had the luster of slate. Roofs were flat and covered with tar *(brea)* from seeps that oozed and bubbled four miles west of town. Indian laborers brought hardened chunks of the stuff into the pueblo and scattered them about on whatever earth-covered roofs needed treatment. The *brea* melted in the sun, to form a waterproof sheet. Overflow dripped in gooey streamers onto the narrow, crooked streets beneath.

Most furniture and utensils were homemade. Beds were either spread out on the floor or on a cowhide stretched across a wooden frame. Meals were cooked outdoors in stone or adobe ovens and — except during winter's pelting rains — eaten in the shade of a *ramada* set on poles and thatched with long coarse reeds called *tules.*

Reeds were abundant. Floods pouring out of the mountains after heavy storms created wide marshes on the low-lying lands west and south of the pueblo. On this featureless plain, overflowing rivers changed course from time to time. In 1815, due to heavy continuous rains, the Los Angeles River shifted its channel from San Pedro Bay to Santa Monica Bay. During the winter of 1824-25, it abandoned its channel to Santa Monica Bay and returned to its original one — to San Pedro Bay along a course roughly parallel to that of the San Gabriel River. Between the streams — (where Downey, Bellflower, Lakewood and Long Beach now stand) were swampy forests of alder, willow and sycamore. In those thickets, wild cattle and horses hid from men and were preyed on by grizzly bears.

A favorite but brutal sport from the early 1850s was "correr el gallo" or "scratching the rooster." The roosters, necks well-greased, were partially buried along a public road. Then, riders on horseback would dash by at full speed and try to grab the roosters, pulling them out of the earth.

Bears furnished a favorite sport. On moonlit nights *vaqueros* ("cowboys") would leave the carcass of a cow where a bear would find it and then spring from ambush and lasso the grizzly as it gorged on the meat. After binding the thrashing creature with ropes, they dragged it on a bullock hide to an enclosure in the town plaza. There, goaded to frenzy, it was matched in a fight to the death with an equally maddened bull. Men, women and children watched enthralled. Afterwards they talked over every detail of the contest — generally the bear won — until another battle was staged to relieve the monotony of their lives. In time the disturbance created by the performances grew so great that the sport had to be moved to a ring outside town.

THE PLAZA

A plaza was laid out in 1815 during construction of the Plaza Church, center of life in early-day Los Angeles. On a site where today Sunset Boulevard meets Main Street, the town houses of the rancheros were located prominently around the plaza, while other homes were built on streets leading away. During the 1830s and 1840s, the plaza was fenced off every Sunday for bull fights, during which the bulls were rarely killed. The first known photograph of the plaza (lower left) was taken in 1857; twelve years later, it was officially dedicated as a public park. It did not assume its familiar circular form until the 1870s (upper left), and through the years, it has been redesigned and relandscaped; its circular shape became even more defined by 1890 (upper right). In 1931, the people of Chihuahua, Mexico, presented a statue of Felipe de Neve for the plaza, commemorating the 150th anniversary of the founding of Los Angeles. Declared an historic cultural monument in 1970, the plaza is also a State Historical Landmark.

Richard Henry Dana, Jr., in 1842

I also learned, to my surprise, that the desolate-looking place we were in furnished more hides than any port on the coast. It was the only port for a distance of eighty miles, and about thirty miles in the interior was a fine plane country, filled with herds of cattle, in the center of which was the Pueblo de los Angeles — the largest town in California — and several of the wealthiest missions; to all of which San Pedro was the seaport.

—*Richard Henry Dana,*
Two Years Before
the Mast (1840)

Abel Stearns went from his native Massachusetts to live in Mexico for three years where he was naturalized before moving to Los Angeles in 1833. There, he became a leading trader and his marriage into the Bandini family made him the largest landowner and cattleman in southern California.

No organized services existed to keep Los Angeles clean. There was no sewage system. Garbage and trash were pitched carelessly into the streets; the plaza was redolent with the manure of scores of horses — and stayed that way until the approach of a major festival (fortunately there were several) led to a general cleanup. Although fines eventually were imposed for swimming, doing laundry or letting animals wallow in ditches from which drinking water was drawn, the regulations were not rigorously enforced.

American infiltration

Mexican independence brought one profound change to California. Instead of having to depend for supplies on government ships (which had not been arriving for some years anyway), the inhabitants could trade with outsiders. The effect was electric, for it gave the province its first sizable market for the one commodity it possessed in abundance — hides from the ranchers' rapidly multiplying herds of lean, long-legged, long-horned cattle.

First English, then American, ship traders hurried to the West Coast in quest of leather for the shoe factories of Great Britain and New England and tallow that could be turned into soap and candles. Their approach was heralded by an advance agent who landed at one of the harbors, bought a horse and rode overland from mission to mission and ranch to ranch, lining up customers by displaying a list of the trade items available on the vessel he represented.

The *Californios* prepared for the visits by rounding up their herds and slaughtering enough animals to pay for whatever they desired. Indians stripped off the hides and gave the inner sides a rough cleaning. As soon as the skins were dry, they were folded in half with the hair inside and put in storage. Meanwhile fat was sliced off the carcass, melted in a huge iron cauldron and poured into hide bags where it solidified for transportation to the beach.

The harbor for Los Angeles and its neighboring missions of San Gabriel and San Fernando was San Pedro Bay, 20 miles south of the town. At dawn of the day appointed for the vessel's arrival, a great bustle filled the pueblo, the ranches, the missions. Indian roustabouts carried the hides from the storehouses to ox-drawn carts. Males who could afford fancy dress donned short jackets and tight-fitting trousers, both adorned with gilt and emblazoned by a wide, colorful sash. They buckled big silver spurs onto their boots, covered their dark hair with bandanas and added wide-brimmed, flat-topped, silver-banded sombreros. Women chose velvet skirts and low-necked, short-sleeved blouses. Generally each one rode side-saddle, with a man seated behind and reaching his arms around her to manage the reins and keep her steady.

After the customers had dismounted at the shore, they were taken by sailors to waiting dories and rowed to the ship where a room below decks had been fitted out as a store. In it — widening the eyes of the women in particular — was a dazzling assortment of lamplit shawls, ribbons, costume jewelry, combs, mirrors, sugar, coffee, pure white flour, tools, furniture, cart wheels and sawn lumber.

While the buyers exclaimed and debated, the hides to pay for the purchases were stacked in a warehouse near the shore. Before being loaded for the final run around Cape Horn, they would be taken to San Diego. There, where fogs were less prevalent than in the north, they would be soaked in brine and their inner sides scraped whistle-clean. After they were dried and the hair sides beaten with flails to remove dust and insects, they would be stowed aboard the ship. Sometimes a vessel would cruise back and forth for two years before filling its cavernous hold. But the expense could be borne, for a single journey might net the distant owners as much as $50,000.

In time, representatives of the trading firms opened permanent stores in

California. Most colorful of those to settle in Los Angeles was Abel Stearns, a New Englander who arrived in 1833 after a three-year stay in Mexico. He won the *Californios* with his courtly airs and fluent Spanish. He indulged in wholesale smuggling, participated in various revolutions and received such a disfiguring knife scar across his mouth during a fight that his neighbors called him Old Horse Face. In spite of his tempestuous character (or perhaps because of it), he was able, at the age of 43, to win the hand of fourteen-year-old Arcadia Bandini, a noted beauty whose father was rich in land and cattle. For his bride, Stearns built the finest house in Los Angeles.

The sea was not the only route by which Americans arrived. In 1826 fifteen ragged, half-starved beaver trappers were led into San Gabriel by famed mountain man Jedediah Smith. Because the group lacked proper passports, Smith was taken to San Diego for a grilling by the governor. If three ship captains who happened to be in San Diego at the time had not interceded for him, the Americans might well have been arrested and sent to Mexico City. Instead, he and his men were ordered to leave California by the route over which they had come. Disobeying, they journeyed north along the foothills of the Sierra Nevada.

Every year after that, other bands of trappers made their way to the coast. Overland trading companies imitated them. Interestingly enough, the first group of traders was composed of Mexican citizens of Santa Fe, led west across the desert during the winter of 1829–30 by Antonio Armijo. Their route was so difficult, however, that the next year American pioneers under William Wolfskill worked out a longer, easier way from Santa Fe up into central Utah and back through the site of today's Las Vegas, Nevada. Known anachronistically as the Old Spanish Trail, the route was regularly used thereafter by pack trains plodding west with coarse serapes and New Mexico silver to trade for horses and mules. Other commerce was less legitimate. During the late 1830s and early 1840s, Ute Indians and renegade mountain men from the interior used the Old Spanish Trail to escape with livestock plundered from California's ranches and missions.

Weary men, beguiled by the unhurried living on the coast, frequently deserted their ships or dropped out of the trapping and trading caravans to settle in California. Los Angeles received its share. Some were content to hunt sea otter or work as carpenters and millwrights, trades the native *Californios* lacked the training to fill. More ambitious men embraced Catholicism, took out Mexican citizenship and thus made themselves eligible to marry Mexican girls and own land in Mexican California.

Many became leaders in their communities. Trailblazer William Wolfskill was one. In 1841 he planted the first commercial orange grove in California. (Before then the only oranges in the area had been grown at the missions and seldom reached civilians.) Another was William Workman, future rancher, land speculator, banker and, for a time, mayor of Los Angeles. Workman also arrived in 1841 with the first Americans to migrate west by land with the deliberate intention of finding homes in the Los Angeles area.

Troubled times

It is not likely that many *Californios,* or even Americans living in California, grasped the full significance of this slow infiltration. They were engrossed by local problems. Throughout the critical decade of the 1830s, various political

PIONEERS AND ORANGES: Jedediah Smith, New York-born fur trapper, mountain man and explorer, led 15 ragged trappers into San Gabriel (top), the first white men to reach California overland. A pioneer in the city's economy, William Workman (above) was a rancher, land speculator, banker and mayor of Los Angeles. Workman arrived in 1841, the year the first commercial orange grove (below) was planted by William Wolfskill.

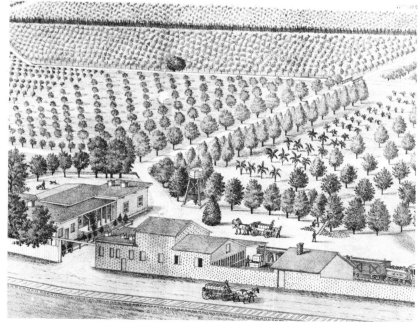

Indian huts at Mission San Gabriel.

Jose Antonio Carrillo was an alcalde of Los Angeles who joined Carlos, his brother who was governor of California, in a revolt against Governor Victoria in 1831. During the Mexican War, Jose defeated American troops in their battle to seize Los Angeles, but soon capitulated and signed the Cahuenga Treaty. Carlos married Maria Josefa Castro, and Jose in succession married two sisters of Pio Pico. Carlos' son Juan Jose was the first mayor of Santa Monica, and three of his daughters married U.S. citizens, one of them being William G. Dana. Juan Jose's son Leo was a motion picture star whose role as a partner of the Cisco Kid glorified the romantic tradition of Spanish California.

factions fought each other for control of the province. Young liberals hoping to obtain self-government for California constantly intrigued against the officials sent north from Mexico. Los Angeles endeavored to wrench the capital away from Monterey. Ragged armies marched back and forth. Each side bombarded the other with fiery proclamation, and at intervals there was even a little shooting. Although the "wars" seem mild from today's perspective, at the time they filled Los Angeles with seething excitement.

Adding to the unrest was the secularization of the missions. Originally the mission program was designed to turn Indians into productive Spanish citizens. That goal achieved, the mission lands, herds and equipment were to be distributed among the neophytes. Their settlements were to become towns open to all Spanish (later Mexican) citizens, and the missions themselves were to be turned into ordinary parish churches.

At the beginning of the effort, government leaders supposed that the process could be completed in ten years. Experience showed, however, that the Indians' own deeply ingrained culture could not be eradicated that quickly. Knowing this, the missionaries (particularly in California) had resisted secularization for many years.

The delay infuriated Mexican liberals. To them it seemed that the missionaries were deliberately perpetuating themselves in order to keep large blocks of land out of civilian hands. Meanwhile (so the argument ran) the Indians continued living under the dominance of the church.

Agitation reached such a point that in the mid-1830s the central administration in Mexico City ordered California's governor, José Figueroa, to oversee the dissolution of the province's 21 missions. Half of each establishment's property would be distributed among the Indians. Civil administrators would manage the rest for the benefit of the town in which the freed natives were to live. The missionaries would be permitted to stay on as parish priests if they wished.

Results were chaotic. San Gabriel was particularly hard hit. Looters — some from as far away as Sonora — swarmed in. Equipment was stolen; thousands of cattle were wantonly butchered. Even the roofs were ripped from some of the buildings for firewood.

Many Indians (already prone to gambling and drinking) lost their share of the property during wild sprees and then, fearing that they would be called to account, ran away to some other district. Soon all coastal California was afloat with cheap, hungry labor. Other Indians, bewildered by what was happening, clustered around the remnants of the missions, the only homes they knew. For months the padre at San Gabriel provided for many of them out of his own pocket.

Dishonest or incompetent administrators compounded the problem by lining their own pockets or letting swindlers bilk them out of sheep, cattle, horses, grain, wine and other stores at a fraction of their value. When the government encouraged citizens to apply for grants of former mission land, several Americans acquired extensive holdings. Only a small portion of the available acreage went to the Indians who supposedly were to receive most of it.

Unsavory backwashes of all this engulfed Los Angeles. Until the mid-1830s, the pueblo was a relatively quiet place. When the wife of rancher Domingo Féliz upset normal standards by helping her lover (a cowboy from Sonora) murder her husband, local inhabitants under the leadership of transplanted American John Temple formed a vigilance committee to set things right. The group took the pair from the jail, shot them and left their bodies on display for two hours as a warning to other would-be malefactors.

Such tactics did not work for long. The plundering of the missions drew a number of gamblers, saloonkeepers and prostitutes into the town. Soon the little pueblo — in 1840 roughly 1,100 people lived there — became known as a den of thieves, a sinkhole of vice. Whatever dominance it might have achieved as a result of the removal of mission power was lost, and for a few years influence passed into the hands of the ranchers.

Conquest

It is tempting to look back on the days of the rancheros as a time of unruffled contentment. A mild climate — broken only by the excitement of a rare flood or earthquake — let people spend most of their time outdoors at ease. Raising cattle was simple. There were no fences to build or repair, no hay to put up. Annual roundups, when cows were gathered and calves branded, were festive occasions. The thrust and bitterness of economic competition was unknown.

Families were large, and younger members paid the patriarch the deference his gray hair deserved. Everyone knew and respected the social and religious forms that gave coherence to the widely separated haciendas. Hospitality was a virtue, personal dignity an innate characteristic. Even a peon delivering a message from horseback (wrote Richard Henry Dana in *Two Years Before the Mast*) sounded "like an ambassador at an audience." Conversation was sprightly and flair was important, for life was meant to be enjoyed.

But it was also a time of widespread ignorance and almost total lack of cultural opportunities. Medicine was primitive, epidemics frequent. Sports were often barbaric; rituals seemed at times to emphasize form rather than substance. Politics was corrupt. Social distinctions were rigid, and military protection rested in the hands of a small army composed mostly of convicts swept up from the streets of Old Mexico's poverty-stricken cities. To those few *Californios* who understood the expansionist tendencies of the United States and who noticed the energy with which American immigrants were elbowing into all the province's economic activities (especially in the north), the future was not reassuring.

The war that came in May 1846 was not of the *Californios'* making but was triggered by animosities between the United States and Mexico over Texas. American strategy called for a two-pronged invasion of the West Coast, one by an army marching overland through Santa Fe, the other by warships already on alert in the Pacific.

At first the naval units seemed to need no help. Monterey toppled on July 7 and San Francisco two days later. Meanwhile most of the American immigrants living in the north flocked to Sonoma to join the California battalion of John Charles Fremont, an American army explorer who had managed to maneuver himself into the vicinity at that convenient time.

If resistance were to be mounted, it would have to be in the south. Earlier that year, Pio Pico had become governor with headquarters at Los Angeles. After the fall of the north, he was joined there by the province's military comandante, José Castro, and about a hundred soldiers. Throughout this time, Pico busied himself selling huge land grants to all Mexican applicants for ridiculously low sums. His intent was to raise revenue while keeping as much acreage as possible out of American hands. By the time the conquerors of Monterey sailed south to attend to Los Angeles, California was blanketed (on paper) with more than 800 grants totalling more than twelve million acres.

That rock having been rolled into the garden of American dreams, Castro and Pico fled with their soldiers to Mexico. The only defense remaining to the pueblo was a four-pounder cannon, 44 inches long, normally used for firing salutes in the plaza during fiestas. As a precaution, the citizens buried it in the yard of an elderly widow who lived on the outskirts of town, then stood back to see what the conquerors had to offer. On August 13, 1846, the Americans marched into Los Angeles without a shot being fired.

Thinking all was well, the main forces moved on, leaving the town in charge of Lieutenant Archibald Gillespie and a handful of troopers. Except

Jonathan Temple, known after he acquired Mexican citizenship as Don Juan Temple, built the house now known as La Casa de Rancho de Los Cerritos in 1844. The adobe and redwood house (above, circa 1910) was located on a bluff overlooking the Los Angeles River; from here, Temple operated his rancho, pasturing 15,000 cattle, 7,000 sheep and 3,000 horses. The great drought of 1863-64 all but ruined his cattle business and in 1866, he sold the rancho to Flint, Bixby and Company — 27,000 acres for $20,000.

John C. Fremont, circa 1850.

33

PICO ON THE PLAZA: Don Pio Pico, the last Mexican governor of California, was photographed (right) with his wife Nachita Alvarado de Pico and nieces, Marinata Alvarado and Trinidad de la Guerra. In an attempt to recapture the glory of California under Mexican rule, he built the Pico House (far right, circa 1875), the first three-story masonry building in the city. The hotel facing the plaza was completed in 1869, the finest in southern California, and cost Pico $50,000 for the building and another $35,000 for the furnishings of the 80-plus room house.

In Rancho Cahuenga's adobe house, Colonel John C. Fremont and General Andreas Pico signed the treaty ending the Mexican-American war.

Avila Adobe (above, circa 1896) was built circa 1818 by Francisco Avila who served a term as alcalde of the pueblo. During the Mexican-American War, the adobe served briefly as the residence of Commodore Robert F. Stockton, commander of the U.S. Pacific Fleet. Although it later fell to neglect, the Avila building was restored in the late 1920s and as the city's oldest existing residence, is part of El Pueblo de Los Angeles State Historic Park.

for Gillespie's overbearing conduct, all might have stayed well, but his petty tyrannies and his constant bragging about his easy victory soon led 50 or so wine-inspired patriots to lay siege to his camp.

After several hungry days, the Americans surrendered. The Angelenos allowed them to march to San Pedro on Gillespie's promise that when a relief ship arrived (shortly after the siege began, a messenger had slipped through the Mexican lines with a plea for help) the invaders would depart.

The promise was not kept. As soon as the relief ship appeared on October 7, its men and Gillespie's marched grimly back toward Los Angeles. They were afoot. The *Californios* who advanced against them were riding top horses and using lariats to drag along with them the little cannon, which they had dug up from the widow's yard and had mounted on the running gears of a wagon. Heat, dust, skillful feinting by the impromptu cavalry and blasting by the cannon — affectionately known to its tenders as the Old Woman's Gun — caused several casualties and forced the Americans to retreat.

The triumph could not last. Fremont marched south with his California battalion. Sea-borne forces gathered at San Diego. An overland column from Santa Fe commanded by General Stephen Watts Kearny approached from the east. Although Mexican lancers sorely pummeled Kearny at Rancho San Pasqual near today's Escondido, they failed to press their advantage. Rested and reinforced, the Americans moved north during the early days of 1847.

The end came quickly. Defeated at two skirmishes south of the pueblo, the *Californios* retreated northwest to Cahuenga Pass leading into the San Fernando Valley and surrendered to Fremont in the hope of receiving better terms. They may have been unnecessarily apprehensive. Chagrinned by Gillespie's fiasco, the Americans were not inclined to be vindictive, and on January 13 both invading generals accepted the capitulation with a generosity that honored the valor of their opponents. All California was now in American hands.

Belated prosperity

The first public school in the San Fernando Valley (above, circa 1884) was established in 1869 under the direction of Mr. and Mrs. Geronimo Lopez.

Unwilling tagalong

Throughout the 1850s, sparsely populated southern California tried to disassociate itself from the fevered north. The interests of the two sections simply were not the same. This difference first showed itself in 1849 when delegates of the entire newly conquered region met at a constitutional convention in Monterey to determine what sort of government they wished to establish within the American framework.

The northerners urged immediate statehood — not so the delegates from the south. Several of them were Hispanos, and it was clear to them that the northern miners would resist a tax on gold claims. This meant the costs of state government would fall most heavily on ordinary real estate — cattle ranches, for instance. The southern delegates argued for a territorial form of government whose expenses would be met for the most part by the federal treasury in Washington.

Wasted breath — the majority pushed through a state constitution that Congress approved (after much bickering) in 1850.

Financial results were exactly what the south had feared. In 1852 the six so-called cow counties stretching from San Luis Obispo down to San Diego had a population of only 6,000 but paid $42,000 in property taxes. In the north, 120,000 people paid $21,000. In return, the south received almost no help from either the state or federal governments in establishing school systems, improving Los Angeles's miserable harbor at San Pedro, solving the Indian problem or combatting violence and outlawry.

Furious at their treatment, southern landowners met in Los Angeles in 1850 to consider remedies. Their decision was a resolution demanding that the new state be cut across its waist and a territory be established in the south, probably with Los Angeles as its capital. Although the effort failed, agitation continued, and in 1859 the state Legislature finally passed a bill authorizing the separation if Congress approved.

Absorbed instead by the mounting tensions over slavery, Congress paid no heed. Los Angeles and its neighbors were forced to continue competing on unequal terms with the north for the funds and population they needed to achieve even a fraction of the prosperity for which they yearned. Considering the history of the preceding decade, their chances did not look good.

Fading hopes

At first blush it seems strange indeed that Los Angeles was unable to lay hold of a reasonable share of the hundreds of millions of dollars in gold dust that poured out of the foothills of the Sierra Nevada during the 1850s. The town was one of the first places outside of northern California to learn of James Marshall's fabulous discovery at Sutter's Mill in the Sierra foothills. Los Angeles was also in a position to tap the services of some of the world's best miners — the tough, white-trousered, floppy-hatted *gambusinos* of Sonora, Mexico, some of whom had been drifting back and forth along Anza's desert crossing ever since it had been reopened in the 1830s.

Los Angeles had already experienced a small gold rush of its own. In 1842, a rancher named Francisco López had discovered placer deposits in Placeritas Canyon, a shaggy spot 35 miles north of the pueblo. Digging began immediately, and by the time the war with Mexico interrupted the work, a mingling of Sonoran prospectors, Indian laborers and young adventurers from the town had taken an estimated $100,000 from the dry gulch.

Among those who labored in the diggings was Antonio Francisco Coronel, age 17, who had come to California from Mexico in 1834. Because of his experience, Coronel was chosen in the late summer of 1848 to lead a mixed

Stephen Clark Foster, born in Maine and alumnus of Yale, was alcalde of Los Angeles, later its mayor and served in the Constitutional Convention of 1849.

HATS OFF: In Placerita Canyon, a simple felt hat marks the spot (above) where, in 1842, Francisco Lopez first discovered gold in California. And since all that glitters can be spent, faro games (below) became the favorite activity in mining camps and gambling dens.

THE OLD
SPANISH AND MEXICAN
RANCHOS
of LOS ANGELES COUNTY

Prepared by
TITLE INSURANCE
AND TRUST COMPANY
TITLE INSURANCE BUILDING
433 SO. SPRING STREET · LOS ANGELES

COPYRIGHT, 1937—TITLE INSURANCE AND TRUST COMPANY, LOS ANGELES

group of 30 Indians, Sonorans and *Californios* to the new goldfields in the Sierra. During the few weeks of good weather, the party reaped well, but when Coronel tried to repeat the success in 1849, a gang of roughnecks from Oregon drove the party out of the mountains on the grounds that they were "greasers" and thus ineligible to take gold from American soil.

It was a specious argument. The treaty of Guadalupe-Hidalgo between the United States and Mexico gave Hispanic residents of the conquered Southwest full rights of citizenship. But paper could not stand against fists and guns. Battered physically and psychologically, Coronel and hundreds of

HOME ON THE RANGE: Ranch hands mount up (above) for a day of herding cattle in California, which inevitably brought a stop at the chuck wagon (left inset) and probably some calf roping (right inset).

other *Californios* withdrew from the mountains, empty-handed and in despair. The Sonorans, having invested heavily in hardship in order to cross the desert from Mexico, hung on a little longer — the town of Sonora in the southern Sierra still commemorates their presence — but the imposition in 1852-53 of special mining taxes on foreigners eventually drove them out, too. Whatever money they might have spent for supplies with Los Angeles merchants went back to Mexico with them.

But perhaps cattle could siphon gold out of the north. During the early years of the rush more stampeders had poured into San Francisco and the mountain camps than could be readily fed. The boniest sort of cattle brought as much as $200 a head — and southern California was full of massive-horned, hollow-flanked animals that a hide trader valued at no more than $2 each.

But in the north — as soon as winter's rain turned the brown land green, trail herds began winding across the Tehachapi Mountains and along the San Joaquin Valley. Rustlers and Indians occasionally made trouble, but most of the animals reached their destination. The ranchers rode home with leather saddlebags stuffed either with raw gold or with the $50 gold slugs that private mints in San Francisco were issuing in order to fill the inordinate demands for currency.

The difference in the regions was immense. Oregonians who sent lumber, wheat and wool to California also reaped well. The money that flowed back they invested in additional mills, foundries, steamboats and wharves. These things in return produced still more wealth and lured in settlers eager to share in the new prosperity.

In southern California, however, the *rancheros* spent their money on imported luxury goods — racehorses, saddles and bridles studded with precious metal, French wines, Italian lace from which their women could sew exquisite mantillas for covering their dark hair, silver table service and ornate furniture that they placed on the earthen floors of their adobe *salas*. They gambled recklessly and entertained lavishly. A Los Angeles wedding between members of leading *ranchero* families (most had town as well as country houses) might be celebrated for a week and attract guests and retinues of servants, all on horseback, from as far away as Santa Barbara and San Diego.

Meanwhile, better breeding stock was not brought in to improve the herds. Gardens were abandoned — it was easier to buy milk and beans than to raise them — and Los Angeles residents continued to dip household water out of the irrigation ditches with buckets.

The prosperity did not last. Gold production peaked in 1852, and thereafter money was not so free in the north. At the same time, better breeds of cattle and sheep were being trailed across the continent to help meet market demands. The *rancheros'* second-rate stock lost favor, and soon returns were little better than they had been during the time of the hide trade.

Expenses soared, however. On top of property taxes, came the problem of defending land titles. Although the United States had promised to respect all legitimate claims, the burden of proving a grant's validity fell on the owner.

It was an onerous process. Casualness had been a hallmark of Mexican property affairs. Documents were lost, surveys were careless, and filings with the proper officials — who often lived far from the proposed grant — were frequently skipped. To fill these voids, the grantee had to rely on the testimony of witnesses. Except for a short period in 1852 when the three-man board of land commissioners met in Los Angeles, these people had to be taken to San Francisco at the defendant's expense. There the Spanish-speaking claimant had to hire interpreters and American lawyers. If his claim was declared valid — and every major grant in the Los Angeles area was honored — the owner then had to have its boundaries surveyed according to American standards.

Since very few ranchers had been provident enough to build up reserves of capital, they met these expenses by selling additional numbers of cattle, surrendering part of their real estate to their lawyers in payment of fees or mortgaging their holdings to Los Angeles moneylenders at monthly interest rates of three to five percent.

Since the lenders were often Anglos who had married into the owner's family, there was generally no great pressure about repayment. For what could a creditor do with the land if he foreclosed? Cattle were a drug on the market, and the thousands of stampeders from the American South who crossed the Los Angeles Basin on their way to the goldfields were not interested in buying even small parts of it to use as farms.

It was ironic — that blind rush for fortune straight across some of the nation's most productive soil. But the gold seekers were from humid climates and were accustomed to judge a land's fertility by its trees. No forests grew near Los Angeles. There was no rain, either, especially during the late spring and summer when growing crops needed water. And so an unknown number of experienced agriculturists hurried on to the north, generally to wind up empty-handed.

It need not have been so. Treeless land can be productive when water is brought to it — and ample water was available in the basin. The high mountains lining it on the north wrung prodigious amounts of moisture from the winter storms and then released it throughout the year into easily diverted streams. At the missions and throughout the land around Los Angeles, thousands of acres of vegetables, grapes and citrus were brought to fruit just that way. But preconceptions are hard to break, even when

RANCHERO	RANCHO	BRAND	DATE
Juan Avila	El Niguel		1833
Maria Ygnacio Verdugo	Los Verdugos		1836
John Roland	La Puente	I R	1852
Jose Sepulveda	San Joaquin		1839
Diego Sepulveda	Palos Verdes		1839
Abel Stearns	Alamitos		1839
Tomas Sanches	La Cienega		1842
John Temple	Los Cerritos		1844
Bernardo Yorba	Santiago de Santa Ana		1844
Ramon Yorba	Santiago de Santa Ana		1844
Teodocio Yorba	Santiago de Santa Ana		1844
Ygnacio del Valle	Camulos		1850
Augustin Machado	La Ballona		1844
Andres Pico	Ex-Mission San Fernando		1851
Francisco Ocampo	San Bartolo		1847

A group of early southern California ranchos and rancheros and the facsimiles of the brands under which they registered their stock.

Peter Burnett, the first American governor of California; after leaving that post in 1851, he was appointed a justice of the state supreme court and later served as the president of the Pacific Bank in San Francisco.

In the 1870s, the city's fuel — wood — was often brought in by donkey.

evidence is clear. Irrigation techniques were unfamiliar to American farmers, and no one tried to enlighten them.

As a result, only two small groups — both working communally — bucked the trend by purchasing California ranches and dividing up the land themselves. One was a party of Mormons who in 1851 prepared the way for the thriving city of San Bernardino, 60 miles east of Los Angeles. Germans fleeing from hectic San Francisco were the other. Their intensively cultivated vineyards launched the town of Anaheim in 1857. Only those two — the rest of the *rancheros* sat tight with their mountains of debt and wistful hopes that next year — surely — the crippled cattle market would revive again. It never did — not in their time.

The shape of the town

Like the *rancheros*, the city fathers of Los Angeles were constantly strapped for cash. As one means of attacking the problem, the city council decided to auction at intervals all the still uninhabited, untilled parts of the pueblo's original grant of four square leagues (28.1 square miles). Before that could be done, however, the town boundaries had to be surveyed according to American standards. Ditch right-of-ways had to be determined and streets aligned — no small problem inasmuch as the original Hispanic settlers clustered their houses around the plaza without predetermined plan and then let canals and thoroughfares wander among the buildings as seemed convenient at the time.

The job of restructuring the haphazard arrangement fell on an American army lieutenant, Edward O.C. Ord. During 1849, Ord strong-armed property lines and streets into congruity and marked into neat rectangles all the parcels that were available for purchase. Although the first auction went well enough to relieve immediate pressures, there was still a great deal of land left over. So the town sought to lure residents by giving away 35-acre plots to any newcomer who would spend $200 in a year's time improving the property. The program must have had some effect, for between 1850 and 1860 the pueblo's population jumped from 1,610 to 4,385. But the tripling of a small figure does not necessarily indicate a big future. In 1858 when merchant Harris Newmark was offered either two loads of firewood or 110 acres on the outskirts of town as payment of a debt, he chose the wood.

The growing population was polyglot. The newly arrived Americans gathered on the west side of town and reminded themselves of their origins by building houses of white clapboards.

Surprisingly numerous were the French, many of whom had fled to California from their mother country during its political upheavals of 1848. They operated some of the finest vineyards in southern California.

Map of the first Ord survey of Los Angeles, 1849, with street names in both Spanish and English. The original orientation of the town was northeast-southwest; later, real estate developments were laid out truer to the cardinal points. Thus, odd jogs and bends in the streets were created wherever the new plats butted against the original pueblo.

Sonoratown was Los Angeles' first barrio, around New High and Republic Streets (left, circa 1885). Here Mexican Americans congregated not only because rent was cheap, but they also gained a sense of ethnic camaraderie.

A thoroughfare leading from Aliso Street to the plaza was known in the late 1800s (left, circa 1875) as Nigger Alley because several black families lived there. It was lined with saloons, gambling houses and brothels, and killings were frequent. Gradually, the Chinese came to occupy the "alley."

The city's main population base remained the Spanish-speaking *pobladores* and their numerous offspring. Sonorans, also Spanish speaking, formed a colorful, crowded colony north of the plaza. Some were transients, traveling between northern Mexico and the goldfields. Others became permanent residents of the pueblo. They lived in close-packed adobe houses shaded by occasional trees. The streets teemed with goats, dogs, chickens, horses and children. Gambling and cockfighting were favorite diversions. Although many of the Sonorans were gainfully employed as common laborers and domestics, many outlaws and prostitutes congregated in Sonoratown with them, and the streets were regularly scoured for wanted men by Los Angeles' vigilante groups.

HIGH SCHOOLS AND HOSPITAL: State law required public education and with it came the Los Angeles High School (above left, being moved) built in 1873 and the State Normal School (above right, circa 1890). The first county hospital in Los Angeles (below) was built in 1858; conducted by the Sisters of Charity, it was located at 1416 Naud Street between Ann and Sotello Streets.

A carretta driven between Mexico and El Pueblo de Los Angeles.

Gradually the more thrifty Chinese, many of them railroad workers, crowded into the odorous section and replaced the Sonorans. In 1871 a race riot that shocked the nation broke out among these interlopers. Americans triggered it by interfering in a struggle between two tongs over a woman. By the time the uproar was over, at least eighteen Orientals were dead; the exact number was never determined.

Census takers did not count Indians though they were still the town's principal source of labor and mercilessly exploited. Hopelessness had made many of them alcoholics. Men, women and children caroused every weekend then were locked up for a Monday morning sale. Anyone in need of workers came to the municipal corral, paid the fines of as many Indians as he needed in his kitchens or fields and took them away. When the week was over, the employer deducted the amount of their fines from their wages and turned them loose. Most returned to the town's tenderloin, where they drank, screeched, danced and fought their way back into the same degradation as before. Although bull-and-bear fights were outlawed as immoral in 1860, the Indian work force continued to be exploited for several more years.

Change of any sort came slowly. Because state law required public education, a two-story brick elementary school was completed in 1855 on the northeast corner of Second and Spring streets. There was no high school, however, until 1873, when Los Angeles High was erected proudly atop Pound Cake Hill at Temple and Broadway. Seven years later, in 1880, the Methodist-supported University of Southern California opened its doors on an eight-acre campus near 34th Street and Exposition Boulevard. Funds for construction purposes were raised from land donated by Protestants, Jews and Catholics alike.

Mañana — why do today what can be put off until tomorrow? Everyone took a noon siesta. The sleepy adobe stores downtown were shaded by wooden awnings resting on slim posts. They were identified by signs hand-lettered on cloth and framed with wood. Merchants whiled away their time waiting for customers by playing cards through an open window — one sitting inside, the other outside — on upended barrels. Whole families plodded to the shops in ancient carretas whose solid wooden wheels shrieked agonizingly on ungreased wooden axles. The first horse and buggy did not dash through the unpaved streets until 1853. A bilingual newspaper The Los Angeles Star, with Spanish pages called La Estrella folded inside, was founded in 1851 and continued in California for a decade.

Hospitality remained a high art and common bond. Old family unities reached into the new politics brought by the conquerors. Because a rico could control the votes of his workers, he had a voice in electoral decisions. Generally the ricos aligned themselves with Democrats who controlled the region. But although they placed Spanish-speaking candidates in many local

CRIME AND VIOLENCE: The late 1800s brought such unsavory happenings as stage robberies (top left, circa 1885), bizarre side shows (top right) and lynchings (above right). The site of the hanging of Lachenia for the killing of Jacob Bell (above right, circa 1870) was later the site of the court house, now the location of the Criminal Courts Building at Temple and New High Streets. As late as 1874, Tiburcio Vasquez (above left) and his gang of Mexican ruffians were committing so many robberies that the governor offered an $8,000 reward for his capture.

offices, they exerted relatively little influence on the state level.

There was a rudimentary sewer system but no municipal delivery of water. People either fetched it home themselves from the irrigating ditches or, if they lived at a distance, bought it from a private carrier who delivered one bucket per day from his ox-drawn cart at a cost of 50 cents a week.

Firefighting and police work were handled by volunteer organizations with a decided social rather than racial cast. Only if an Anglo or Hispano possessed proper status (one account declared), was he deemed worthy to throw water on flames or arrest his errant brethren of any race.

There were plenty of the latter, many of them derelicts who had failed in the mines or criminals who had been driven out of the north by vigilance committees. The scofflaws were not finicky about their targets. When not preying on the gentry, they were given to brutal quarrels with each other over cards and women.

Outraged by 1851's 44 murders without a conviction, the mayor and city council asked several leading Anglo and *Californio* residents to form a

STAGE LINES: *General Phineas Banning (above, standing), with the help of investors, established stage lines out of Los Angeles. The Banning Stage, driven by its founder (right), pulls away from Wilmington, the town Banning founded and named for his Delaware birthplace.*

Juan Bandini (below, with one of his daughters), born in Peru, came to California circa 1822 to become a ranchero and became a social and political leader in San Diego and Los Angeles.

vigilante group capable of restoring order. Later a mounted force of lancers extended the activity throughout the county. During the next several years, these para-military forces fought pitched battles with outlaw gangs and summarily executed close to three dozen suspects — too summarily at times, for it developed later that a few of the victims had not been guilty of the crimes for which they were charged.

The wholesale executions did not end brigandage. As late as 1874, Tiburcio Vásquez and his gang of alienated, dispossessed Mexicans were committing so many robberies that the governor offered a reward of $8,000 for his capture. This lure resulted in a tip that let a posse surprise Vásquez in a ranchhouse near the site of today's Hollywood. When he tried to flee through a back window, the lawmen wounded him. Then, instead of lynching him, as probably would have happened during the 1850s, they let him receive a stream of visitors in his cell before sending him north to San Jose to stand trial.

The energy displayed in this quest for order was one contradiction to the town's apparent languor. Another was the growing determination of a handful of merchants to force Los Angeles into prominence as the supply center of southern California. Their initial motivation came from several sources — a short-lived gold rush to the Kern River east of Bakersfield; the desire of the Mormons in Salt Lake City to have an outlet to the sea and the establishment of Army posts at Yuma on the Colorado River and at Tejon on the north side of the pass leading over the mountains to the San Joaquin Valley.

Each of those happenings created demands for supplies and transportation. The obstacle was a lack of facilities for funneling into the city the goods and people destined for the hinterlands. There were no railroads, and the only harbor was shallow San Pedro Bay, long cursed by hide traders as the worst on the Pacific Coast. Although sidewheel steamers plying between Panama and San Francisco occasionally stopped by San Pedro to unload mail and passengers, freighters never did. They went straight to San Francisco. There Eastern merchandise consigned to Los Angeles was reloaded onto rickety coastal vessels and brought all the way back. Unloading was chaotic, haulage into town archaic.

To the cool eyes of 20-year-old Phineas Banning of Wilmington, Delaware, who disembarked at San Pedro in 1851, the disorder looked like opportunity. He was an extraordinary individual — more than six feet tall,

round-faced, curly-haired. He was also persuasive and soon talked an investor named D. W. Alexander into helping him finance a 21-mile stage and freight line from San Pedro to Los Angeles. He built a town a short distance from the shore — at first it consisted only of Banning's home, barns and corrals — named it Wilmington after his birthplace and watered it with a nine-mile ditch from the Los Angeles River. He dredged out a channel from San Pedro's shallow road into an island-protected inner harbor where lighters transferring goods and passengers from ocean ships could find adequate berths.

While this was going on, Banning also found time to spin stage lines along the coast — up to Ventura and down to San Diego, with another tentacle reaching out to the Kern River goldfields. He talked Army officers into awarding him haulage contracts to their new posts and then set about smoothing out the roads necessary for his enterprises. By the middle of the 1850s, he and Alexander owned 500 mules, 15 stagecoaches and 40 highwheeled wagons. During the winter of 1855-56, he began using some of that equipment on the long haul to Salt Lake City.

In his own mind, Banning was pointing the way to the future, but it took a series of natural disasters to awaken some of his more complacent contemporaries to the economic logic of what he was doing.

The merry-go-round

The Civil War, which devastated the rest of the nation, was scarcely a diversion in southern California. *The Los Angeles Star* joined a few other of the state's newspapers in advocating that California reject both the Confederacy and the Union in favor of an independent Bear Flag Republic. Response was lukewarm. Demonstrations by Southern sympathizers in El Monte and San Bernardino ended with the arrival of federal troops from the north. The distant war, in short, stirred only echoes in the Southland, gripped as it was by severe troubles closer to home.

Repeated deluges of rain throughout the winter of 1861-62 launched southern California's great cataclysm. Cattle drowned, houses tumbled. Vineyards and groves were either washed away or smothered under water-borne sand. Then came two years of baking drought accompanied by a virulent epidemic of smallpox. Enfeebled ranch families watched starved cattle die by the hundreds of thousands. Taxes became delinquent on five-sixths of the property in Los Angeles County. *Rancheros* everywhere defaulted on their debts, yet creditors remained reluctant to foreclose for fear that the land would simply be a burden.

ENTER VICTORIA: At New High Street where Sunset Boulevard cuts in (top), the new was overtaking the old in 1887. The adobes in the foreground were traditional, and the hillside residences showed the Victorian influence. At the Casa Verdugo (above), adobe bricks were made.

EARLY UTILITIES: The first gas works (above), built in 1867, and Pico House, in 1871. An early-day fire department contingent (top) rushes up the First Street hill to a fire.

Then, as the country dried out, relief came from unexpected sources. Congress chartered a southern transcontinental railroad known as the Atlantic & Pacific. Excited by the prospect of being on the ground when the line reached the West Coast, soldiers of the defeated Confederacy trickled into the Los Angeles Basin, hoping to remake their shattered lives. Simultaneously, the growth of huge wheat ranches in the northern California squeezed numbers of small farmers south. And Eastern health seekers, advised by their doctors of southern California's benign climate, began wandering into the area looking for places to stay.

As this quiet invasion was gathering headway, lightning struck — rich silver mines were discovered at Cerro Gordo on the far edge of the Owens Valley, 200 miles to the north. Demands for freight leaped and were met principally by Remi Nadeau, Phineas Banning's most bitter competitor.

Everyone benefited. The miners needed food; the hundreds of freight teams needed barley and hay. As for Phineas Banning, he countered Nadeau's success by persuading Los Angeles to buy half of an offer of $500,000 in stocks and bonds so that he could build southern California's first railroad between the town and San Pedro, where the federal government was at last scratching out a few improvements to the harbor. By the fall of 1869, the trains were running — two a day, hauling ingots of solid silver along with the rest of their cargo.

Ripples grew to waves. In 1868 Los Angeles acquired her first two banks. The first — Hayward & Company — occupied the site of today's United States Courthouse. Its owners were John Hayward and former governor of California John G. Downey. The second was Hellman, Temple and Company, opened by merchants Isaiah Hellman and John Temple. That

46

same year, the city had her first street lights, activated by gas distilled from the same sort of tar the original inhabitants had used for covering their roofs. Two- and three-story brick buildings went up, developers opened new subdivisions on the hills overlooking the plaza and the Los Angeles Water Company — granted a 30-year franchise by the city — began laying its first pipes. At that, the fire department (a city-supervised volunteer organization came into being in 1871 and graduated to full-pay status in 1885) gave up its bucket brigades in favor of a bright new engine.

Out in the country, John Downey divided his 17,000-acre ranch into agricultural plots for sale to the incoming farmers. Water? — plenty. He proved it by drilling southern California's first artesian well in 1868 and thus showed prospective purchasers that most of the Los Angeles Basin was underlaid by a giant aquifer.

Aggressive though Downey was, his efforts paled in comparison to the high-pressured sales work of what was called the Robinson Trust. Basis of the trust's activities was 177,796 acres acquired from debt-ridden old Abel Stearns who had lost 30,000 head of cattle during the drought of the mid-1860s. Townsites were laid out, bales of brochures printed and an alliance formed with San Francisco's Immigrant Union.

The Union was the brainchild of the Central Pacific Railroad which, in conjunction with the Union Pacific, had brought the first transcontinental train to the San Francisco area in May 1869. Propaganda was needed to create traffic. The Immigrant Union supplied some. More came from a spate of travel books, notably Charles Nordhoff's railroad-inspired and widely-read *California for Health, Pleasure and Residence,* of which three millions copies sold in ten years. All this benefited southern as well as northern California.

Exuberance swept Los Angeles County. Pasadena and Riverside took shape. Fine new strains of oranges were developed. The town expanded so far that shoppers and businessmen demanded — and in 1875 received — the service of horse-drawn street cars. A second shortline railroad, the Los Angeles & Independence — its eyes on newly-discovered silver mines near Death Valley — laid its first stretch of track due east from Santa Monica on through Los Angeles toward San Pedro Street. Convinced that Santa Monica would soon pass San Pedro as a handler of freight, hundreds of people snapped up real estate offerings in the new beachside village.

Shortlines were fine for moving traffic to the ocean, but what most Angelenos craved was an overland railroad connection with the rest of the nation. To this end, a group of citizens formed the first Los Angeles Chamber of Commerce in the 1870s. The Southern Pacific, a subsidiary of the Central Pacific, was driving southward through the San Joaquin Valley toward the Colorado River with every intention of keeping rival transcontinental lines out of California. Its shortest route to the Colorado River passed approximately a hundred miles east of Los Angeles, but if the townspeople wanted a connection with San Francisco and the East, the railroad's owners said blandly, they could have it — at a price. The Southern Pacific agreed to swing its rails through Los Angeles in exchange for the maximum subsidy allowed by law — five percent of the county's assessed valuation or $602,000. Part of that sum, moreover, would have to consist of the securities the town held in Banning's Los Angeles & San Pedro Railroad. With control of the shortline secured by this device, the Southern Pacific could then set its rates sky high and choke off competition by water.

Swallowing hard, the citizens trooped to the polls on November 5, 1872 and authorized the subsidy, only to have construction of the line start late and limp slowly. The nation was entering the depression of 1873, and despite Los Angeles' gift, the Southern Pacific was almost out of funds. The stagnation spread to other industries, and on August 27, 1875, a wild run by depositors forced the pueblo's banks to close their doors. The land boom died — and so did one of the town's pioneer bankers, 77-year-old William Workman, who shot himself through the head with a pistol.

Another casualty was the Los Angeles & Independence Railroad whose

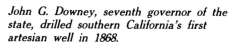

WATER WORKS: *City water tanks in the plaza (top) and horse-driven irrigation system (above), both circa 1875.*

John G. Downey, seventh governor of the state, drilled southern California's first artesian well in 1868.

SANTA MONICA: The Santa Monica beach, with the North Beach Bath House and Arcadia Hotel (above), quickly became one of southern California's most popular picnicking and bathing resorts. In 1874, Colonel R. S. Baker sold some of his land holdings in Santa Monica Canyon to Senator John P. Jones of Nevada; together, they planned a railroad, wharf and town. Less than two years later, some 1,000 people resided in the town's 60 houses (left, bird's eye view northeast from the Arcadia Hotel).

ON TRACK: The arrival of the Southern Pacific tourist train from the East in the "boom days" of 1885 (left) and the first departure of a cable car to east Los Angeles down Downey Avenue (above).

treasurer, F.P.J. Temple, was Workman's banking partner. Late in 1875, the once-feisty shortline to Santa Monica surrendered to the Southern Pacific. That railroad now held the entire basin's steam transportation system in its iron fist.

But at least the Southern Pacific was finally moving toward Los Angeles. Thousands of Chinese coolies attacked the rugged Tehachapi Mountains with horse carts and scrapers. Rails serpentined upward to the mouths of what was then the fourth longest tunnel in the world. On September 5, 1876, the first train rolled into a town bedecked with garlands and wild with joy over the prospect of becoming (as one newspaper reporter ecstatically predicted) "the most extensive and beautiful city this side of the Atlantic." As a more solid indication of what the connection could mean to the southland's fruit growers, William Wolfskill promptly shipped an entire carload of oranges to St. Louis.

It was just a beginning. During the ensuing years, the Southern Pacific pushed east across the Colorado River and in 1882 reached New Orleans. Los Angeles now had direct land and sea connections with every major section of the United States.

As prosperity returned during the early 1880s, the town ceased being a village. Adobe buildings disappeared. (During this period, also, the southland's Spanish-speaking population lost its numerical superiority and became a minority group.) Telephones and electric lights appeared in 1882. Cable cars carried passengers up steep hills to the newest subdivisions — Anglo subdivisions. To handle the perennial problem of water, reservoirs appeared here and there on commanding heights. Sewers and storm drains were laid 20-plus miles to an outfall at the ocean — out of sight, out of mind, although there were some people who thought that in a land afflicted with intermittent droughts, every bit of waste water ought to be filtered and reused for irrigation.

By then, however, any suggestion of restraint was unpopular. In 1883 the Atchison, Topeka & Santa Fe Railroad, which had acquired the charter of the old Atlantic & Pacific, broke through the Southern Pacific's barrier at the Colorado River and two years later rolled into Los Angeles on its own tracks. The antagonistic roads thereupon switched their warfare from financial battlings in Wall Street to conflicts of propaganda and rate cutting. As roundtrip fares plummeted — for part of one day they reached $1 per person — tens of thousands of happy vacationers from the East and Midwest rode the cars to Los Angeles County — five trains a day during the winter of 1886-87.

There the bemused visitors — most of them conservative citizens who ran solid businesses in their home towns — were swooped up by armies of real estate salesman. They were promptly overwhelmed by hoopla. Flag-draped buggies and railroad flatcars carried them free of charge to the

Nicholas Martinez sold ice cream in the summer and tamales in the fall and winter as he strolled the main streets of Los Angeles every evening. Of Mexican-Indian heritage, Martinez always wore a white canvas suit and carried a huge bucket on his head.

FOR SALE: A real estate promotional poster advertising the sale of lots in "Garvanzo" (above), in the northeastern portion of Los Angeles, actually "Garvanza," in 1887. Lots also were sold in Monrovia (right) during the boom of the 1880s.

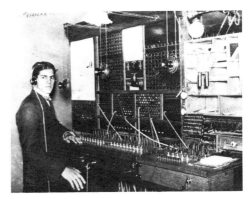

HELLO OPERATOR: By 1886, the telephone had more than 1,000 subscribers in Los Angeles; it started out with seven subscribers and three operators in 1882.

newest paper cities. While they gulped free lunches, brass bands blared and daredevils risked the balmy skies with balloon ascensions. A mania seized them. Why not buy building lots on credit, then resell a few days later at a profit?

Why not indeed? The newspapers were flooded with ads such as this one in the *Los Angeles Times* for the embryo town of Santa Ana:

. . . Beautiful! Busy!
Bustling! Booming!
. . . A great Big Boom! And You Can Accumulate Ducats
by Investing!

The banks went as crazy as the people. By the summer of 1887 when the frenzy peaked, they had 80 percent of their deposits out on loan to real estate speculators. But then memories of the depression of '73 returned, credit tightened, doubts grew, and suddenly the fever cooled.

Fortunately the banks had acted in time. There were no runs, no crashes. Although thousands of would-be profiteers went home with empty pockets, many others decided to stay. Los Angeles had entered the decade of the 1880s with a population of 11,183. It ended it with 50,395 — plus nearly 90 miles of paved streets where there had been none in 1887. Houses, meanwhile, had gone up so rapidly that, of the pueblo's original grant of 17,172 acres, only 450 remained as open space. They were salvaged in the nick of time and today form Elysian Park. Two other permanent gains were the founding of Pomona College in the suburb of Claremont in 1887, and Occidental College in Eagle Rock in 1888.

Contemplating the good that came from the excitement, an official of the Santa Fe Railroad sought to reassure the city by declaring, "People will continue to come here until the whole country becomes one of the most densely populated sections of the United States." The city fathers, however, were not content to count on predictions alone. The Los Angeles Chamber of Commerce (founded in 1888) set to work analyzing what steps were needed to end the brief depression and to make growth a positive aspect of the city's future.

Chapter 4

Full steam ahead

*Spring Street, looking north from Third,
circa 1905.*

The dynamics of growth

The Chamber of Commerce promoted Los Angeles as a "garden of Eden" at major fairs across the nation.

I n Europe, America was presented as the land where everyone had a chance to better himself. In America, the frontier was offered as the hope of the future. Go west, young man, Horace Greeley had advocated, and grow with the country. And certainly people were going west, pouring by the tens of thousands into Kansas City, Denver, Portland, Seattle, San Francisco and scores of hamlets in between.

How could they be prevailed upon to go to Los Angeles rather than somewhere else?

At first the Los Angeles Chamber of Commerce concentrated on available opportunities. It mailed out (mostly to the eastern states) bushels of statistics about the low price of land, high agricultural output, the availability of water, the ease of transportation, the potentials of trade. These written evidences of opportunity were reinforced by tempting displays of produce at every major fair in the nation.

The appeal worked. Despite the depression of the 1890s, the census takers of 1900 found 69,000 additional people in Los Angeles County. Of that increase, 52,000 had crowded into the city, giving it a population of 102,000, nearly 96 percent of them whites. A portion of the newcomers were unemployed laborers seeking a warm climate in which to winter. The city's growth rate for the decade was a whopping 103 percent.

Partly in response to this vigorous expansionism, new enterprises took shape even amidst the depression. In 1893 Thaddeus S.C. Lowe (who during the Civil War had served the Union Army as the world's first military balloonist) financed the construction of a twisting railroad to the top of Mount Lowe north of Pasadena. The hotels the railroad fed stood on ground leased from the U.S. government's Angeles National Forest, the first of its kind in California. (Angeles Forest had been established in 1892 to

PROFESSOR'S PROJECTS: Thaddeus Sobieski Coalincourt Lowe — with his family, circa 1890 (standing in back in the middle) — was one of those creative, determined individuals who saw southern California as the perfect place to fulfill his fantasies. He tried to establish a balloon ferry to ascend the 6,000-foot mountain, Mount Lowe. After this scheme was grounded, he proposed the construction of a narrow gauge one-car railroad to travel up the mount. On July 4, 1892, the first car (right) ascended and descended the incline; two years later, the Mount Lowe Astronomical Observatory was built. Both became major tourist attractions in the San Gabriels.

protect the watersheds that nurtured the towns and orange groves lying between the San Gabriel Mountains and the ocean.) Later, in 1904, the Carnegie Institute established its famed Mount Wilson astronomical observatories in the same national forest, not far from the terminus of Thaddeus Lowe's spectacular railroad.

New colleges were inaugurated. Throop Polytechnic Institute of Pasadena, founded in 1890, blossomed 30 years later into the world-famous California Institute of Technology. Another innovation was Whittier College, launched in 1891 in the small Quaker town of the same name. Architecture, too, felt the new energy, particularly as manifested in the work of the brothers Charles and Henry Greene of Pasadena. Although the Greenes in general followed the pattern of so-called Spanish-style ranch houses, they turned to California redwood for material and produced a highly functional "bungalow" built around courtyards and pergolás. Unfortunately the Greenes' classic lines were so successful that they spawned a host of gimcrack imitations.

Meanwhile, far to the east, a new kind of demographic yeast was at work.

Although the United States in 1900 was still primarily rural and although popular philosophy still insisted that virtue and strength were drawn ultimately from contact with the nourishing earth, increasing numbers of young people from the Midwest's big farm families were refusing to listen. America's basic land-use pattern — one family on each 160-acre homestead — had caused them to live in isolation. Winters were harsh, roads next to impassable. Summer's labor was grinding; agricultural prices fluctuated erratically. Meanwhile the new industrial cities offered jobs, companionship, cultural releases — and alluring temptations. Off the children flocked, leaving their parents uncertain and equally dissatisfied.

Oranges and trolley cars

Once awareness of the Midwest's discontent had dawned in the years following 1900, Los Angeles boosters supplemented their promotional emphasis on economic opportunities with the pleasure of living in sunny southern California, where snow was perched not on rooftops but on the far-off mountains — as a hundred thousand picture postcards made clear. Soon glamour was added to the allure. Why go to Italy? America had its own Mediterranean climate — right on the shores of the Pacific.

The region also had its own romantic history in its Spanish missions. Now that "base" Indian workers and "swarthy" Mexicans had almost disappeared from the scene (the census of 1900 showed only 817 Mexicans in Los Angeles), regional writers by and large forgot the Mexican interlude and turned instead to the rancheros and the devout Franciscan padres of an earlier era, training gentle Indians in the arts of civilization.

A leading figure in the romanticizing of southern California was a tourist, Helen Hunt Jackson. Her first California-inspired book — written after a brief visit to the Los Angeles area in 1880 — was *A Century of Dishonor*, a biting condemnation of the United States government's treatment of the Indians. While working on the book, she became enamored of the Spanish ranches and their Indian retainers and decided to center a novel around them. The book that resulted, *Ramona*, was published in 1884 and became an instant and long-lasting bestseller. For years other authors and many towns capitalized on the interest by pretending to know the full facts about and even the actual birthplace of the fictitious heroine and her Indian sweetheart, Allesandro. In 1921 the Ramona industry became institutionalized with the inauguration of a lavish pageant at the town of Hemet.

Charles Lummis, editor of a magazine called "The Land of Sunshine," and author George Wharton James joined Mrs. Jackson's efforts to better

OF INDIANS AND AUTHORS: *Helen Hunt Jackson (above), a novelist living in Colorado, found a captivating subject in the Indians' mistreatment and, in 1881, her A Century of Dishonor was published, documenting the U.S. government's treatment of native Americans. Her phenomenally popular Ramona was published in 1884, a more romantic look at Indian life. She also helped write a report, sponsored by the U.S. Department of the Interior, on the California mission Indians' needs. Characteristically clad in a corduroy suit and sash, Charles Fletcher Lummis (below) drew notice in Los Angeles after he walked from Ohio to California in 1884-85. He became a foremost promoter of the Southwest, edited a promotional magazine, organized the Sequoyah League to improve the lot of the Indians, created the Landmarks Club preservation group and founded the Southwest Museum.*

PURSUIT, PRESERVATION: The Arroyo Seco area was southern California's first art center. The gently rolling hills covered with sycamore trees were known as the home of Charles Lummis, founder of the Southwest Museum (above) there, and the Judson studios (Professor Judson at work, top right) in the College of Fine Arts (right inset).

Professor George W. James (right) was concerned with preservation of California's heritage — its Indians and missions — as well as its natural resources, such as those in the Sierra Madre forest, where he traveled with study parties (right).

Palm trees, like this one on Figueroa Street, grow from 20 to 75 feet tall in southern California and all but one of its 1,200 species are native to the state.

the conditions of the Indians. Results were meager — how meager is still a point of debate. Far greater success attended her travel book, *Glimpses of California and the Missions* which started a new trend in 1883. In 1895 James penned his own best seller, *In and Out of the Old Missions,* and the next year Lummis formed the Landmark Club dedicated to preserving the collapsing buildings.

The importance of Ramona and the mission tales in luring settlers to California can hardly be overemphasized. In time this literary trend changed California architecture, drawing builders away from Victorian towers, cupolas and bays to red tile roofs, arched colonnades and walls of pastel-color stucco. Mixed easily in with all this were miles and miles of palm trees along the streets of the new subdivisions. Palms were not really Spanish — or native to Los Angeles either — (they came from the deserts and the tropics) but never mind. They certainly were not midwestern, and that was what counted.

The great symbol, though, was the orange. Unlike grapes (which had been wiped out of large sections of the south by a fungus), the golden fruit was saved from its great enemy, cushion scale, by the introduction of Australian ladybugs in 1891. Within eighteen months the ravenous, black-spotted, red little beetles had all but eliminated scale from the groves, and by the mid-1890s California growers were producing more oranges than the West could consume.

Improved refrigerator cars allowed shipment by rail to the East, but people there were indifferent. They regarded oranges as luxury items,

SWEET CITRUS: Boxing fruit took many hands at the packing house in Ontario (top) and just as many picking at Richards' Ranch in Pomona (left), both circa 1905. King Orange (above) reigns over the Thirteenth National Orange Show in San Bernardino, February 1923.

FRUIT HARVEST: Workers pitted apricots at Owensmouth in Canoga Park (top), in July 1924, gathered grapes (above) and harvested dates (below).

something to put in Christmas stockings or to exclaim over at weddings but not to incorporate into daily diet. Because demand was small, produce brokers and commission men handled shipments casually, letting the fruit pile up beside Florida oranges rather than move it on to markets where there was no immediate competition.

In an effort to overcome the lethargy — and also to help farmers with pest control, picking and packaging — southland orchardists formed a series of cooperatives that blossomed in 1905 into the Los Angeles-based California Fruit Growers' Exchange. After deciding to do its own marketing, the Exchange hired a high-powered advertising agency and set about promoting California oranges as assiduously as the Chamber of Commerce was promoting Los Angeles. In fact, the campaigns were soon intertwined.

A third participant in the effort was the Southern Pacific Railroad. Double motives activated its directors — sell the tens of thousands of acres of grant land the railroad received from the federal government as an aid to construction and increase freight volume by stimulating agricultural activity. Its California agents accompanied display trains carrying all kinds of produce throughout the nation. They provided potential immigrants with accurate information about soils, horticultural practices in a subtropic environment and the mysteries of irrigation.

It seems likely that these far-traveled Southern Pacific agents were the first to discover the yearning that many people had for small farms that would enable them to live in communities rather than in isolation and at the same time would let them make money by the intense cultivation of high-value crops. Hoping to cash in on the desire, the railroad snipped its lands in the southern part of the San Joaquin Valley into ten- and twenty-acre parcels and advised citrus and figs as the ideal crops for concentrated farming. Since Los Angeles intended to be the supply center for as much of the San Joaquin Valley as it could reach, the city approved the campaign. Indeed, it adapted the yearning for small-scale citrus farms to its own county situation.

But how was a market for so many oranges to be found? In 1906 the railroad and the Fruit Growers' Exchange joined hands and funds in a determined effort to create a demand that did not yet exist. The Midwestern state picked as the locale for the campaign was Iowa. "Health" was selected as the main theme, and prizes were announced for the drawings, essays and poems that best emphasized the point. The unrhymed poem that went off with top honors read, in part, as follows:

> If long life you would have,
> Knowing naught of human ills,
> Daily eat at least one orange
> Brought from California's groves.

The governor of Iowa was prevailed upon to proclaim Orange Week. Newspapers were fed reams of copy, most of it so skillfully prepared that it was used verbatim. But the big triumph was the fruit trains rocketing through the countryside, each car draped with huge banners that read "ORANGES FOR HEALTH — CALIFORNIA FOR WEALTH." A 50-percent rise in sales followed, and the delighted promoters quickly spread the campaign to other sections of the country, further aided by one of the most effective brand names ever coined, *Sunkist*.

Timing could not have been more auspicious. The nation's long agricultural depression had ended. The price of midwestern land soared; farmers and small-town merchants who had clung grimly to their properties during the bleak years sold out to optimistic newcomers and trooped west to enjoy their repaired fortunes in a land — the subtropical Los Angeles Basin — that had become ineradicably associated in their minds with that glossy, warmly shining emblem of comfortable living — the orange. Between 1900 and 1910, the county population jumped from 170,000 to 504,000, the city from 102,000 to 319,000 — a staggering 212 percent gain. Of those 319,000 people, only 7,600 were blacks, 5,600 were Mexicans

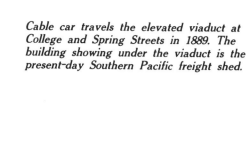
Cable car travels the elevated viaduct at College and Spring Streets in 1889. The building showing under the viaduct is the present-day Southern Pacific freight shed.

(Mexicans were being brought back to work in the groves and on interurban rail beds), and 4,000 were Orientals, mostly Japanese truck farmers and abalone fishermen. Los Angeles, in short, was still more than nine-tenths white.

Placing this large influx of relatively prosperous, middle-class immigrants in the low-roofed, single-family, tree-shaded bungalows they wanted was almost magically facilitated by a remarkable network of electric railways, both urban and interurban. Ownership of the lines was entwined and complex. Basically, until 1911 Henry E. Huntington and railroad president Edward H. Harriman each controlled a sizable piece of the Los Angeles city system (with its yellow cars) and the county system (with its 600 big red cars). In 1911 they separated amicably. Huntington thereafter concentrated his Los Angeles Railway Corporation on the city's lines and Harriman promoted the interurban system with what he called the Pacific Electric Railway Corporation.

Neither owner was an originator. Electric trolleys had begun replacing old horse-drawn and cable-pulled cars late in the 1880s. None of the pioneering companies succeeded, however. Their owners were not wealthy and relied heavily for construction funds on property holders who were willing to give them subsidies in exchange for service.

Henry Huntington's situation was different. He was a nephew and understudy of Collis P. Huntington, one of the builders of the powerful Central Pacific-Southern Pacific transcontinental railroad network. Shortly after Collis's death in 1900, Henry sold the bulk of his own (and his inherited) stock in the railroads to the Union Pacific, of which Harriman was president. Then he took his tremendous fortune to Los Angeles County to speculate in real estate. Efficient transportation was, to him, merely a means of increasing the value of the land he had acquired.

Huntington's program suited President Harriman of the new Union Pacific-Southern Pacific combine. Although the railroad did not own a great deal of land in Los Angeles County (its grants lay farther north and east), it did want to stimulate freight and passenger traffic. One way of doing it was to use their own and Huntington's trolley systems for spreading people throughout the region.

Both Huntington and Harriman commanded enough money to build where and when they wanted and then wait for results. After scooping up the region's existing lines, they spun tracks for yellow cars throughout the city (by 1910 Los Angeles' area had expanded from 28 to 89 square miles) and, more gradually, a thousand miles of rails and overhead power lines for the bigger red cars that served the county. Electricity came from each system's own power plants, and they even built water companies to serve their subdivisions.

Organizing to make a city grow

There was no way to make the city grow without a connection to the rest of the continent — and that meant a railroad.

Getting one was not that easy in those early days. It meant strong support from the local community. In an effort to see that the Southern Pacific built into the city, a group of civic-minded citizens founded the first Los Angeles Chamber of Commerce in 1873. The group was led by Judge Robert M. Widney. There were over 100 people present, and they signed up to pay $1 monthly dues.

Not everyone wanted a railroad, however. Opposition ranged from general public suspicion of the "soul-less, selfish" railway companies to San Diego interests that wanted the terminus in their city.

Judge Widney called the first Chamber meeting in his courthouse after a bill was sent to Congress from Southern Pacific. The bill sought authority to curve the tracks away from Los Angeles. Widney wrote, printed and mailed pamphlets against the bill to every member of Congress. The bill subsequently died and the terminus was built.

After that, Chamber meetings were called whenever the need arose. Some of the first activities included instigating the first appropriation by Congress for the survey and improvement of San Pedro Harbor, promoting trade with Arizona and promoting other commercial interest in southern California.

The activities of the first Chamber ceased after several years of local droughts and disasters.

TO AND FROM THE CITY:
Transportation lines trolleyed citizens back and forth, such as the 401 on Baldwin Avenue and Sierra Madre Boulevard (above), 1908. On a holiday in the country, people pick poppies in Altadena (right inset), 1904, and take in the view from the first hotel at Long Beach (left inset), 1887. The palatial oceanside hotel burned in 1888.

One of the two first police women in Los Angeles, Lucy Gray, proudly displays her badge, 1890.

By 1910 the cooperating lines had become the glue that held 42 towns and dozens of unincorporated districts together into what one contemporary called "the healthiest and most rapidly growing body in America."

Homes and their adjuncts — lawns, porches, rose gardens, citrus, palm trees — all were boxed by streets or roads that intersected at precise right angles, all zoned to bar commercial hurly-burly and undesirable ethnics. To shop, draw books from the central library or attend the symphony (the Los Angeles Symphony, founded in 1895, was the fifth in the nation), citizens simply boarded a big red car in the suburbs and, on reaching the city, transferred as necessary to a yellow one. In the spring, they picked wildflowers in the foothills and in the summer bathed at one of several beaches. There were special events, most notable the famed Tournament of Roses, first held in Pasadena in 1889. In 1902, the year of the first football game (Michigan beat Stanford 49-0), the big red cars brought throngs to Pasadena that the game did not get underway until two hours after its scheduled starting time.

Lawn sprinkling, rose clipping, tree pruning — not every visitor was impressed. Cynics found the scene bland, complacent, conservative, rootless, insecure, rigidly moralistic and overrun with innumerable off-beat religious organizations and philosophic cults. "Iowa on the loose," some scoffed. "Suburbs in search of a city," some mocked. But just the same, a new dynamics of urbanism was taking form on the southern California coastal

ROSES, ROSES, ROSES: In 1889, members of the Valley Hunt Club decided to celebrate New Year's Day with a parade of decorated horses and carriages at a park in Pasadena. Their wish was to emphasize the midwinter abundance of fruit and flowers in California. There was to be a "Tournament of Roses" too, with foot and bicycle races and a tug-of-war, then in 1902, an East-West football game. Michigan met Stanford on a slightly disastrous afternoon in Tournament Park — there were traffic jams, three times as many spectators as seating capacity and consequently, a late kickoff. The final score: Michigan 49, Stanford 0. There were no more football games for 14 years; instead, a polo match, then chariot races in the spirit of those described in a current bestseller, Ben Hur. The first queen was crowned in 1905 to reign over the famous rose parade.

plain. Well before the advent of the automobile and for better or worse, Los Angeles had invented suburban living. Perhaps figures say it best. Each weekday during the early 1900s (and numbers were higher on weekends), 225,000 passengers — many of them duplicates — rode trolley cars a total of 73,000 miles, often at exhilarating speeds of from 40 to 60 miles an hour, into the city or to the mountains and beaches and back at a cost of less than a penny a mile.

Partly because of this efficient trolley system, downtown Los Angeles experienced a heady burst of construction between 1902 and 1908. One beloved off-shoot of the growth was a block-long cable car system known as Angel's Flight. Built in 1901, the two-car railway — one car descended while the other climbed — undertook to move passengers up or down the steep slope of Bunker Hill between Hill and Olive streets. (So enshrined did Angel's Flight become in the hearts of its users that after the line was abandoned in 1969, the two orange-and-black cars were placed on exhibition in the Heritage Museum at 1200 Olive Street.) Another product of the early-century boom and one that still endures is the *Los Angeles Examiner* (combined now with the old *Herald*) founded in 1903 to compete with the powerful *Los Angeles Times.*

The growth of new towns mirrored the vigor of the central city. Long Beach, which 60 Methodist colonists had founded precariously in 1882, finally incorporated as a city in 1897. Beverly Hills began its opulent existence in 1907. Three years earlier, an entrepreneur named Albert

From 1901 to 1969, the two orange and black cars of Angels Flight, Olivet and Sinai, delighted passengers with the ascent and descent of the miniature cable car line. As one car ascended, the other descended and they met midway. Located on Third Street between Hill and Olive in Bunker Hill, the construction of the arch at the entrance of Angel's Flight was just beginning in 1909.

Beach scene at Venice, which started in 1905 as a cultural center, complete with canals, gondoliers and a restaurant shaped like a ship. But in the 1920s, public tastes changed and Venice was turned into an amusement park.

Kinney built fifteen miles of concrete canals radiating from a core he hoped to turn into a cultural showcase named Venice. Alas for plans — people stayed away in droves until Kinney replaced high artistry with vaudeville acts and sideshow freaks. Then Venice throve. Another slow beginner was Avalon on Santa Catalina Island, 27 miles from the harbor at Wilmington. Success remained elusive until 1919. That year William Wrigley Jr. took over, started glass-bottom boats plying the harbor, lined the crescent-shaped shore with palm trees and Spanish-style houses and hotels and put troubadors dressed in Spanish clothing in strategic places. One more southern California success story was begun. But there were even bigger success stories in that energetic era.

The fight for a harbor

During the earlier boom of the late 1880s, Los Angeles' civic leaders noticed that the region was rapidly outgrowing the facilities of its patchwork harbor at San Pedro Bay. If improvements were not made, commerce might swing to the superlative natural port at San Diego. What then would happen to Los Angeles' dream of being southern California's chief supply center?

The temporary collapse of the boom did not silence the question. To the contrary — improving the harbor became an integral part of the Los Angeles Chamber of Commerce's strategy to revitalize the region's growth. In 1890 the organization prevailed upon the federal government to send a group of Army engineers to California to study the feasibility of dredging out a harbor to accommodate the largest existing ships and protecting the artificial port with a two-mile-long breakwater of massive stones. Although costs were estimated at $4 million — a chilling sum for the time and place — the engineers reported favorably. Rejoicing proved premature, however;

The Seventh Regiment before departure for the Spanish-American war in 1898.

for as soon as the plan was announced, it ran head-on into the opposition of Collis P. Huntington, president of the Southern Pacific Railroad. Water traffic was one development the otherwise cooperative rail line did not want fostered.

Early in the 1870s, the Southern Pacific had obtained control of Phineas Banning's Los Angeles & San Pedro Railroad as part of its price for giving the city of Los Angeles transcontinental connections. The Southern Pacific had also purchased the tracks of the little Los Angeles & Independence Railroad that ran east from Santa Monica Bay to the city and had torn up the tracks. The destruction completed, ocean traffic could reach Los Angeles only over the company's rails from San Pedro.

The railroad used its monopoly like an ax. For one instance, freight rates across the Pacific from Hong Kong were lower than the costs the Southern Pacific demanded for hauling the same cargo a mere twenty miles by land from San Pedro to Los Angeles. Such manipulations kept ocean competition from holding land rates to reasonable levels and acted as one more damper on the Chamber's plans for turning Los Angeles into a major supply center.

Hope of breaking the stranglehold came unexpectedly from an upstart line called the Terminal Railroad. Although few people realized it at the time, the Terminal was a front for the Union Pacific, which hoped to reach Los Angeles and the ocean by slanting southwest through Utah and Nevada to southern California. During a careful study of all property deeds in the San Pedro-Wilmington area, the Terminal's scouts found a chink in the collar of land that the Southern Pacific had forged around San Pedro Bay. In 1891, the Terminal people gleefully started running surveys toward the bay for tracks of their own.

To counter the threat, Collis Huntington quietly bought up the beach front at Santa Monica, including the single gap in the bordering bluffs by which a railroad could reach the shore. He then announced that the bay floor at San Pedro was too rocky to hold the pilings needed to support major wharves and that the Southern Pacific was going to shift its operations to a new wharf — the longest in the nation — at Santa Monica. Certainly the federal government would also see the wisdom of transferring its harbor appropriations to the same area. Since Huntington's lobbyists in Washington could apply enormous pressure to many Congressmen, the remark was no idle threat.

SEA AND SAND: Rock is hauled up the Main Channel (top) for the San Pedro Breakwater (above), which was completed in 1912. However, some young Californians took to the sand instead of the sea to do some sailing (below).

Nearly a decade of intense maneuvering followed. A Free Harbor League was formed in 1895 to assist the Chamber in its work to secure the San Pedro site. A prime mover in these efforts was pugnacious Harrison Gray Otis, publisher of the raucous, unrestrained *Los Angeles Times.* Senator Stephen White of California was also won to the cause as was practically every person who owned real estate between Los Angeles and San Pedro. They had plenty of opponents. People who owned property between Los Angeles and Santa Monica and wanted to see the city grow west rather than south leaped to support Huntington. So did many Congressmen and Senators. Although several investigating committees reported in favor of improving San Pedro Harbor rather than Santa Monica, the river and harbor bills that reached the floor of Congress (without ever quite passing) all favored Santa Monica.

Huntington's power was waning, however. He was ill (he would die shortly) and in serious trouble with the government on other fronts. In 1899 the tide turned. The development of the San Pedro-Wilmington complex was authorized, and construction of a huge breakwater began.

The fight was not finished, however. The Southern Pacific still owned enough land in the district to stymie changes it did not like. In exasperation, the businessmen of Los Angeles decided that the harbor could not be completed satisfactorily unless it were municipalized. But political realities presented formidable roadblocks. Neither San Pedro nor Wilmington was capable of handling so great a civic project. Los Angeles, which could, was twenty miles from the waterfront, and state law allowed only contiguous cities to consolidate.

ON THE BEACH: Free parking (top) in 1900 and sheep dipping at Bixby Ranch (above) in 1901, both at Long Beach. Balboa Park (below) boasted an elaborate bath house.

To solve the problem, Los Angeles asked its voters to annex to the city a narrow strip of land running south beside the railroad tracks to the port cities. The proposal was accepted by an overwhelming majority, and — thanks to this shoestring — the cities were now contiguous. Somewhat more reluctantly, San Pedro and Wilmington agreed in 1909 to let themselves be consolidated with their neighbor to the north. The harbor became a Los Angeles municipal project, and in 1912 the huge breakwater was completed.

Again timing was auspicious. Hawaii had been annexed, and the Philippine Islands had been awarded to the United States in 1898. The nation now faced Asia as well as Europe. In 1903 President Theodore Roosevelt showed the importance of this change by winning concessions for a trans-Isthmian canal from the new American-conceived Republic of Panama. After eleven years of work (1904-1914), the Panama Canal opened for traffic. Meanwhile, Los Angeles demonstrated her appreciation by inaugurating the first Los Angeles-Honolulu Transpacific Yacht Race in 1906.

The effects of all this were dazzling. In 1899 when work on the breakwater began, the port at San Pedro Bay had handled 200,000 tons of freight. By 1912, the year the breakwater was completed, the figure had risen to 1.9 million. After that the climb was slow but steady, reaching 4.3 million tons in 1920 — the same year that the census takers confirmed that Los Angeles' population — 577,000 — had leapfrogged past San Francisco's 507,000. Five years later in 1924, the Los Angeles harbor again surpassed San Francisco's, handling 22 million tons. It was the busiest port on the Pacific. Long Beach joined the bustle. Aided by the United States Navy's need for facilities, the two cities kept adding breakwaters until the ponderous stone walls extended for more than eight miles through the bay, furnishing shelter to 6,000 acres of channels and anchorages. Sheer determination had turned an inland city into a major handler of salt water traffic!

The power of water

Among the least noticed of the Los Angeles Basin's many resources is its magnificent aquifer. During the course of millions of years, the erosion of the mountains immediately to the north has created, between the foothills and the ocean, broad beds of sediments and gravels many hundreds of feet deep. Hydraulic engineers have estimated that the tiny interstices among this infinitude of particles can contain 20 million acre-feet of water within economical pumping range. (An acre-foot equals 325,829 gallons, enough to cover one acre one foot deep. Thus there are, in 20 million acre-feet, about 6.5 trillion gallons.) During each "average" year, moreover, another 850,000 acre-feet of rain and snow water percolate into the aquifer, most of it from the bordering mountains, some of which exceed 9,000 in elevation. Whatever part of this inflow cannot be held in the porous sediments leaks out into the ocean.

Such quantities sound inexhaustible, but they are not. By 1900, Los Angeles County held 170,000 people, the bulk of them living south of the mountains. More thousands lived in the adjacent western parts of San Bernardino and Riverside counties and in Orange County, the latter of which had been carved out of the southeastern part of Los Angeles County in 1889. To take care of the population's water needs, 10,000 wells driven by powerful turbine pumps had been drilled into the alluvial plains between San Fernando and Long Beach, and there were more wells in the water-holding gravels to either side of that strip. As for the Los Angeles, San Gabriel and Santa Ana rivers, they had long since been completely utilized.

An inevitable conclusion followed. If the Los Angeles Municipal Water Company ever ran short — it had taken over the private delivery system within the city in 1902 — it would not be able to probe for additional supplies in the vicinity without running into a hornet's nest of lawsuits. Yet if the city grew very much, it most certainly would run dry. What could be done?

Fred Eaton, a man of considerable experience — superintendent of the city's principal private water company until 1886 and mayor of Los Angeles from 1898-1900 — proposed an answer. Far north of Los Angeles a stream called the Owens River ran for a hundred miles through a deep, narrow trough between the eastern slope of the Sierra Nevada and the Inyo and White mountains before losing itself in a landlocked sink called Owens Lake. Inasmuch as Owens Valley lay about 3,000 feet higher than the city, river water turned into a concrete-lined aqueduct could be pulled south by gravity alone, though 53 miles of tunnels and twelve of inverted steel siphons would have to be constructed to carry the stream through intervening mountains and across dozens of chasms. The 3,000-foot drop also meant that considerable hydroelectric power could be generated along the way.

Eaton carried his vision to the business community through the Los Angeles Chamber of Commerce and to a former employee and long-time friend, William Mulholland. Mulholland lacked formal education but possessed a prodigious memory, a flair for mathematics and (behind his walrus mustache) a scathing tongue. He had emigrated as a 19-year-old sailor from his native Ireland to New York City in 1874. Four years of wandering led him to Los Angeles, where Fred Eaton had given him a job as ditch tender for the Los Angeles Water Company. Intensely ambitious, the young laborer spent his spare time studying geology and engineering. He did so well that when Eaton retired as superintendent in 1886, Mulholland stepped into his shoes. When the city acquired the company, the former ditch tender, now in his mid-40s, stayed on as superintendent and chief engineer of the municipal water department.

In September 1904, under a punishing sun, the two men traveled across 240 miles of desert to the lower part of Owens Valley in a buggy drawn

From the beginning, harbor development was one of the main issues of Los Angeles. The Chamber of Commerce set up a harbor campaign. One of the first moves was to invite all senators and representatives to visit Los Angeles and San Pedro. Many responded, and in May 1889, the Chamber hosted a delegation from Washington. The group boarded a boat to tour the coastal area where they could see the need for a deep-water harbor.

Earlier that year the Chamber had pushed for the passage of a Congressional bill that would provide for a special board of Army engineers to examine the coast from Point Dume to Point Capistrano and to recommend construction of a deep-water harbor at some point. The bill was passed in the summer of 1890. By the end of 1891, the engineers filed a report which unequivocally favored San Pedro and advised an appropriation of approximately $3 million for the project.

Local squabbles immediately arose over the site selection, and the proponents of Santa Monica as a site managed to stall any action for several years. In 1894, the Chamber polled its entire membership by secret ballot, confirming that they overwhelmingly favored the location of a deep-water harbor in San Pedro. Over the next four years, the Chamber prepared resolutions and circular letters, organized public meetings, presented the facts about the harbor to the Eastern newspaper publishers and roused public sentiment in favor of the project. A Free Harbor League was formed in 1895 to assist the Chamber in its efforts to secure the San Pedro site. In the spring of 1896, the following appropriation was up for consideration before the House of Representatives: $400,000 for the San Pedro inner harbor; nothing for the outer harbor; $2.9 million for Santa Monica.

Naturally the dispute over location flared up again. The Chamber Board of Directors reaffirmed its position for San Pedro. After a hard-fought battle, California Senator Stephen White succeeded in holding up the appropriation pending another survey by the Board of Engineers. The long fight was won in 1897, when the Board of Engineers reported four-to-one for San Pedro. Construction of a deep-water harbor at San Pedro began in 1899.

William Mulholland once tended the ditch of Los Angeles' antiquated water system. In 1902, when the city overtook the private water company for which he worked, Mulholland became chief engineer. As such, he proposed and oversaw the construction of the Los Angeles Aqueduct.

IN OWENS VALLEY: Bordered by the Sierra and the Inyo mountain ranges, the Owens Valley was verdant before the construction of the Los Angeles Aqueduct which drained the area of its water. Creeks bubbled through the valley (bottom) and ranches flourished (below).

by a pair of horses. The trip convinced Mulholland that the aqueduct was feasible from an engineering standpoint. Other obstacles stood in the way, however. One was the new (1902) federal Reclamation Service, which was contemplating a program of ditch and canal building that would double the 60,000 acres already under irrigation in the valley.

The other hurdle was Fred Eaton himself. He wanted to form a syndicate to buy water rights from valley ranchers and then lease the water to the city. Mulholland demurred. The city's municipal system, he insisted, should not be dependent on private whim for its water. In his opinion, both Eaton and the Reclamation Service would have to be edged out of the way before the aqueduct could be made truly viable.

Both aims were accomplished. J.B. Lippincott, the head of the Reclamation Service's southwestern division was a close friend of both Eaton and Mulholland — and was also drawing a consultant's fee from the city while working for the federal government. Lippincott persuaded the Reclamation Service to withdraw from the valley on the grounds that far more people would be benefited by an urban than by a rural project — a view, incidentally, with which President Theodore Roosevelt was in full accord. Meanwhile, Eaton was consoled for lost water sales — the city paid him $450,000 for a reservoir site that occupied less than one-fifth of his 12,000-acre ranch near the head of the valley. The ranch, along with 5,000 cattle, had cost him $500,000.

Eaton purchased from farmers numerous rights that he turned over to the city — for a fee. Simultaneously ten wealthy Angelenos formed a syndicate to purchase several thousand dry acres in the northeastern part of the San Fernando Valley — the very point where the aqueduct would dump its waters. Among the ten were Henry Huntington and Edward Harriman — whose trolley cars would soon be serving the area — and the editors of three of Los Angeles's leading newspapers. All this time, not one paper breathed a word.

On Saturday, July 29, 1905, one day after the last necessary purchase had been completed, Harrison Gray Otis of the *Los Angeles Daily Times* (the paper's title then) scooped his rivals — and partners — by devoting his entire front page to "the most important movement for the development of Los Angeles in all the city's history."

From then on, events moved at headlong pace. Within six weeks, the city's voters passed — by a margin of 14-1 — a $1.5-million bond issue. This made a $50,000 part payment to Fred Eaton for his reservoir site and for financing detailed surveys for the aqueduct. The next year — in spite of heated lobbying in Congress by electric companies that feared competition from municipal generating plants along the aqueduct's course — the federal government granted the city the necessary right of way across the public domain. That achieved, the voters on June 12, 1907, passed a $23-million bond issue to pay for the most ambitious construction project in the nation, except for the Panama Canal.

Beginning in 1908, 5,000 men labored on the project through five blistering summers and five gale-swept winters. They were inspired by bonuses for exceeding their daily quotas. Supplies came to them over a specially constructed railroad and a paved highway. The city manufactured its own concrete to Mulholland's exacting specifications and built five small generating plants beside small Sierra streams to furnish electricity for power machines. When bills were toted up at the end of the effort in 1913, they came to $24,460,000 — $40,000 less than Mulholland's original estimate.

At first the farming communities of Owens Valley had accepted the Los Angeles expansion in good spirits. Construction opened up jobs and a market for produce and horse feed. It brought in a railroad and a highway. Because the aqueduct intake was in the southern part of the valley, the upstream farmers felt no great pinch although it was evident that, as soon as water began flowing through Mulholland's ditch, agricultural expansion would end.

But if expansion ended in Owens Valley, the reverse was true in Los Angeles. For years residents of the distant city had dreamed of a "Greater Los Angeles" spreading across all but the most mountainous parts of the county. As soon as aqueduct water reached them, they used it as a tool in realizing that desire. Any town that wanted to share in the Owens Valley bonanza had to consent to annexation to Los Angeles. In addition it had to pay, retroactively, its share of the canal's construction plus a four percent "delinquency" fee.

Pasadena, Long Beach, Beverly Hills, Santa Monica and a handful of other vigorous communities disdained the offer. They were confident they had ample water in their aquifers, and they desired to maintain their independence. The rest scrambled, including San Fernando Valley (but not the town of San Fernando) with its 170 square miles. By 1927 Los Angeles had swelled from the old pueblo's 28.1 square miles to 441 — by far the largest area embraced at that time by any city in the United States.

Nor was water the whole story. In 1910 while construction of the aqueduct was still underway, the Los Angeles electorate had increased the city's heavy bonded indebtedness by voting $3.5 million for building hydro-electric generating plants beside the canal. These plants were in addition to and much larger than the ones Mulholland had erected for powering his construction camps. Their purpose was to lure industry to Greater Los Angeles by providing ample electricity at cheap rates.

The city's privately owned power companies offered to buy power from the new stations and distribute it through their own systems. Although the plan would have spared the city the expense of building transmission lines, an advisory referendum in 1911 showed that Los Angeles citizens overwhelmingly endorsed the principal of municipal distribution of power. For that reason, the new Depatment of Water and Power rejected the plan. In 1914 the voters authorized the spending of $6.5 million on a municipal system. The competition that ensued was long and costly; complete victory did not come to the city until 1936.

As the Owens Valley ranchers and merchants watched the growth, second thoughts came. True, Los Angeles had turned over to them the small hydroelectric plants Mulholland had built for use on the aqueduct. True, the valley now had a railroad and an automobile highway that brought increasing numbers of summer tourists to their mountain-girt villages. But they began to analyze more carefully.

When a severe drought occurred early in the 1920s, purchasing agents working for the city moved northward into the heart of the valley, seeking still more water rights. The alarmed local people proposed an alternative. So far no dam had been built on the site the city had purchased from Fred Eaton. But if a big reservoir were created behind a dam 150 feet high, the ranchers felt it would capture enough of the Sierra's heavy spring run-off to provide ample water for every user, including the expensive and critically important canal-side generating plants.

Unhappily for the proposed compromise, a reservoir as large as the ranchers wanted would engulf most of Fred Eaton's ranch. In exchange he asked $1 million. At that Mulholland exploded because Los Angeles had already paid Eaton $450,000. Mulholland maintained the rock at the Eaton site was not satisfactory for a dam of the size the ranchers advocated. As a result, the Department of Water and Power found another reservoir site in San Francisquito Canyon near the head of the Santa Clara Valley, much closer to Los Angeles than Eaton's ranch. There the additional storage dam the city needed was erected in rock that turned out to be no more stable than that at Eaton's site.

Meanwhile the valley ranchers formed a union of sorts in the hope of stabilizing prices for their land and water rights. To compound the problem, the village merchants demanded "reparations" for business they said they had lost when old customers had sold out under Los Angeles' pressure and had moved away.

Cool clear water: The Los Angeles Aqueduct

By 1888, water was becoming more and more scarce. The city was entirely dependent upon the Los Angeles River and local wells for its water supply. After a number of dry years, the river barely met the city's needs. It was evident that a growing population could not be served by these local sources. Los Angeles Chamber of Commerce officials working with civic leaders, including William Mulholland (superintendent of both the privately owned water company and the new municipal water department), developed a plan to bring water from the Owens River, 250 miles northeast of Los Angeles. Plans were formulated to construct an aqueduct which could move water for two million people. Investors, however, rejected the proposals as impracticable.

In spite of numerous set-backs, the Chamber persisted. It spearheaded drives for bond issues including one for $1.5 million approved in 1905 and authorizing the purchase of water rights and rights-of-way. A second bond issue in 1907 passed ten-to-one in favor of $23 million for aqueduct construction.

Of all the developments in this period, the construction of the Los Angeles Aqueduct stands out as the most significant. It was the success in obtaining an ample water supply that made it possible to sustain the steadily growing population.

On November 5, 1913, approximately 30,000 people gathered in the northern part of the San Fernando Valley, recently annexed to Los Angeles, to watch the first waters from the High Sierras plunge down the open aqueduct. It was the culmination of a seemingly impossible project in which Chamber leadership was a moving force.

Opening of the Los Angeles Aqueduct, November 5, 1913.

TENNIS, ANYONE? William Young, an Englishman who moved to Santa Monica in 1879, introduced tennis to California. Within a few years, the sport enjoyed immense popularity, especially among the affluent. Early-day tennis players (top) might have played at Las Tanas Rancho (top right), the state's first tennis club, established circa 1884. Tennis champion Malla Mallory (above) played at Long Beach, 1910.

BEFORE DISNEYLAND: Famous Polish-born actress Helen Modjeska moved to the Anaheim area in 1876 where she helped found a Utopian colony. After the colony began to fail, she successfully resumed her acting career.

Ill-will sparked into violence. To call attention to their plight, armed bands of valley people first blew up a section of the aqueduct in 1924. Later they opened a key waste gate and for four days dumped the canal water onto the desert. State investigators poured in to study the situation, and Greater Los Angeles — which by then was feeling the pinch of the drought — resumed negotiations.

Believing that their strategy was working, the ranchers hiked their prices still higher. When Los Angeles resisted, more dynamite exploded. Armed guards rushed in from the city, and newspapers across the nation — most of them sympathetic to the toilers of the valley — began turning out sensational copy about California's "Little Civil War." Fortunately, no blood was ever shed.

It was a short war. Leaders of the rancher opposition were the brothers Mark and Wilfred Watterson, owners of five small banks in the valley. During the uproars, they had embezzled their depositors' funds — the better to defend the valley, they said. When caught, the Wattersons were sentenced to prison. Nearly every valley resident lost something in the debacle, and opposition crumbled.

Not even this ended the sorry tale. On March 12, 1928, the San Francisquito Canyon dam collapsed. A thunder of water smashed through the towns of the Santa Clara Valley, killing at least 385 people (an indeterminate number more were buried under debris or washed out into the sea). There were tens of millions of dollars worth of damage. The shaken city paid every claim presented to it without contest. In the Owens Valley where property values had dropped drastically, purchasing agents continued buying land and water at inflated 1923 prices. Soon Los Angeles owned more than 95 percent of the valley farmlands and town plots. Most of it was leased back to the original occupants.

Not every Owens Valley resident considered the program as generous as did the city's Department of Water and Power. In effect the tenants had no voice in Los Angeles' political and community matters that concerned them, no way to control the land and the water on which the livelihood of so many of them depended.

Los Angeles residents reacted differently. Though valley stubbornness and dynamite (plus the devastation wrought by the San Francisquito disaster) had ballooned costs far higher than anyone could have anticipated, the assurance of water and hydroelectric power had helped create the new industrial boom for which Los Angeles residents yearned.

LA FIESTA: In April 1894, the Merchants Association began promoting La Fiesta de Los Angeles to help the city overcome economic difficulties and attract visitors from San Francisco's Mid-winter Fair. Costumed Fiesta-goers marched to city hall and usurped control from the city council, paraded with decorated floats and elected a queen. The Fiesta was so successful that young and old alike (right) celebrated it for several years, as an 1897 poster (above) indicates.

OLE! Ranch life of Spanish southern California was romanticized during the latter part of the nineteenth century with folk music and dancing (right inset) and festive barbecues, for which a steer was traditionally killed (above), at Plummer's Ranch in Hollywood.

CAMPING IN CALIFORNIA: Angelenos began to invade the mountains around their city as early as the 1860s. In San Bernadino County, a mountain auto line trucked tourists on holiday (right) bound for Big Bear Lodge (below), Big Bear Lake (bottom) and Bartlett's Camp (bottom right, facing page). A pony trip wound its way to the summit of Mount Lowe (bottom left, facing page). In the Sierra Madres, a mountain camp was established on the west side of Buck Horn Hill (top, facing page).

PALOS VERDES: In 1914, Frank
Vanderlip acquired 16,000 acres
comprising almost all of the Palos
Verdes Peninsula. His plan to turn it
into countryside estates was thwarted by
the depression. An inn (above), 1927,
and a ranch (right), 1935, had been
established before part of the struggling
development was incorporated into Palos
Verdes Estates in 1939.

VAN NUYS: Harvesters worked the
ranches in the San Fernando Valley
(right), circa 1898. However, as
subdivision of the land began in the
early twentieth century, tract offices
began to pop up, like the one at
Sherman Way and Virginia Streets
(above) in Van Nuys, 1912.

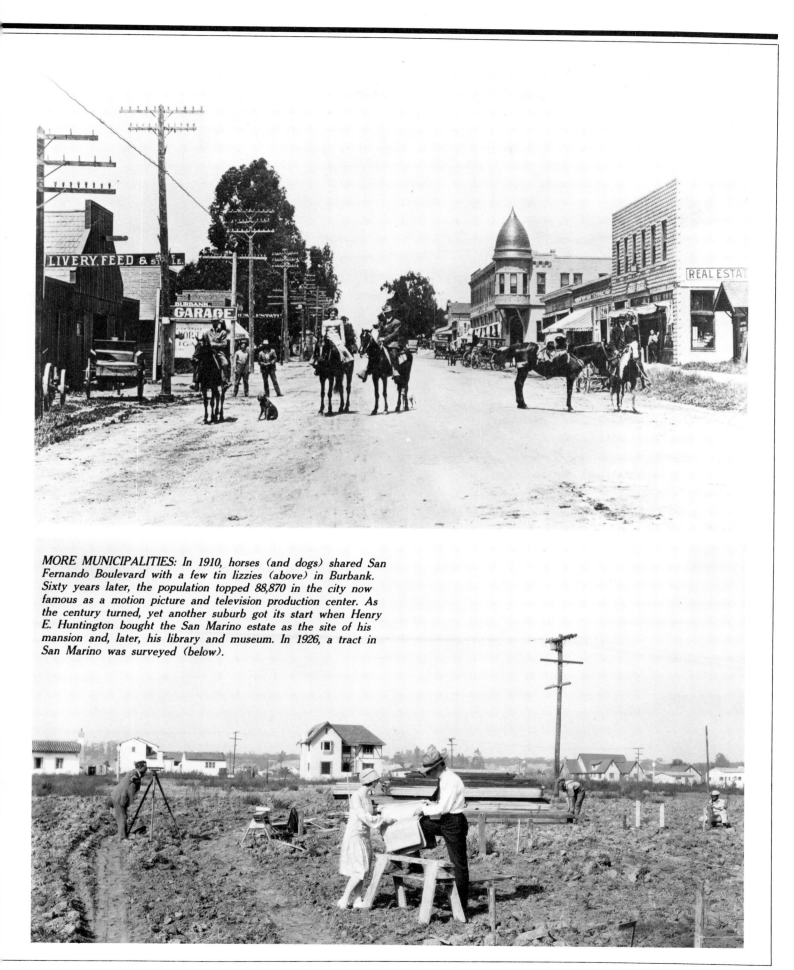

MORE MUNICIPALITIES: In 1910, horses (and dogs) shared San Fernando Boulevard with a few tin lizzies (above) in Burbank. Sixty years later, the population topped 88,870 in the city now famous as a motion picture and television production center. As the century turned, yet another suburb got its start when Henry E. Huntington bought the San Marino estate as the site of his mansion and, later, his library and museum. In 1926, a tract in San Marino was surveyed (below).

THE WAR: Post office workers round the corner of Third and Broadway as they march in a "preparedness day" parade in 1916 (above). In 1920, Los Angeles gives members of the 364th Infantry a hearty welcome home from World War I (top).

Chapter 5

Scrambling for prosperity

A 1908 Tourist car successfully drives through the water at East Lake Park, now known as Lincoln Park.

AerialTrolley Car Co. Inc   Burbank, Cal.
L.W. & E.C. Fawkes, Patentees.

TROLLEY CARS: The "Aerial Swallow"
(above) was a short-lived experiment in
monorail transportation in Burbank in 1907.
The electric trolley, such as those in
Pasadena (below), was a more successful
mode of early-day transportation.

Growing pains

Harrison Gray Otis, owner of the *Los Angeles Times,* was southern California's self-appointed defender of individual liberty. He staunchly opposed the efforts of the Southern Pacific Railroad to establish a harbor monopoly at either San Pedro or Santa Monica because such a monopoly would retard the development of his city — and he really thought of it as *his.* By the same token, he supported the Owens Valley aqueduct because more water would further city growth. It would also produce water for land that he, his son-in-law Harry Chandler and their associates owned in the San Fernando Valley.

It was characteristic, therefore, (and typical of the journalistic style of the day) for Otis to hurl his bitterest invectives — "corpse defacers," "shuffling, shouting scavengers," "putrescent pustules" — and his awesome civic power at anyone attempting to unionize Los Angeles labor. In his opinion, cheap labor was not only good for the *Times* but would also lure industry to the city.

Born in the small town of Marietta, Ohio, on February 10, 1837, Otis obtained some education at a commercial college and much more as a printer's devil. Shortly after his marriage at the age of 22, he enlisted as a private in the Union Army. He fought in fifteen Civil War engagements, was wounded twice, rose to a captaincy and was given the brevet rank of lieutenant colonel in recognition of meritorious service.

Real authority was slow coming to him, however. He worked in the patent office in Washington, edited one newspaper for Army veterans and another in the then-backward village of Santa Barbara, California. Afterwards he spent three years in Alaska — where he was thoroughly miserable — as a government agent trying to run down seal poachers and bootleggers. In 1882 he obtained a part interest in the *Los Angeles Times* (founded the year before), fell out with his partners and in 1886 took over sole control of the struggling morning paper. The boom of the late 1880s filled his paper with real estate ads and opened the way to lucrative speculations on the side.

His first serious clash with union labor came in 1890. The land frenzy had faded, and as business grew dull, the town's four newspapers cut wages by 20 percent. During the strike that resulted, three of the papers came to terms. Otis did not, and by hiring scab labor managed to stay open. Resentments still rankled on both sides four years later when a nationwide strike was called against the Pullman Company that provided sleeping cars for railroads. Trains throughout the West stopped running.

The disruption to local economy led Otis to publish a series of editorial attacks against the whole philosophy of striking. His theme, expressed in vitriolic language, was that every citizen had a full right to pursue any lawful occupation he chose free from outside interference. Unionists retorted by ringing the *Times* building with pickets, intimidating its carriers and destroying as many papers as they could find. They also boycotted firms that advertised in the *Times.* That tactic really made Otis's juices boil. Organized labor, he vowed, would have to be driven out of Los Angeles and kept out.

To shore up his force, Otis prevailed on the area's leading firms to join together in 1896 in one grand employers' body called The Merchants and Manufacturers Association (commonly M & M). Any business that broke ranks by truckling with any union answered to either Otis or the M & M. While opponents criticized their methods, strong arguments were advanced in favor of their strategies. Supporters believed that the city would not grow without industry, and industry would not come unless it was offered cheaper labor than was available elsewhere in California — most specifically San Francisco.

The Bay City had long been the leading manufacturing center of the

FOURTH ESTATE: *Harrison Gray Otis (above) and partners purchased Mirror Printing, Binding and Ruling (below) in the early 1880s, along with the* Los Angeles Times *newspaper. Nathan Cole was the first editor of the* Times *which was housed in a building at First and Broadway Streets (bottom) until it was blown up in 1910.*

EVIDENCE OF UNREST: The Los Angeles Times building (above) was dynamited in September 1910, killing 22 employees. Controlling social unrest was one of the duties of mounted policemen (below), circa 1900.

west coast, and its industries were thoroughly unionized. Wages averaged 30 percent higher than in Los Angeles, where a constant inflow of uprooted homeseekers and job hunters provided employers with a ready pool of workers who lacked a substantial base of support in their attempts to better conditions. As a matter of self-protection, San Francisco labor decided to supply that base. Otherwise (so the northern workers feared), San Francisco employers would try to cut wages to Los Angeles levels. Failing in that, some employers might migrate south, taking their jobs with them. As a counter, labor organizers decided to invade Otis's country.

The political mix

The confrontations between union labor and the Merchants and Manufacturers Association took place against a confused political background. Throughout the nation, reformers who called themselves Progressive Republicans were challenging the conservatives of their own party, and Socialists were pulling into their ranks the disenchanted Populists and Democrats. Able representatives of both groups were keeping Los Angeles in a ferment, and inevitably the labor problem became intangled with their activities.

Leader of the Progressives was a wealthy physician, Dr. John Randolph Haynes. His goal, like that of his fellow believers, was to reestablish honest and efficient government by breaking what he considered to be corrupt alliances between business interests and political machines. The weapon on which Progressives everywhere relied was the restoration of power to the people by means of the initiative (the passage of legislation by popular ballot), the referendum (the right to veto, by popular ballot, acts passed by the legislature) and the recall (the removal, by ballot, of an official before his term had expired).

Los Angeles' contribution to this program was the nation's first use of the recall in 1904 to depose a city councilman who had voted to award municipal printing to the *Times* even though that paper's bid had been $15,000 higher than its nearest competitor. Five years later a corrupt Democratic politician, Mayor Arthur Harper, received similar treatment for forcing underworld characters — especially prostitutes — to buy protection by investing in worthless stock he was selling. As Harper's replacement, the reformers elected a bewhiskered innocent named George Alexander.

The victories had a painful side effect — they threw the old-line Democratic and Republican parties into disarray. Chief beneficiaries of the breakdown were the Socialists, led by a young labor lawyer, Job Harriman.

In Los Angeles, as elsewhere in the nation, workers — outraged by economic inequities arising from the country's rapid rush into industrialization — were joining the Socialist party and shouting approval of inflammatory talk about class warfare. To complicate matters in the city, the surge coincided with the arrival of union organizers from San Francisco and other union centers. Although many workers were not Socialists and some Socialists were not laborers, they often participated in each other's rallies and marched together in noisy parades.

The summer of 1910 brought tensions to a head. California's Progressive Republicans picked as their candidate for governor stocky, round-faced Hiram Johnson whose main claim to attention was his successful prosecution of San Francisco's leading grafters. While campaigning in Los Angeles, Johnson rocked conservative Republicans back on their heels with a vicious personal attack on Harrison Otis. "In San Francisco," Johnson declaimed during a major speech (in typical vituperative style of the day), "we have drunk to the very dregs of infamy . . . But we have nothing so vile, nothing so low, nothing so debased, as Harrison Gray Otis."

During this bitter and (for Johnson) successful campaign, a mounting wave of strikes swept Los Angeles. Upset by the blows, Otis and the M & M persuaded the city council and the mayor, George Alexander, to

pass an anti-picketing law that allowed the police to arrest not only pickets but even persons caught "speaking in public streets in loud or unusual tones." Hundreds of arrests and convictions followed.

To counter the move, John Joseph McNamara, secretary-treasurer of the militant International Association of Bridge and Structural Iron Workers Union, decided on violence. (Although McNamara's headquarters were in Indianapolis, his interest in the Los Angeles situation was direct, for the Iron Workers local there was on strike.) He ordered his brother James and associate Ortie McManigal to travel to southern California and teach them that the unions, too, could play rough.

Shortly before midnight on September 30, 1910, James McNamara placed a suitcase filled with dynamite in a narrow passageway separating two sections of the *Times* plant. Many employees — the actual count was close to a hundred — were inside preparing the morning edition. He tripped the timing device and ran for cover.

At 1:07 a.m. on October 1, the dynamite exploded. The force of the blast caused several tons of ink stored nearby to erupt into flame. Instantly the building was an inferno. Residents who rushed out to watch the spectacle felt it was a wonder that only 17 persons were hurt and 20 killed.

Recriminations flew. Otis roared that unionists were to blame. Union members who knew nothing more definite about causes than Otis did, placed the blame on a leaky gas line that the *Times* had neglected to repair. Some even suggested that the publisher had been callous enough to destroy his own plant in order to discredit the labor movement.

The district attorney's office, the Merchant and Manufacturers Association and Mayor Alexander hired top-notch detectives to ferret out the truth. The most successful was the mayor's sleuth William J. Burns who had done yeoman work for Hiram Johnson and the other prosecutors during the San Francisco graft cases. Burns caught up with Ortie McManigal, secured a confession from him in exchange for a promise of immunity, then arranged for the arrest of the McNamara brothers and hustled them back to Los Angeles without regard for the niceties of the law. Both men pleaded not guilty.

Crying frame-up, labor throughout the United States rallied behind the McNamaras. Contributions poured in to a defense fund. Famed lawyer Clarence Darrow was prevailed on to take the case for a $50,000 fee and a war chest of $200,000 to cover expenses. As his chief assistant, he chose Job Harriman. Harriman's involvement in the case was gall to Otis and his supporters.

The Los Angeles city elections came a year after the general election of 1910. At the primaries Harriman (the Socialists' candidate for mayor) had picked up so many votes that he had almost clinched the office then and

H. Gaylord Wilshire was 23 when he moved to California from Ohio in 1884. On the West Coast, he raised oranges and walnuts, mined gold, patented a therapeutic electric belt and, at one point, had a monopoly on all Los Angeles billboards. His most significant investment in real estate was the land he bought near MacArthur Park; the boulevard bearing his name was to become one of the city's most prominent. When the real estate boom collapsed, Wilshire found himself a great deal poorer and, like many others of that day, turned to socialism; he issued "Wilshire's Journal" to support that cause, ran for Congress and lost.

At 3050 Wilshire Boulevard was Bullocks Wilshire, the nation's first surburban department store, which opened in September 1929. Co-founders John G. Bullock and P.G. Winnett had faith that the auto age would speed the migration west and encourage shoppers to patronize the store then surrounded by undeveloped land. The art deco structure featured a distinctive rear entrance where attendants met patrons and parked their cars.

there. Politicians of all persuasions were freely predicting that he would complete his victory at a run-off election against Alexander on December 5, 1911.

To businessmen the prospect was disheartening. Anti-labor legislation would be revoked if Harriman won, and widespread unionization would follow. Equally distressing were the probable financial consequences. Approximately $17 million dollars worth of aqueduct, harbor and hydroelectric bonds remained unsold in the city's vaults. When Eastern investors learned that labor-plagued Los Angeles had elected a Socialist as mayor, what chance would those bonds have of being sold?

Clarence Darrow was equally disheartened. He had soon grown convinced that his clients were guilty and that the best service he could render them — he was philosophically opposed to the death penalty — was to save their lives. But Darrow feared that the prosecution was building an airtight case, and he was further depressed when one of his associates was caught trying to bribe prospective jurors, and Darrow himself was indicted for the crime. (Later, after a highly emotional trial, he was acquitted on one charge of bribery and escaped the other when the jurors hearing the case were unable to reach a verdict.)

Shortly before the McNamara trial was due to open, journalist Lincoln Steffens — in Los Angeles to cover the story for Eastern newspapers — suggested that prosecutors and defendants negotiate a deal that would spare the city an inflammatory confrontation. Darrow agreed.

Exactly what went on behind the scenes will never be known. Apparently the prosecution did not want to make martyrs out of the McNamaras by executing them on charges that many people believed were fabricated. Here, too, was a way to discredit Harriman. And so, with the judge's acquiescence, the deal was made. Four days before the run-off election for mayor, the McNamaras entered a jammed courtroom and changed their pleas to guilty. John Joseph McNamara, the secretary-treasurer of the Iron Workers Union, was sentenced to 15 years in prison for conspiring to destroy the newspaper building. His brother James who had planted the dynamite, was given life. Harriman lost the election. Labor's efforts to organize the city were routed.

Largely because of World War I and the Russian Revolution, organized labor stayed discredited in Los Angeles for another quarter of a century. About 1920 a "Red scare" swept the United States, and California, like 23 other states, passed a Criminal Syndicalism Act that made a felony out of even belonging to an organization that advocated sabotage, violence or terrorism to effect changes in the country's industrial or political order. Most states soon dropped the measure. After several years, California followed suit. The law dovetailed with the fears of the conservative small farmers, village lawyers and merchants and retiring country preachers who flocked into the area during the renewed boom of the early 1920s. For them, "Red" acted as a code word that bound strangers together in a common cause and gave them a defense against their own insecurities.

In 1923 an IWW strike at the San Pedro harbor led to repressive action by the police. During a single roundup, more than 700 persons were arrested and herded into a stockade at Griffith Park. Socialist writer Upton Sinclair was clapped into jail for mounting a podium on private land near an inderdicted gathering place and reading from the Constitution of the United States. Citizen vigilante groups reinforced the police, and within a month the strike was broken.

If anything, success intensified the hysteria. The Los Angeles police department formed a special "Red Squad" to maintain control over the situation. Membership in unions fell drastically and did not improve until the advent in the mid-1930s of New Deal laws that protected labor's right to organize. The special squad stayed on the job until 1938 when it was abolished by reform mayor Fletcher Bowron who had been elected to the office after his vice-tainted predecessor had been ousted by the use of the second recall in the city's history.

Wilshire Boulevard

The eastern portion of Wilshire was probably a thoroughfare of sorts as early as the days of Spanish settlement. The Spaniards' military road, the Camino Real, roughly followed the present Wilshire to La Brea where it then veered north to the Cahuenga Pass into the San Fernando Valley. When, in 1895, H. Gaylord Wilshire laid out a one-quarter mile tract west of the present MacArthur Park, Wilshire was a dusty country road. Gradually, the road became a boulevard: the segments were joined so the street stretched from Grand Avenue downtown to the ocean in Santa Monica, and the names of the segments (El Camino Viejo, Orange Street, Sixth Street, Los Angeles Avenue, and Nevada Avenue) gave way to "Wilshire Boulevard."

ALONG WILSHIRE: Before its intensive commercial development in the late 1920s, the corner of Wilshire Boulevard and Fairfax Avenue was the site of an airport (bottom right) owned by Charlie Chaplin's brother Sidney. However, by 1929, the "Miracle Mile" along Wilshire between Fairfax and La Brea Avenues (top) was well on its way to becoming one of Los Angeles' major commercial centers. Another early-day landmark of the area was the Ambassador

Hotel (center right), which opened in 1921 on a 23-acre tract facing north on Wilshire, then a dirt road; its fame spread with the Coconut Grove nightclubs there. The hotel also served as the site of the Academy Awards and was where Senator Robert F. Kennedy was shot. The streamlined art deco style of architecture of the late 1930s and early 1940s was popular along Wilshire, seen in Sontag Drug Store (center left) and Coulter's department store (bottom left).

WITH OIL: An early-day oil refinery (below) was erected in 1876, one of the first in the Newhall area. Oil wells sprung up among the residences on Court Street (top right), circa 1901. In 1928, an oil well fire (above) was fought at Santa Fe Springs. The Gilmore Company sold gasoline with labels in Chinese (bottom).

The rise of industry

By 1929 the annual value of manufactured products turned out by the Los Angeles work force had jumped past that of the San Francisco-Oakland area $1.32 billion to $1.17 billion.

No doubt cheap labor had some effect, but more came from other assets the city had been struggling to gain since the turn of the century — cheap water, cheap electricity, good rail connections and a deep-water harbor. Added to those benefits were others that had little to do with wage levels. One was the region's extraordinary growth. During each of the first four years of the 1920s, more than 100,000 new residents had poured into the city alone. Although the influx slowed somewhat thereafter, it and natural increase together had ballooned the county's population from 936,000 in 1920 to 2,208,000 in 1930 — a growth rate (136 percent) that was far greater than that of any other American metropolitan region during the same decade. (The closest rivals were the Detroit metropolitan area with a 68 percent increase and the San Francisco area with 34 percent.) No less important were Los Angeles County's three new, indigenous industries — oil, motion pictures and aviation. They would have drawn workers and their dependents no matter what the union situation was.

Everyone knew that petroleum was a major constituent of the asphalt seeps that bubbled up here and there throughout California. Phineas Banning had tried at an early date to capitalize on some springs on his Wilmington property, and during the 1860s several productive wells had been drilled in Ventura County northwest of Los Angeles. Because of its heavy asphaltum base, however, that first oil had been hard to refine. The kerosene that resulted (provided that there were no explosions along the way) sooted up lamp chimneys and smelled atrocious. Most householders preferred to continue combatting darkness with whale oil from the fleets that still plied the coast and maintained a rendering station near the Palos Verdes Hills southwest of the city.

Heaviness did have one virtue, however. Thick asphalt oil mixed with sand formed good paving material and much was shipped to San Francisco for that purpose. Without sand it could be burned smokily in furnaces as a substitute for the coal that California lacked. Thus there was an oil industry of sorts in the state quite early, but it had next to no impact in Los

Angeles until a gold prospector down on his luck, Edward Doheny, showed up in 1892.

When Doheny learned that there was a market for crude oil, he decided to try to find some close enough to the city to handle with the horse-and-wagon transportation then prevailing. Apparently he did not even travel four miles west to look at the region's most famous tar pits at La Brea beside the dusty road that became Wilshire Boulevard. In addition to being an hour away, that source was locked up inside the old La Brea land grant then owned by the Hancock family. Instead Doheny stayed within the limits of the original pueblo, and in a residential district near Westlake (now MacArthur) Park, he found a small vacant lot that he thought offered promise.

A long-time friend, Charles Canfield, joined him in putting up $400 to buy the property. With pick, shovel and windlass the two men started digging a 4-by-6 foot mine shaft, as ordinary prospectors would. Not until oil fumes threatened to asphyxiate them did they switch to a primitive drill. Eventually they opened up a self-renewing puddle whose contents they dipped up in barrels — about seven a day at first — and then hauled into town to sell as fuel, as a lubricating agent and as a coating to help keep steel pipes from rusting.

At first selling was as hard as digging but soon markets widened. Refining techniques perfected in the East allowed the relatively safe distillation of gasoline. It could be sold as paint thinner, fuel for cooking stoves and as a propellant for motors, mostly on water pumps, but now and then for a new-fangled invention called the automobile with which people were beginning to tinker. California inventors meanwhile produced an improved burner that let train locomotives use diesel oil in place of costly imported coal.

Although Doheny and Canfield soon left Los Angeles to open new fields elsewhere, hundreds of others rushed to the city to exploit the new resource they had found. Empty lots were snapped up first, then houses were bought and moved out of the way, or, if that was inconvenient, clanking derricks were erected in yards. Eight- and ten-horse teams and wide-wheeled freight wagons tore up streets and lawns. A pervasive stink of oil lay over the district, to practically no one's distress.

By fits and starts — for a time overproduction dropped prices from $1.80 a barrel to fifteen cents — the field expanded westward until it surrounded La Brea Ranch. The Hancocks thereupon put down some 70 wells of their own and made a great deal of money. What perpetuated their name, though, was the park that they later presented to the county for the sake of the tar pits which scientists had come to regard as a priceless paleontological treasure house filled with the bones of extinct animals. (Today Hancock Park is also the site of an architecturally imposing complex that houses the Los Angeles County Museum of Art and the George C. Page Museum of La Brea Discoveries which dramatically illustrates the area as it was in the days when dinosaurs roamed the land.)

From about 1900 to 1919, other sections of the state outperformed the county as producers of oil. The laurels returned with a rush, however, thanks to an anticlinal formation that slants along the coast south and southeast of the city. Known as the Newport-Inglewood Fault zone, this area of geologic deformation produced the Long Beach earthquake late in the afternoon of March 10, 1933. In that city and at Compton to the north, the temblor killed 120 people. The tumbling of brick school buildings caused the greatest part of the $50-million damage. But as a balance to that sum are the billions of barrels of oil that lay (much still lies) in the fault zone where the Santa Fe Springs, Huntington Beach, Signal Hill and Wilmington fields geysered into being. Wilmington, the last to be developed, became California's richest and the United States' second richest producer of petroleum.

By the end of 1933, Santa Fe Springs, Huntington Beach and Signal Hill

The Doheny residence, built in the early 1920s, typified the Tudor Revival style of architecture.

Salvation Army workers help the destitute after the 1933 earthquake at Long Beach.

MAKING MOVIES: A new industry thrived on the West Coast — making motion pictures — and it seemed everyone was doing it (top left and right) by the 1920s. From 1927 to 1931, First National Pictures, now Warner Brothers, was at home in Burbank (above). Charlie Chaplin's studio (right), constructed in 1918, was one of Hollywood's first complete motion picture studios.

were producing 689,000 barrels a day. To help move the flood, more than a thousand tankers a year shuttled back and forth through the Panama Canal. Hundreds of freighters brought to the Long Beach and San Pedro harbors the enormous quantities of lumber needed for the quillwork of derricks that sprang up during the frantic race for wealth. In such a situation it did not matter a great deal whether or not unions were around to demand better wages and shorter hours.

The flicks

The movie industry centered on Los Angeles for several reasons. The neighborhood offered a variety of scenic backgrounds — urban streets, mountain trails, Sahara-like deserts and storm-tossed oceans. Another advantage was sunny winters. Because the cameras of the time could not handle indoor lighting, interior scenes were shot in rooms that had no roofs. Obviously a region whose skies were blue most of the year increased working hours manyfold. By the same token, construction crews unhampered by snow and wind could build flimsy sets in quick, money-saving time.

Cheap rents, cheap materials and cheap overhead (including cheap labor), also drew moviemakers to Los Angeles from the East. But the main cost the newcomers wanted to avoid was one imposed by the Motion Picture Patent Company, a would-be monopoly that sought to dominate the industry by forcing producers to buy its film and lease its patented cameras and projectors. To rebels against the high charges, remote California looked attractive indeed, and the westward flight began about 1907.

Many of the newcomers concentrated in the village of Hollywood, west of Los Angeles and north of the La Brea tar pits. It was founded in 1887 as a temperance colony. In 1910 it joined its four square miles and 5,000 people to Los Angeles in order to obtain Owens Valley water. After the consolidation had taken place and the two towns began to intermingle physically, costs rose. This prompted several film makers to seek new locations. One notable migrant was Carl Laemmle, who in 1914 crossed Cahuenga Pass to the edge of San Fernando Valley. There he created Universal City, where producers in a hurry could rent every necessity for standard productions — sets for Western towns, city mansions, rural hovels, barns for cowboy horses, even housing for temporary employees — just step in, gentlemen and for a small fee begin to shoot. (For a small fee tourists, too, can still tour the constantly updated version of Laemmle's vision.)

In spite of the dispersal of the industry, Hollywood and movies became inseparable in the popular mind. If not all the stars lived there, at least those who amounted to anything left their hand and footprints in the cement sidewalk outside Grauman's Chinese Theater. The breathless tales of the gossip magazines revolved around Hollywood, and it was to Hollywood that busloads of tourists went to gape from behind velvet ropes at stars bedecked in diamonds under klieg lights streaking the evening sky.

Profits snowballed unbelievably. As they did, moviemakers quit depending on novelty to attract customers and with dazzling technical skill switched to story-telling. They talked much of art, but the force that guided nine-tenths of their productions was popular desire. The company that first took advantage of the constantly changing technology was the one that waxed fattest, at least until another change started a stampede in a new direction. the most thunderous stampede was the rush to sound, launched in 1927 by Warner Brothers' production of Al Jolson in "The Jazz Singer."

In the mid-1920s even before "The Jazz Singer" had turned the silver screen into a new kind of gold, the motion picture industry of Los Angeles was employing more than 20,000 people and paying them close to $1.5 million each week. Trade journals claimed that the easily shipped, easily handled cans of film accounted for 20 percent of the value of the *entire state's* manufacturing output.

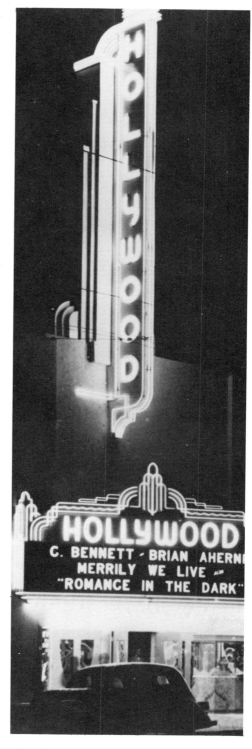

Art deco streamlines are highlighted in neon at the Hollywood Theater.

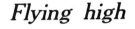

AVIATION HISTORY: A veteran of covered wagon days, Ezra Meeker (above) was photographed on his arrival from New York by oxcart to witness the country's first great air meet. The air carnival was staged in 1910 at Dominguez Field near Los Angeles (top) and drew early-day flyers of all kinds (right and below) bound for blue skies and open air.

Flying high

As in the case of movie making, aviation was drawn to the Los Angeles area by sunny weather that reduced construction costs for hangars and subjected work and flying time to minimal interruptions. To prove the virtue of that sunshine, enthusiasts decided to hold America's first international aviation meet at Dominguez Field, a part of the first Spanish land grant awarded in southern California. The show was scheduled for January 1910, a mere six years after Orville and Wilbur Wright had lifted the world's original motor-driven plane above the beach at Kitty Hawk, North Carolina, for a few heart-stopping seconds. Since French daredevil Louis Paulhon was prevailed upon to attend (bringing his plane with him in a crate), the event truly was international.

The competition went on for ten days to the ecstatic plaudits of constantly swelling throngs. Glen Curtiss broke the world's speed record by flying sixteen miles in just under 24 minutes. Paulhon of France set a world altitude record of 4,140 feet and also dumfounded tens of thousands of people along his route by flying from Dominguez directly over Los Angeles to Arcadia and back — a nonstop roundtrip flight of 45 miles.

From then on, visionaries were convinced that aviation had a future, but though they experimented energetically for many years, financial success eluded them. World War I probably hurt the infant industry more than it helped, for it ended with a glut of planes on the market and no buyers. Donald Douglas went to the financiers of the city to raise $15,000 as a first step toward meeting a post-war Navy contract for three advanced-type flying torpedo carriers. Another trio of Douglas planes called "World Cruisers" drew wide praise for circling the globe successfully in 1924, but in spite of the triumph Douglas did not find his metier until the early 1930s when he entered the commercial field with his famed D-C (Douglas Commercial) series.

By that time, some of the early companies had failed, some had moved away, some had consolidated. Out of the ruck came four that were strong enough to survive the Depression and — at its end — help meet the unprecedented demands of World War II. The four were: Douglas; its hard-driving competitor Lockheed with its pace-setting, all-metal Electra series; Northrop and, last to be incorporated prior to the war, North American. As employers and generators of wealth, the four aviation companies did not compare with either the oil or motion picture industries during the 1920s. But like them, aviation had glamour. It helped assure Angelenos that their city was not only in step with the times but was also looking toward the future.

Future prospects — ultimately that was Los Angeles' main appeal for industry. The Goodyear Tire and Rubber Company, which was thoroughly versed in the field of labor relations, did not care about the open shop when it decided, in 1919, to build a huge branch plant south of the city. Its plans revolved instead around such compelling facts as these — there were more cars per capita in Los Angeles County than in any other comparable region in the United States; an energetically maintained harbor opened a way to the rubber plantations of Asia; a rapidly developing highway network led to ample supplies of cotton and agricultural products in the nearby San Joaquin and Imperial valleys.

Similar reasoning swayed other tire companies to follow Goodyear's suit. Ready markets and cheap transport were the main items prompting the Ford Motor Company and Union Oil Company to erect ultramodern plants in Long Beach. In addition, the Merchants and Manufacturers Association and the Los Angeles Chamber of Commerce sang the virtues of the open shop in attracting industry. The dynamic resource (in addition to climate, water, power and transportation) was people, people, ever growing numbers of people.

Sprawl

The influx of outsiders into the Los Angeles metropolitan area during the 1920s has been called the "flivver migration." For the first time, considerable numbers of new residents arrived by automobile, compounding the congestion already occasioned by the hundreds of thousands of cars (500,000 in 1924) already registered in the county. Excited by the potentials inherent in the migration, business interests and county governments sought to increase momentum by forming in 1920 the All Year Club of Southern California, dedicated to developing the area as a summer as well as a winter resort and drawing visitors other than a wealthy leisured class. The drive worked. Although the new throngs contained several millionaires eyeing homesites along Pasadena's opulent Orange Grove Avenue or the valuable slopes of Beverly Hills, the great majority possessed modest incomes and modest educational backgrounds. They were pigeonholed as lower middle class — owners of small businesses, wage earners and small farmers.

By 1930 Los Angeles spread across 441.7 square miles and cradled a population of 1,238,000, almost double that of San Francisco. Of that number, 66,000 came from Europe, 30,000 of them from Italy, Greece and the Slavic nations. Although Mexico was much closer to California, only

GROWTH ON THE HOME FRONT: The early twentieth century growth of Los Angeles was phenomenal, as Garland real estate advertisement illustrates (top).

Birth of an airport

Aviation was still a novelty when plans of a municipal airport in Los Angeles were envisioned. But as airmail contracts were awarded and airlines began to offer passenger service, the future of this new industry became more evident. It was clear that if Los Angeles could not provide an adequate and safe place to land, pilots would bypass the city.

During the 1920s, the Los Angeles Chamber of Commerce vigorously promoted a municipal airport. Since federal laws specifically forbid federal funds to build or develop airports, it had to be done by local government and citizens.

The 1928 National Air Races were scheduled to be held at Mines Field, which became the site for the Los Angeles Municipal Airport. The airport consisted of one short dirt runway and no buildings, surrounded by bean fields. Its traffic was a few single engine planes flown by aviators whose exploits represented high adventure to most.

By 1929, the airport had two permanent hangars and a 2,000-foot-long runway, graded and covered with decomposed granite and oil. The highlight for that year, though, was the landing of the world famous Graf Zeppeline, the newest and largest aircraft in existence, which stopped to refuel in Los Angeles on a trip around the world.

HOLLYWOOD HILLS: In 1897, Cahuenga Boulevard (above) was a dusty trail leading into the mountains where bicyclers rode through the pass to picnic. In 1926, at a cost of $500,000, the boulevard was completed, joining Hollywood with the San Fernando Valley. Mr. and Mrs. Horace Wilcox (below) of Topeka platted the town of Hollywood in the late 1890s; Mrs. Wilcox named it for the "Mass of the Holy Wood of the Cross," said by early-day missionary Junipero Serra near the site. By 1926, the Hollywood homes in the hills, such as those along Franklin Avenue (left center) were luxurious tributes to their residents who worked in the movie industry. The California version of "The Great White Way" glowed from Hollywood in 1946 (bottom left).

53,000 Mexicans claimed Los Angeles as home. There were 39,000 black residents and 18,000 Orientals, the majority of them Japanese. In other words, Los Angeles was still roughly 90 percent white in 1930. The largest block of whites still came from the Midwest, although the points of origin were tilting somewhat from the Indiana-Illinois-Iowa axis toward Texas, Oklahoma and Colorado. One mildly curious statistic is that females outnumbered males 100 to 96, whereas San Francisco offered 114 men to each 100 women.

Except for unmarried people (who tended to seek out apartment houses in Hollywood or in the Wilshire district), the migrants of the 1920s, as those before them, wanted single residences in suburbs filled with sunshine and hibiscus bushes. The city leaped to accommodate them. In the years 1921-1928, it authorized 3,233 subdivisions embracing 49,608 acres chipped apart into 246,612 building lots. Having purchased his lot, the buyer had to contract for a home to be built on it.

Although both the city and county by then had created planning commissions (the former dating from 1920), neither group was inclined to impose regulations that seriously inhibited private developers. Public beaches slowly vanished. Because wide streets took up saleable land, main traffic arteries seldom were as beautiful as parkways, and parks rarely appeared unless civic-minded individuals donated the land. Even then the city and the outlying towns fretted because such acreage was removed from the tax rolls.

Loose zoning ordinances allowed for the division of scores of residential districts with slice after slice of unplanned commercial strips. And though public zoning laws were silent on the problem of segregated housing, minorities seldom made their way into the city's newer units.

King auto

The big red interurban cars that had started to serve the county as a binding force were soon strangled by automobile traffic. Barely able to move in the downtown streets during rush hours and unable to go directly from one suburb to another as automobiles could, they lost riders, cut service, persuaded the public utility commission to let them raise their fares and thus hastened their own demise. This process quickened with the introduction of buses in 1923.

The automobile was king — make way for the car! In 1920 a gaseous protest-parade of honking vehicles forced the city fathers to rescind an ordinance against parking on downtown streets. Westlake Park (now MacArthur Park) was sliced through the middle by the completion of Wilshire Boulevard so that motorists would not have to drive around it. Reluctance to interrupt traffic delayed plans for an ambitious civic center dominated by a towered city hall 28 stories high. The center shrank in on itself and did not become a viable core for the city's civic energies until redevelopment plans gained new momentum during the 1960s.

Increasing traffic congestion during the 1920s led major downtown department stores to move to, or establish branches in, the suburbs, at first along Wilshire Boulevard. With merchants having made the jump in establishing other major centers, support for a system of subways or elevated tracks to relieve downtown tieups naturally waned.

Suburban fears of a downtown revitalization program by means of improved public transit probably were baseless. The trolley companies could not raise enough funds themselves for the changeover, and the penurious city would not. Besides, manufacturers of buses were talking persuasively about how efficiently their products could perform if the trolley tracks were torn up and their buses given free rein. Buses (being blood brothers to automobiles) carried the day. As a consequence, Los Angeles entered the 1980s with its sights still focused on improvements for its public transit system.

No dogs or actors allowed: The motion picture industry

The sign was tacked to Los Angeles apartment buildings and rooming houses in the early 1900s. Los Angeles was then a pious, self-righteous community whose residents regarded members of the movie colony as threats to the community's tranquility and — even more — its morality.

The movie makers began to arrive as early as 1906. George Van Guysling and Otis M. Grove established a studio in Los Angeles and shot their first film on a ranch near Hollywood. Two years later, William Selig finished the first full-length film completed in Los Angeles — "The Count of Monte Cristo." The actors reportedly "whooped while off the set" and shot at bar fixtures as well as palm trees.

City residents were relieved when the movie colony moved from Edendale (near Dodger Stadium) to Hollywood in 1911. Al Christie, along with David and Bill Horsley, inaugurated the move when they rented the Blondeau Tavern at Gower and Sunset and shot a movie the following day. Like their Los Angeles neighbors, they fumed at the invasion.

Resentment decreased as the industry proved profitable and respectable. The triumphant premiere of "The Birth of a Nation" demonstrated that the movie makers were engaged in a worthwhile enterprise. Studios such as Fox, Metro, Paramount, RKO and Warner Brothers became an important social and economic force in the area. Not only did they employ such stars as Mary Pickford, Douglas Fairbanks and Charles Chaplin, they also had less well-known actors and a growing number of technicians on their payrolls. The movie industry's active support of the United States during World War I also helped to win good will.

After the advent of sound movies in 1925, the character of the industry changed. Prior to that time, it was common to see crews filming in Los Angeles; by then crews moved inside the studios. If sound movies resulted in a less picturesque city, they produced a more profitable industry. The motion picture business mushroomed into one of Los Angeles' leading industries.

According to historian Carey McWilliams, the decision of the movie makers to locate in Los Angeles was a "providential dispensation" — a way of providing the lotus land the means to attain its promise. It was further confirmation that "God has always smiled on southern California," that "a special halo has always circled this island on the land."

The automobile: Wheels of fortune

"Whatever glass and steel monuments may be built downtown, the essence of Los Angeles, its true identifying characteristic, is mobility," wrote Richard Austin Smith in the March 1965 issue of *Fortune*. Though fifteen years old, the statement remains true. "Freedom of movement has long given life a special flavor there," Smith continued. "It has liberated the individual to enjoy the sun and space that his environment so abundantly offered as well as put the manifold advantages of a great metropolitan area within his grasp." And in Los Angeles, citizens partake of the city's advantages and express their freedom of movement with the help of a car.

Los Angeles is the capital of the world's car culture. While Detroit produces automobiles, Los Angeles celebrates them and the culture they promote. This preeminence is a result of many factors. The sheer abundance of land encouraged settlers to disperse. Early railroad promoters founded towns along tracks far from downtown and spurred the development of a linear city. Car travel was encouraged by the climate, the novelty of tourist attractions to new residents, the affordability of gasoline, the privacy of cars and the psychological satisfactions of auto ownership. Not only was driving practical, convenient and liberating. To many, the type of car owned became an expression of personality, if not social class.

Automobiles changed lives and landscapes. Parking meters, lights and freeways became commonplace, as did a panoply of drive-in structures. Though the drive-in was not invented in Los Angeles, drive-in architecture may well have reached its stylistic pinnacle in the city. Mobility became a dominant design metaphor in the '20s and '30s, particularly in Los Angeles where premier examples of "Streamline Moderne" architecture still stand.

Today, the fuel shortage, smog and congestion are forcing Angelenos to relinquish their reliance on the automobile. The challenge will be to retain the sense of mobility that has been an energizing and affirmative force throughout much of the city's history.

ALL ON WHEELS: The first automobile hit Los Angeles in 1897 (top left), with J. Philip Erie at the controls and W.W. Workman along for the ride. Soon, everything was on wheels — the California Dairy Council (top right), Moxie soft drink (center left), a mobile ministry (center right), Beachwood Automotive Service (above left), Mandarin food products (above right) and Love Nest Candy (below).

MOBILE SOCIETY: With the age of the automobile came drive-in establishments for gasoline (left top and center), sandwiches (right center), movies (right top), automobile clubs (left), plus multi-lanes and loops of expressway (above).

Merchants and movie moguls: the Jewish community

Jews were among the first immigrants to settle in Los Angeles in the mid-nineteenth century. The federal census for Los Angeles County indicated that eight males of Jewish descent (out of a total county population of 1,610) lived in Los Angeles in 1850. All were merchants in Bell's Row (later Mellus Row) at Alison and Los Angeles streets. Two were from Poland, six from Germany. The federal census for 1870 listed 330 Jews in the city out of the total population of 5,728; most came from Germany and Poland.

Unlike the Jews of San Francisco, who segregated themselves according to nation of origin, the Jewish community of Los Angeles was united until the mid-1880s, when differences caused its members to form separate organizations. For those 30 years, Los Angeles was a "one synagogue town" — and that synagogue was B'nai B'rith, built on Fort Street between Second and Third in 1873. They also established the Hebrew Benevolent Society (1854) and a major local newspaper, The *Emanu-El* (1897), later the *B'nai B'rith Messenger*.

During the nineteenth century, Jews enjoyed a position of pre-eminence in Los Angeles. As the city's mercantile leaders, they formed an economic elite. Harris Newmark, merchant, civic leader and author of *Sixty Years in Southern California,* was part of this group as was Isaiah W. Hellman, a prominent banker. Jews also attained considerable political clout. Not only were they often more literate than non-Jews, they could, on occasion, mediate the differences of the gentile religious majorities.

Los Angeles' Jews were not isolated from the larger community. While they generally resided in separate parts of town, Jews and non-Jews were members of the same fraternal organizations, served on the same civic bodies, supported one another's religious causes and married each other's children. One in every four marriages between 1858 and 1876 was between a Jew and a non-Jew.

Serious "social exclusion" began in the 1880s, but Jewish acculturation and accomplishment has continued throughout the twentieth century. Their contributions are especially evident in the field of clothing manufacture and entertainment. Among the leaders in the development of the California sportswear industry were Morris Cohn, Lemuel Goldwater, Daniel J. Brownstein and Henry W. Louis. Those who were pioneers of the motion picture industry include Sol Lesser, Earl Laemmle, the Warner Brothers, Irving Thalberg, Sid Grauman, Louis B. Mayer and William Fox.

JEWISH INSTITUTIONS: The B'nai B'rith Synagogue (above) at Ninth and Hope Streets; the Library of Jewish Alliance (left), circa 1911; and the first Kaspare Cohn Hospital (below).

Brass bands and fast horses

Cultural resources were widely diffused. The central library designed by Bertram Goodhue (vaguely Spanish in style and achieving architecural harmony by means of a fine balance of broad-planed, softly textured masses of concrete) was built downtown in 1925 near nothing in particular. The Los Angeles Philharmonic Orchestra played during the winter in the downtown Philharmonic auditorium and during the summer outdoors under the stars in the hill-girt Hollywood Bowl.

THE OLYMPICS: At the opening ceremonies of the Olympiad in 1932 (top), a capacity crowd of 101,022 packed the Los Angeles Memorial Coliseum. An Olympic Village was built (above left) and banners flew on city streets (above) to celebrate the event.

FOURSQUARE GOSPEL CHURCH: The Angelus Temple (top right) was dedicated in 1923, a monument to the ministry of Aimee Semple McPherson who raised funds for the church during evangelical campaigns (above) from 1918 to 1922.

Henry E. Huntington invested the large fortune inherited from his uncle Collis P. Huntington in Los Angeles' Pacific Electric Railway Company, electric power systems and Southern California real estate. He also became one of the city's leading philanthropists.

The largest park in the nation sprawled northeast of the Bowl, in mountains too rugged for homesites. It was the gift of wealthy Colonel Griffith J. Griffith. Among Griffith Park's major attractions today are a fine Greek Theater and a combined observatory and planetarium. The city almost missed having both. Some years after donating the park, Colonel Griffith was sentenced to prison for two years for trying to murder his wife. After his release, he offered to build an observatory in the park he had donated, but the city was reluctant to deal with the convicted criminal. Undeterred, Griffith used his will to raise the ante to $700,000 including the Greek Theater as well as the observatory, and after his death in 1919, Los Angeles reconsidered. In 1935 the observatory at last opened. It housed a 12-inch telescope, a striking model of the moon that revolves around the observer as if he were the earth and a planetarium equipped (in 1964) with an ultra-fine Zeiss projector for spreading a moving replica of the heavens across the rounded ceiling.

Another magnificent donation — this one from trolley builder and land speculator Henry E. Huntington — was the world-renowned Huntington Library, Art Gallery and Botanical Garden, which opened its doors in 1928 in San Marino, close by Pasadena and the equally famed California Institute of Technology.

Well to the south of the downtown area, near Exposition Park with its museums and in hailing distance of the rapidly growing University of Southern California was a structure that sports-minded Angelenos believed was the biggest arena in the world — the million-dollar Coliseum. Opened in 1923, the Coliseum was later enlarged (at the cost of another million dollars) to host the Olympic Games of 1932. Other sports features developed during this era include the Los Angeles Open Golf Tournament, launched in 1927; flower-bespangled Santa Anita Race track at Arcadia, opened in 1934 and Inglewood's Hollywood Park. Dedicated in 1938 and also devoted to horse racing, Hollywood Park's mile-long oval park surrounds three artificial lakes dotted with ducks, geese and swans.

Not the least of the city's cultural resources in the minds of thousands of devotees was Angelus Temple opened in 1923. Located near Echo Park, the Temple was the creation of a pretty redheaded evangelist, Aimee Semple McPherson who came from San Diego to Los Angeles in 1920. First her followers built her a home and then within two years the Temple. In it a vast organ thundered, brass bands played, elaborately gowned choirs raised hosannahs on high. Consummately theatrical, Aimee herself chased the devil across the stage with a pitchfork, or, dressed as a highway patrolman,

arrested him from the seat of her motorcycle. Those who could not attend services listened to her masterfully staged productions over the Temple radio station. Branch churches proliferated, and thousands of young women flocked to her college near the Temple to learn the craft of evangelical Christianity.

She could do no wrong. In May 1926, a chilly time for swimming, she disappeared after entering the surf at Ocean Park just outside the canal-lined resort town of Venice. Weeks later the grieving faithful were electrified by her appearance in the dreary town of Agua Prieta, Mexico, hundreds of miles away. Although not a curl was displaced and not a scuff appeared on her shoes, she convinced her congregation that she had been kidnapped but had escaped her captors by fleeing afoot through the wilderness. No one believed witnesses who later placed her in Santa Barbara and Carmel with a handsome male ex-employee of the Temple. For two decades, she was a prime show for tourists and a center of stability for unguessable numbers of lonesome, heartsore residents.

GRIFFITH CONTROVERSY: Should the city accept the gifts of Colonel Griffith J. Griffith? In 1896, he presented Los Angeles with 3,015 acres of land; the headwaters of the Los Angeles River (top left) flowed from the north side of the tract that was to become Griffith Park. Some wondered whether the gift was a means of avoiding taxes; others wondered if the imprisonment for the attempted murder of his wife had led Griffith to donate the land . . . perhaps the gift would buy him respectability. Consequently, the city refused Griffith's further donation of $100,000 to build an observatory at the park. However, the city did not refuse the bequest of $700,000 that Griffith had willed at his death in 1919 for an observatory — under construction in 1933 (center left) and completed in 1935 (above) and the Greek Theater (top right) finished in 1930.

HOLLYWOOD BOWL: The first performance in the originally natural amphitheater was in 1922; two years later, a wooden shell was built to improve the carrying power of the sound. In 1928, a second shell elliptical in shape was designed; three years later, it was replaced with a concrete shell which has been remodeled off and on since.

Chapter 6

The seesaw years

Tuesday, December 25, 1934.

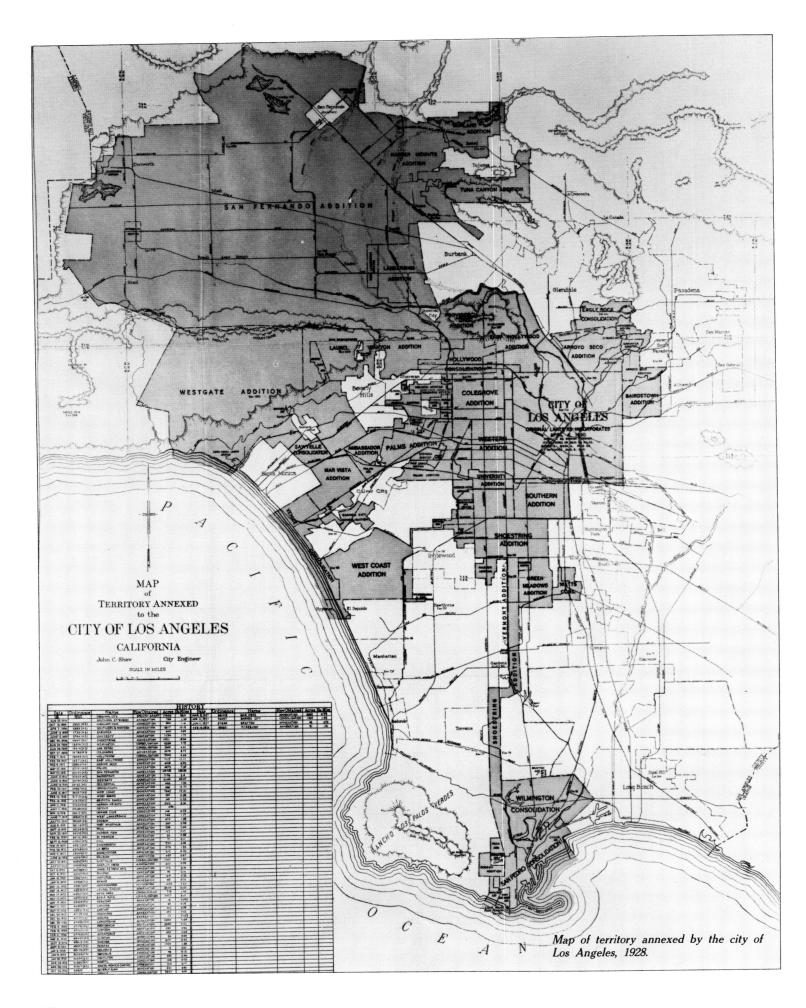

MAP
of
TERRITORY ANNEXED
to the
CITY OF LOS ANGELES
CALIFORNIA

John C. Shaw   City Engineer

SCALE IN MILES

Map of territory annexed by the city of Los Angeles, 1928.

MULHOLLAND DRIVE: Ground was broken by William Mulholland (left) for a highway that would extend from Cahuenga Pass to the Leo Carrillo State Beach. Named for the city engineer instrumental in the construction of the Los Angeles Aqueduct, Mulholland Drive's opening day was a highlight of 1924 (above).

Blind confidence

MEMORABLE EVENTS: Opening day at Union Station, May 7, 1939 (top, facing page); snow in Los Angeles settles on Pico Street, January 9, 1930 (bottom, facing page); and the home of the Los Angeles Stock Exchange (above).

Firmly in the grips of its boom psychology, Los Angeles — as the rest of the United States — overlooked the signs of the approaching depression of the 1930s. Europe's chronic instability seemed too far away to matter. Instead of reading portents in the nation's persistent post-war agricultural slump, Angelenos noticed only that their county continued to lead all others in farm production, shrunken though the total was. The decline in real estate sales and construction work in the late 1920s was deemed to be only temporary. Although wages stayed low, the stock market soared high, fueled by borrowed money.

As usual, the area's approach to water problems typified its attitudes. During the first half of the 1920s, the heavy influx of population into Los Angeles coincided with drought in the Sierra Nevada. Prophets cried out that if trends continued, city and county would face another crisis by 1940. Something had to be done.

Promoters led by William Mulholland launched a search for new sources of water. Two existed, both difficult. One was the Colorado River 240 miles to the east across barren mountains and sun-smitten wastes. Ninety-two miles of tunnels and batteries of massive electric pumps would be needed to move the hard salt-laden river water to the coastal plains. Because Los Angeles alone could not handle the costs involved, help would have to come from neighboring municipalities — if they would agree.

The other source of water was Mono Basin, more than 100 miles northwest of the mouth of the already-completed Owens Valley Aqueduct. If the city were to build a storage reservoir (Crowley Lake) on Fred Eaton's once-rejected ranch and then tunnel eleven miles into Mono Basin, it could tap additional Sierra streams and thus add an appreciable flow of good mountain water to the Owens Valley canal. Instead of having to be pumped, this water would pour downhill and could be harnessed to hydroelectric generators along its course. Unhappily the struggle with the embattled farmers of the Owens Valley and the devastating collapse of the San Francisquito Dam was drawing such unfavorable attention at that time that even Los Angeles voters might be reluctant to authorize the necessary bonds.

Instead of debating choices, the Los Angeles Chamber of Commerce decided to push for both projects. They persuaded the governments of neighboring cities to join Los Angeles in financing the cost of the Colorado River aqueduct through the sale of municipal bonds. To make the plan legally and politically feasible, the city joined with other southern California communities to form the Metropolitan Water District (MWD) in 1928. They also persuaded the voters of the city to authorize the Mono extension. Thus as the Depression closed in, the metropolitan area was committed to two necessary yet difficult building programs.

Citizens voted a bond issue of $200-million for MWD aqueduct construction in 1931. Work began the following year. Meanwhile, voters authorized a number of bond issues, much of the funds earmarked for the Mono Basin project. (The project was completed in 1940 and increased the system's yield by approximately 35 percent. Grant Lake and Bouquet Reservoirs were added.)

Nor was that all. There were other plans afoot — an enlarged Coliseum for the 1932 Olympic Games and a huge new Union Railway station. In 1919 the southern branch of the University of California had taken over the Vermont Avenue campus of the old Los Angeles State Normal School. Now they were preparing to erect a dazzling new cluster of Italian-style red brick buildings on a 383-acre campus in Westwood at the foot of the Santa Monica Mountains — the genesis of today's UCLA. It was formally dedicated in 1926.

Private industry was equally exuberant. The Goodrich Rubber Company

announced plans for a major expansion program in the southern part of the city, and in early October 1929, ground was broken with much ceremony for a $1.5 million stock exchange building in the heart of the business district.

Crash

During this free-wheeling time, when the more scandalous women of the movie colony and their imitators took to shortening their skirts, bobbing their hair, smoking cigarettes and drinking bootleg liquor from the thin silver flasks their escorts carried in their hip pockets, Europe's fragile economy fell apart. The panic spread across the Atlantic, and on October 29, 1929, the American stock market began its abysmal plunge.

In Los Angeles, as elsewhere, sales skidded, banks closed, businesses failed, many because of wholesale frauds committed during the speculative frenzies of the preceding years. Within twelve months, building permits in the city dropped by two-thirds, and 51,000 men lost their jobs. To the distress of the Hollywood Boulevard Association, beggars appeared on the street corners to panhandle the few tourists that still appeared in the hope of glimpsing some famous countenance. They had to entreat the police for aid.

The crash also dampened Los Angeles Municipal Airport development. Major airlines refused to locate at the new field when they had better facilities at Grand Central Airport in Glendale and at United Terminal in Burbank. Municipal investments dropped from $35 million in 1930 to $1 million in 1933.

THE THIRTIES: The United Air Terminal (top, facing page), now Lockheed Air Terminal, was dedicated May 30, 1930; Simon's Drive-in (bottom, facing page) was a popular spot at Sunset Boulevard and Vine Street, 1932; an earthquake shook Long Beach (above) in 1933.

Mayor John C. Porter — a car salesman who had been elected on the strength of his promise to promote morality and enforce prohibition — had no background in dealing with the economic paralysis. Others had. Dr. Francis Townsend, an elderly physician of Long Beach, was distressed by the suffering of senior citizens. He proposed a two percent tax on commercial transactions so that every person over 60 could be given $200 a month if he or she promised to spend the sum within that time. A variant of the plan, California Revolving Pensions — better known as "Ham 'n Eggs" or "Thirty Dollars Every Thursday" — stirred up even more excitement. It garnered more than a million votes in the election of 1938 and probably would have carried except for last-minute revelations about the corrupt practices of its promoters.

Even more terrifying than pension plans to conservative Californians was Upton Sinclair, a frail-looking writer and resident of the Los Angeles County suburb of Altadena. Sinclair had long been a highly visible member of the Socialist Party. But he left it and offered himself as Democratic candidate for the governorship in 1933. He presented his program in the form of a novel entitled *I, Governor of California, and How I Ended Poverty.* He, too, advocated pensions for the elderly. He also proposed that the state establish communal farms on tax-delinquent land and end unemployment by means of state-operated factories. All this and more he wrapped up in the acronym EPIC — End Poverty in California.

In August 1934 — thanks partly to picking up 54 percent of Los Angeles' Democratic vote — Sinclair won his party's nomination over two strong rivals. Republicans led by movie mogul Louis B. Mayer concocted a slashing campaign of vilification. One of the most effective devices (along with labeling Sinclair as an advocate of free love) was an artfully staged newsreel shot of tramps piling out of boxcars and telling interviewers that they were the vanguard of an army of hoboes coming to California to share the wealth with "Uppie." Townsend opposed Sinclair's $50 pension proposal and endorsed the incumbent Republican Governor Frank Merriam of Long Beach, who favored Townsend's $200 plan. That stopped Sinclair — 1,143,620 votes to 879,557.

Hordes of poverty-stricken Americans — attracted by decades of Edenesque propaganda — were indeed descending on California. Most were farmers fleeing in ramshackle jalopies from the dustbowl of the southern plains, the "Okies" and "Arkies" of John Steinbeck's searing novel, *The Grapes of Wrath.* In the struggle for jobs, they displaced thousands of Mexicans as underpaid agricultural workers. They loaded the relief rolls in the cities, especially in Los Angeles County and so alarmed the Legislature that it passed a law closing the California border to all persons who had no identifiable means of support.

On February 4, 1936, squadrons of Los Angeles County patrolmen sought to enforce the order. They took up positions at the points where main highways crossed the state line into southern California. The blockade lasted two months before the American Civil Liberties Union obtained an injunction staying it, and in 1941 the United States Supreme Court voided the law. But by that time, the United States was on the verge of entering World War II, and once again California was begging for immigration.

Resurgence

Dismal though the Depression was in southern California, it was more endurable there than in other sections of the country. Winters — though not as balmy as advertised by the All-Year Club of Southern California — were less rigorous than those in many regions, and some jobs did exist. The motion picture industry stayed afloat, for people the world around always seemed able to afford a ticket to a well ballyhooed film. Financed largely by agencies of the federal government which purchased many of the bonds authorized by the electorate, 11,000 men went to work in 1933

GREAT DEPRESSION: *Los Angeles celebrated its 150th birthday September 4, 1931, with "La Fiesta" activities (above), in spite of the decade's depression. The End Poverty League, Inc., (top, facing page) was born in the dismal 1930s, as were bread lines (bottom, facing page) to help the destitute.*

The S.S. Rex, a gambling ship, at sea in 1939.

building a prodigious 242-mile ditch between the Colorado River and Lake Mathews near the city of Riverside. From there another 150 miles of distribution canals wound through the thirteen cities that then made up the main Metropolitan Water District of Southern California. The first water flowed into Lake Mathews in November 1939.

Meanwhile parabolic high tension lines swung on steel legs across the desert to bring power from Hoover Dam to the aqueduct's pumps and to the industrial wheels of the Los Angeles metropolitan area. The Owens Valley Aqueduct was extended into Mono Basin — water was turned into the canal in 1940 — and its generators produced still more energy for the city.

There were no commercial airlines based at Los Angeles Municipal Airport, but aircraft manufacturers moved into the area in 1932 — first Douglas, then Northrup and in 1936, North American and allied manufacturers. The city received federal relief funds for improvements, and the Works Progress Administration (WPA) did the work. The five major airlines — which had outgrown surrounding airports — agreed to relocate to Los Angeles Municipal when the work was completed.

After squabbling for years about an appropriate site, the railroads combined forces to erect a majestic, airy, mission-revival style Union Passenger Terminal next to the old plaza. The Terminal handled the 64 trains that still carried passengers into and out of Los Angeles in 1939. The next year, a $5-million dual highway was opened between the city and Pasadena. Today its curves, narrow lanes, rare pullouts and abrupt entrances seem archaic almost to the point of quaintness. But it was the state's first freeway and evidence that in spite of the Depression, Los

Angeles' always mobile population had swelled during the decade by another quarter of a million people — from 1,238,048 in 1930 to 1,504,277 in 1940.

What all this meant was that when the demands of World War II fell across the land, Los Angeles, more than many cities, was ready to meet them.

Even before the war broke out, demand in rearming Europe and Japan for American products had started pushing economic indicators upward. As far as Los Angeles County was concerned, the resurgence came first to the makers of airframes. (Most engines were imported from the East to be added to the craft in western assembly plants.) The initial benefits went to Lockheed Aircraft Company whose main factories were in Burbank in the San Fernando Valley. Lockheed's all-metal, twin-engined Electra — enthusiastically endorsed by such popular idols as Charles Lindbergh, Wiley Post and Amelia Earhart — had enabled the company to weather the Depression in sound shape. When England ordered two hundred Electras modified for use as bombers early in 1939, the boom began. It swelled with the Allies' declaration of war against Germany in the fall and in 1940 became almost a frenzy when President Roosevelt called on the nation's companies to turn out 50,000 planes each year.

American participation, brought on by the Japanese bombing of Pearl Harbor, Hawaii, on December 7, 1941, soon made the 50,000 figure obsolete. In 1944 American plane manufacturers — eight of them in southern California — turned out 96,000 aircraft of all types. Lockheed alone, with a work force of 90,000, accounted for nearly ten percent of the total. By war's end, the intertwined, closely cooperating aircraft makers of Los Angeles County had been awarded seven billion dollars in contracts. More millions

WAR EFFORTS: A "Los Angeles Attack" parade in 1944 featured a float (top) sponsored by rubber companies; tanks roll in a freedom parade, 1944 (center); and an "Army Ordinance Show" was presented in the Coliseum, 1943 (above).

went into the building of airports, training camps and maintenance facilities. Petroleum refineries meanwhile had to expand at breakneck speed in order to meet the demand for aviation gasoline and the fuels being gobbled up by tanks and military trucks.

The war halted commercial airport development. The site became a military complex occupied by the U.S. Army and Navy. (Even though wartime conditions prevailed, a master plan was developed in 1944. It called for an additional 2,000 acres for a terminal complex and runway extensions.)

Although the San Francisco Bay area received the lion's share of the West's shipbuilding contracts, the facilities at San Pedro and Long Beach were also busy turning out troop transports, freighters and landing craft. A huge Kaiser steel mill — the first blast-furnace installed in California — appeared at Fontana east of Los Angeles. The demand for farm products tripled, and service industries of all kinds were created to care for the needs of the battalions of troops that received their training in the state's military installations before being sent to the front.

Acute social dislocations accompanied the production effort. Tens of thousands of southern California's young workers were drawn into the military services. Non-military construction all but ceased, and those of the industry's workers that escaped the draft had to shift to new and often unfamiliar jobs. They could not begin to meet the demand, and new sources of labor had to be tapped. The once-destitute, floating population of Okies and Arkies now found themselves being solicited to go to work in factories and fields. Mexican laborers flowed back across the international border, and blacks poured west from the cotton-planting South. Of equal significance was the startling shift of women into war work from their traditional roles as secretaries, teachers and homemakers.

There was never enough of anything. Gasoline was rationed. Housing was desperately short in spite of the hasty erection of thousands of trailers and

WORLD WAR II: Support on the home front included victory gardens (top, facing page) at the corner of Toberman and Eighteenth Streets, 1943, and a defense plant (bottom, facing page) dedicated at Long Beach in 1941. U.S. Army anti-aircraft guns (above) were stationed at Westwood.

boxlike prefabricated homes. Schools were crowded, utilities overstrained. Even the fabled climate of the Los Angeles basin suffered from the fumes being poured into it by factories, refineries and nearly 1.5 million automobile exhausts. On several occasions during 1943, palls of eye-watering, brown-gray smog sheathed the skies and became a recurrent and widely noted feature of the regional scene.

Mass hysteria accompanied these social dislocations. The West Coast was poorly defended; and after the bombing of Pearl Harbor, it seemed to the frightened residents of Los Angeles that their factories were the next logical targets for attack. Sensitive buildings were hastily camouflaged, antiaircraft guns were placed amid sandbags on strategic hilltops. Window lights and automobile headlights were ordered blacked out at night. Thousands of civilian plane spotters and air raid wardens were recruited to stand vigil on behalf of the nervous populace.

Three days after Pearl Harbor, warning sirens screamed out in Los Angeles for the first time. Though no danger followed, alarms continued intermittently for several weeks. Rumors that sounded fantastic but nevertheless spread rapidly achieved sudden credibility on February 23, 1942, when a Japanese submarine surfaced off the coast of Santa Barbara County and lobbed a few ineffective shells at a minor oil installation. Or perhaps, as some people still believe, it was really an American submarine trying to scare people into greater vigilance.

Whatever the truth, vigilance did mount to the point that someone detected mysterious objects above the city in the early morning of February 26. Signals chattered, antiaircraft guns thundered, shrapnel from the exploding shells rained down. Hundreds of thousands of citizens rushed recklessly outside their homes to watch tracer shells draw golden arcs against the night sky. Zealous airraid wardens fell down stairs and over curbs as they rushed about their duties. Speeding cars collided in the blackened streets, and three persons died. They were the only casualties. What, if anything, was aloft in that wintry darkness has never been learned.

But there were real Japanese available who could be turned into scapegoats. Of the 100,000 or so who lived in California, the great majority had congregated in the Los Angeles area. Most had been born in the United States; the rest were immigrants. In spite of discriminatory laws concerning school attendance and the ownership of property, they were by and large model citizens. No matter — the military decided that they were potential traitors, a view backed by such civilian notables as Governor Olson, the state's popular Attorney General Earl Warren and Los Angeles' reform mayor, Fletcher Bowron. In March 1942, shortly after the Los Angeles air "attack" had shaken the nation, President Franklin D. Roosevelt issued the order for every person of Japanese descent to be interred in relocation camps in the desert. Bewildered but obedient, the Japanese sold their land, homes and possessions for whatever they could get — aggregate losses approached half a billion dollars. They spent most of the rest of the war behind barbed wire, wondering why this total disregard of their personal rights had occurred.

Emotionalism was carried to the Mexican community. During the summer of 1942, white jurors considering scraps of circumstantial evidence found seventeen members of a Mexican-American gang guilty of murdering a youth named José Diaz in what achieved notoriety as the Sleepy Lagoon case. (Sleepy Lagoon was a gravel pit in East Los Angeles.) The District Court of Appeals overturned the convictions but not before the prejudices that had led to the imprisonments flared up in the "zoot suit" riots.

Most local Mexicans, including thousands who were American citizens, had congregated in a *barrio* that spilled out of the east central part of the city into the county. The older residents had been content to stay there. The younger were not and took to roaming in groups through the downtown dance halls, movie houses and beer joints. They called

DISPLAY OF SUPPORT: "His morale means victory - write" was the message of 1943 UFO window displays at Bullocks (top, facing page); Foreman & Clark shoppers were reminded in 1941 to "Buy U.S. defense bonds," "Remember Pearl Harbor" and "Give to the Red Cross" (bottom, facing page).

A Spanish home gathering of Maria Florentina Silvae de Ibarra (center, right of dove cote) and her family, circa 1890; she was the widow of Hilario Ibarra.

Maintaining the first culture: Los Angeles Hispanics

Los Angeles' Hispanic heritage is part of the city's distinctive character. The band of *pobladores* who settled Los Angeles were Mexican. Spaniards ruled all of California during the Mexican period and owned all the region's private lands. Their descendents have played an important part in the area's economic, social and cultural life.

Prior to the arrival of the Anglo, Hispanic colonizers had developed a rigid class structure in California. At the top of the hierarchy was the *gente de razon* — Spanish Franciscans, Spanish officials and Spanish officers of the troop garrisoned in California (which included some Mexicans). At the bottom of this structure were the *paisanos* who consisted of artisans, colonists, Mexican troops and the Sonorans who migrated to California to work in the gold mines. The *gente de razon* lived a relatively splendorous and languid life, while the *paisano* class knew few luxuries but were well acquainted with hard work.

America's conquest of California altered this system. The *gente de razon* initially endorsed the new regime, for they had been against Mexico since its independence from Spain. The grandees claimed to possess pure Spanish blood and to speak unadulterated Castilian, so they had not adapted well to Mexico's rule. Consequently, they welcomed America's victory. The Americans recognized the *gente de razon's* status by appointing seven of them out of 48 delegates to the first constitutional convention. The *paisanos* were not represented. Gradually, resentment toward Anglo-Americans grew as both grandees and *paisanos* lost their land to the new government.

With the breaking up of the ranchos, vaqueros lost their jobs. So did Hispanic shepherds who were replaced by Basques moving in to southern California. Consequently, Hispanics began to work as ranch hands and general laborers. Their influence and visibility were further diminished by the immense Anglo migration to the area in the 1880s. At the turn of the century, increased jobs in agriculture and on the railroad construction brought a new migration of Hispanics. By 1945, Los Angeles possessed a larger Mexican population than all the cities in the world except Mexico City.

Antagonism between Anglos and Hispanics culminated in the mid-1940s with the Sleepy Lagoon murder trial and the zoot suit riots. Since then, conflict between Anglos and Hispanics has decreased. While Hispanics lagged behind blacks in developing political clout, they gained ground in the '60s. Bilingual education is now widely offered, and Hispanics have a greater opportunity for higher education and superior jobs. Maintenance of their language and cultural ties has created a solidarity among Hispanics and enriched their lives. Broadway Street, El Mercado, Olvera Street and Plaza de la Raza are among the vibrant social, economic and cultural centers of Hispanic life in Los Angeles today.

themselves *pachucos,* and to further identify themselves, the boys combed
their hair into duck tails and wore what amounted to a uniform — wide
hats, broad-shouldered coats, trousers with high waists and peg bottoms and
long, heavy key chains.

Soldiers who frequented the same bars and movie houses took umbrage
at these "drape shapes" or "zoot suits." In addition, the military personnel
resented rubbing shoulders with youths who were not in military uniform. A
higher percentage of Mexican-Americans than of whites was actually
inducted during the conflict, but the concentration of brown-skinned civilians
along a few blocks of the downtown tenderloin obscured the reality. On top
of those explosive elements were boredom and racial animosities seeking
outlets.

On June 3, 1943, several Mexican youths jumped and robbed some
sailors. The next evening nearly a hundred Navy men armed with clubs
invaded the Mexican district. They began beating and stripping the clothing
off any dark-skinned male they could catch. City police stepped into the
affray and arrested 44 badly pummelled Mexicans for inciting the riot. This
convinced many sailors, soldiers, marines and some civilians that they had
been granted *carte blanche* to continue the assaults. The rioting lasted four
more days, fortunately without deaths, until finally the Navy dampened it
by declaring all Los Angeles out of bounds, a stiff blow to firms dealing
with military personnel on leave.

Nationwide condemnation followed the episode. The county supervisors
investigated, committees on community relations were established, and the
police department was reminded to train its officers to treat all citizens
equally.

The frantic years passed, filled with tensions, shortages, crowding,
frustrations and a growing weariness brought on by a war that seemed
closer and more urgent than any foreign conflict America had yet known. It
was also a time of intense creativity and of searching reevaluations of what
life should be like after the shooting ended. News of Japan's surrender
reached the city on the afternoon of August 14, 1945. The streets clogged
with a monstrous traffic jam through which pedestrians weaved deliriously,
weeping, whooping, embracing total strangers. It was not a time for

*V.J. Day is celebrated in Los Angeles,
August 14, 1945.*

111

Music Corporation of America, built in 1940.

wondering. Those who did must have realized that the city, like themselves, had experienced the greatest upheaval of its 164-year-old career and was faced with making adaptations whose eventual impact could scarcely be imagined.

Pioneering the new affluence

Eager for peace, the United States demobilized both militarily and economically with reckless haste. Millions of young men were hurried back into civilian life without jobs. War contracts were cancelled and layoffs mounted as industry groped to retool for peacetime production.

Civic leaders, prepared for a population exodus, found there had not really been an exodus at all. Hundreds of thousands of war workers and military personnel had been drawn to or through California during the conflict. Many had fallen in love with Los Angeles' beaches, mountains, generally mild weather, casual life styles and promises of opportunity. When they were laid off or discharged, they returned to their former homes, straightened out their affairs, married the girls who had been waiting for them or collected their families, then headed west again, straight into the confusions of conversion.

Materials of all kinds were hard to come by; even the motion picture industry had difficulty obtaining film. The scarcest commodity of all was housing. According to a report by one of Los Angeles' Congressional representatives, Helen Gahagan Douglas, 162,000 families — 50,000 of them veterans — could find no better shelter than tents, garages, ramshackle trailers and firetrap hotels.

These were not destitute people. Most could have afforded better accommodations if anything better had been available. Because there had been relatively little on which to spend money during the war years, savings had accumulated prodigiously. Veterans, in addition, could readily obtain low-interest federal loans for building homes, starting small businesses or completing their educations. And since many would-be students were also married (in itself a unique social change), they too needed homes.

The result was a new kind of housing boom for Los Angeles. Once developers had simply graded a tract, put in sewer and utility lines and let the buyer of a lot erect his own house. Now — financed by loans from the federal government or from the area's proliferating savings and loan institutions — developers undertook to build acres of homes as well. House plans and construction procedures were standardized; structures were put together like automobiles on an assembly line. Using nearly nine million in borrowed money, one developer, Louis Boyar, bought 3,375 acres of farm land at the southern edge of the city, paved 133 miles of streets, erected 17,000 homes, called his instant city Lakewood and began taking orders. People stood in lines for a chance to buy. During one fabulous 60 minutes, Boyar's salesmen sold 107 houses. Except for size, Lakewood was not unique. Similar scenes on a smaller scale were reenacted throughout the county. There was one immediate side effect of the colossal building spurt. So much farm land was swallowed that Los Angeles County lost its long-held position as the richest agricultural county in the nation.

Statistics grow mind-numbing. During the 1950s, nearly two million people poured into the Los Angeles metropolitan area. Early in 1962 (according to estimates by the state government) or 1964, (according to the federal government's Census Bureau), California moved ahead of New York as the most heavily populated state in the union. Of the state's total population, nearly half — some ten million people — were stuffed into the Los Angeles Basin which occupied only one-sixth of California's area. Six million people resided in Los Angeles County alone.

As far as the average newcomer was concerned, county lines practically ceased to exist. "Greater Los Angeles" spread until it blanketed not only

Westchester Tracts, 1942.

Los Angeles and Orange counties, but also the southeastern part of Ventura County and the western parts of San Bernardino and Riverside counties (in the latter, the University of California opened a new campus in 1954). That same year, the city that had given its name to this vast conglomeration had become the third largest in population in the United States, trailing only New York and Chicago.

What prompted so many people to pack their possessions and move en masse to one comparatively small, unfamiliar locality? One of the impulses was the national trend toward ever increasing urbanization. Another was a continuation of the familiar yearning for a more satisfying life — that same search that had been bringing migrants to southern California ever since the advent of the railroads in the 1880s. During the 1950s and 1960s, that same hope for a more pleasant existence — beaches, mountains, sunshine — still fired imaginations but among a different age group. For although few elderly people still sought out southern California as a place in which to retire, increasing numbers of younger men and women saw it as a desirable spot in which to work and raise families.

Their reasons were varied and complex, but one reason was that the land was still economically young and flexible. Its corporations, big and small, had not let their procedures harden into set ways. During the war, management had been willing — indeed had been compelled — to experiment and innovate. The preponderance of light industries for the most part were mobile — not tied to nearby natural resources. Ongoing research and experimentation were energetically fostered at such places as Pasadena's Jet Propulsion Laboratories and Santa Monica's famed RAND Corporation whose very name was an acronym for research and development.

And so restless young adventurers came by the tens of thousands, eager for challenging work in a milieu that years of propaganda and their own brief experiences during the war had assured them was rewarding. But they came into a restless, shifting economy. Traditional industries faced major shakeups as they struggled to maintain accustomed roles of leadership. The Long Beach-San Pedro Harbor, for example, had to entirely revamp its

113

114

methods of handling cargo to keep abreast of competition from Oakland. The oil industry adopted new techniques in order to hold third place in production behind Texas and Louisiana. The once gold-plated movies staggered under haymaker blows from television (the first semi-commercial station had begun in 1939) but then fought back to solvency by realizing their own potential. As television programming expanded, studios produced both movie and television projects. In addition, the invention of cross-country cables allowed the development of new kinds of motion picture entertainment (laced with advertising commercials) to reach into practically every home in the land, subtly implanting on the nation's group consciousness the Los Angeles vision of the world.

Ambitious men could go far by joining old industries adapting to new challenges. Or, if the workers preferred, they could try new fields. National acceptance of casual California sportswear helped to make the city one of the country's leading centers of styling and clothing manufacture. Producers of plastics that could be adapted to almost endless uses, makers of furniture, of increasingly sophisticated toys and of arcane oil-well drilling tools achieved nation-wide stature. Real estate and tourism still hummed, the latter fostered by such ingenious developments as Disneyland, Marineland and Olvera Street near the city's old plaza. But the greatest challenges came from head-long changes in the aircraft and electronics industries — changes brought about by a continuing sequence of international crises.

During the late 1940s, a hastily demobilized America was confronted around the world by a cynical Russia whose aggressions in eastern Europe violated the amicable terms of the Yalta Treaty, signed by the Allied Powers during the closing year of the war. The Soviets, moreover, when they exploded an atomic bomb in 1949, ended the United States' monopoly of that awesome force. The Cold War followed and in 1950 changed into heated conflict when a North Korean army (supplied and directed by the Soviet Union) invaded South Korea. Although that war ended in 1953 with an uneasy return to the *status quo,* the arms race went on, receiving new urgency in 1957 from Russia's success in putting the world's first satellite, Sputnik, into orbit. By 1960, California was receiving 40 percent of all governmental contracts related to aerospace research and development (including jet aircraft and missiles) and 24 percent of all defense-oriented contracts. Of California's total share, the Greater Los Angeles area received roughly 70 percent.

The impact can hardly be exaggerated. Between 1950 and 1960, employment in manufacturing in Los Angeles grew at ten times the national rate. As a result, the city shot into third-place standing in the value of manufactured products as well as population. And because the United States had committed itself to maintaining wartime strength without curtailing peacetime spending, the income that Los Angeles workers received from defense-related jobs enabled them to push the city into second place among the country's retail markets. In short, there were few places on earth where more money flowed from one hand to another during the course of ordinary commercial transactions.

Meanwhile, Vietnam — a name scarcely known at the time to most Americans — was emerging as yet another trouble spot. Again hundreds of thousands of troops poured through California on their way to the Asian Front. Their sinew now was provided by ultrasophisticated military hardware manipulated by electronic and computer systems of increasing complexity. To keep materiel flowing to the front, the federal government poured billions of dollars into new defense contracts.

It was not entirely a stable situation. Contractions and expansions regularly billowed through the region's economy. In many ways, Los Angeles adjusted to its new situation by developing radically new responses. And yet, at the same time, it paradoxically maintained certain social patterns that had been in evidence since the days of the horse and buggy.

1940s HOUSING: *Southern Los Angeles housing projects (top, facing page), Rolling Knolls Apartments in Harbor City, 1945; F.H. Dolan "box houses" (bottom, facing page) at Manhattan Beach, 1943.*

115

That's entertainment

Metro cameramen at work with director Sam Wood.

Grauman's Chinese Theater, built in 1927 in Hollywood, now Mann's Chinese Theater.

Premier at Carthay Circle, 1938.

THEATERS: Free talking pictures were possible with a portable sound theater (above left) with viewing from the open rear (above right). The elaborate baroque interior (below) was as fascinating as the entertainment at the Los Angeles Theater, built in 1931 on South Broadway.

FOR ENTERTAINMENT: When the Hollywood Palladium (above) opened in 1940, it was the world's largest dining and dancing emporium; CBS broadcasting studios (below), 1940.

SUNSET'S STUDIOS: Warner Brothers studios (above) in 1934 and the NBC studios (below) with Tommy Dorsey performing in 1944.

Olvera Street

In 1928, Mrs. Christine Sterling, with the assistance of other influential Angelenos, saw that a dirty alley in Los Angeles' historic pueblo district was transformed into a "typical Mexican marketplace."

First known as Wine or Vine Street, it was renamed to honor Augustin Olvera, the first county judge, nephew of Ignacio Coronel and signer of the treaty of Cahuenga.

Prisoners provided the labor for the construction of the paseo and Mrs. Sterling prayed that a bricklayer or plumber would be arrested to provide technical assistance. The street they built opened to the public April 20, 1930. It has become an integral part of Hispanic culture in Los Angeles and is the scene of the annual Blessing of the Animals the day before Easter and the Christmas celebration of Las Posadas.

Mrs. Christine Sterling (far right), Judge Augustin Olvera (right). Traditional shops (bottom) and restaurants attract shoppers to the area.

Chapter 7

Megalopolis

Pershing Square, downtown Los Angeles.

Westwood, home of the University of California at Los Angeles.

Sprawl

In 1950 the United States Bureau of the Census invented the jawbreaking term "Standard Metropolitan Statistical Area" (SMSA) to describe places like Los Angeles. What this meant was that national living patterns had changed so radically that old labels — "rural" and "urban" were two of them — no longer sufficed. Cities had burst through their politically-drawn boundaries and had become regions composed of many units. They needed a broader designation.

By 1970 the number of SMSAs in the United States had swelled to 233. Of that total, Los Angeles was second only to New York in population. It sprawled completely around such lesser entities as Beverly Hills, Burbank and Culver City. It contained multitudes of unrelated, commercially-oriented strip boulevards festooned with overhead wires and visually polluted by monstrous billboards and garish neon signs. Self-contained cores like Century City had mushroomed into prominence. In that city-within-a-city, 12,000 people lived in 22 high-rise apartments, worked in nearby skyscrapers, housed visitors in a huge curved hotel and found amusement in their own ultrasophisticated theaters, restaurants and nightclubs. Elsewhere in the metropolitan sprawl were legendary districts like Hollywood, tightly circumscribed ghettos like Watts, dormitory complexes at several universities, and specialized areas like the rapidly growing International Airport with approximately 110,000 primary and secondary employees in 1980 and the narrow strip City of Industry, which held almost no residential dwellers but had been incorporated along eighteen miles of railroad track to serve more than 300 manufacturing and warehousing concerns.

During this period, air traffic in Los Angeles also felt the influx of people traveling to southern California. In 1950, the city council renamed the airport Los Angeles International (LAX), signifying a world transportation center. Projections of future passengers indicated a drastic need to expand the facilities. A bond issue for $59.7 million passed with 86 percent in favor of the new airport.

By the end of the decade, the dawn of the jet age arrived as American Airlines inaugurated its New York to Los Angeles jet service with Boeing 707-123 aircraft early in 1959. Meanwhile, architectural and construction work began, launching the new jet-age terminal in 1961. By the following year, 21 airlines were servicing LAX, 11 of which were international lines. As the giant airport complex passed the 10-million passenger mark in the mid-1960s, LAX proved to be a primary contributor to the economy of the entire Los Angeles area.

Beyond the city limits were subsidiary conglomerations that elsewhere would have been SMSAs in their own right — Long Beach, Torrance, Glendale, Pasadena, Santa Ana. There were rows upon rows of tracts between the west end of the San Fernando Valley and San Bernardino 60 miles away. And there were the planned suburbs like Westlake, Valencia and Irvine; and the plush marinas at Newport Beach. Far-off centers were also in effect extensions of the metropolitan area — the huge ski resort at Mammoth Lakes 320 miles to the north where much of the city's Owens Valley water originated; Palm Springs, lying luxuriously at the sunny edge of the interior desert.

Visualizing all that, the eminent historian Daniel Boorstin in his prizewinning *The Americans: The Democratic Experience,* described the Los Angeles Standard Metropolitan Statistical Area as illegible, unfathomable. But do those who live in the region agree? Does the city really defy description?

CALIFORNIA COLLEGES: Amos G. Throop (below) founded the Throop Institute in 1891, also known as the Polytechnic Institute at Pasadena which served as the foundation of the present-day California Institute of Technology (right). Colleges in the Los Angeles area include Whittier College (left center, circa 1905), Occidental College (right center, circa 1910), Scripps College (left bottom) and Pomona College (right bottom).

HALLS OF LEARNING: With the Trojan mascot standing guard (top), University of Southern California students (right) and buildings (College of Medicine Library, above) are integral parts of campus life in Los Angeles. A variety of architecture is evident on Los Angeles area campuses, such as the Spanish flavor at Loyola University (below) and the modern at the University of California at Irvine.

UNIVERSITY LIFE: University of California at Los Angeles students (inset below) attend school in Westwood; in 1933, the campus could be seen from the Bel Air Country Club (bottom). Clean architectural lines are found on the campuses of Ambassador College (below) and Pepperdine University (right).

A TOUCH OF THE UNUSUAL: Institutions with an obvious message are found in doughnut (top), ice cream (center) and hot dog (above) stands in Los Angeles, as well as a pet cemetery (below) for animal friends to rest in peace.

The problem

Famed architect Frank Lloyd Wright once claimed that the American continent is tilted southwest and that everything loose is sliding into southern California. The metaphor contains all that is needed to make it memorable. It is short, clever and oversimplified. By raising images of kooks, con men, promoters and zealots, it turns attention from the broader truth that for 300 years the whole American nation has been pushing steadily westward in one of the great migrations of world history. Pacemakers, too, were in the vanguard, but the crazies were the ones that attracted notice.

Though city watchers say the trend toward bizarre style is not as marked as it was during the southland's earlier boom cycles, it still exists. Even today you can find restaurants shaped like derby hats, drive-ins like Oriental temples. Pet cemeteries continue advertising private chapels and plastic angels that for a fitting price will usher defunct poodles into a fitting eternity. Off-beat religious and psychological cults, their labels modernized, still hold out hope of personal anchors to lonely seekers.

Other seekers strive to establish new identities for themselves by making as much money as possible by whatever means come most readily to hand. It is the land of the hard sell, people on the make, a frenzy for success. To join the ranks ask only two questions: Is it new? Will it sell?

Such talk raises bristles. Civic leaders quickly point out that during the 1950s Los Angeles County was inundated by more than a million newcomers, all clamoring for housing, food, clothing, education of varying sorts, amusements and ease of transit while searching for what they felt they needed. Instead of collapsing under the strain, the region absorbed everyone — Nobel Prize winners (more reside in the Los Angeles area than anywhere else in the world) as well as kooks. With little in the way of guidelines to help (few regions had ever before gone through such an experience), Los Angeles leaders formulated and then began executing plans for the future. The Los Angeles Cultural Heritage Board was established in 1962. New colleges opened — Harvey Mudd (1957) and Pitzer (1963) both in Claremont and another branch of the University of California at Irvine (1965). The work is not finished. Given the nature of the region's dynamics, perhaps it never can be finished. Even so, the planners declare, words like "freaky," "loose" and "greedy" do not define the Los Angeles SMSA as well as words such as "innovative," "creative," and "open for opportunity."

Fending off chaos

By the middle of the 1960s, most residents of the metropolitan area — at least those with white skin — could cite several reasons why they were pleased with the direction the area was taking. Attacks were being launched against yet another water shortage, increased traffic congestion, smog and the creeping decay of Los Angeles' long-neglected downtown center. Voices continually urged support for programs to meet the housing and schooling needs of minority groups. More might have been done, to be sure.

First, there was the water shortage. Throughout the 1950s, the Los Angeles SMSA relied on three sources. One was water pumped from underground aquifers at the base of the Santa Monica and Sierra Madre mountains. The second was tasty Sierra Nevada water brought by gravity flow through aqueducts thrusting northward into the Owens Valley and Mono Basin — high-quality water that went entirely to the city of Los Angeles. The third source was Colorado River water pumped across the desert from Lake Havasu behind Parker Dam and distributed to member units by the Metropolitan Water District of Southern California.

Water

On the completion of the Colorado River Aqueduct in 1941, MWD served only thirteen cities. One year later, the Coastal Municipal Water District joined the system, but even then the huge aqueduct operated at less than two percent of its capacity, and fears were widely expressed that southern California had a white elephant on its hands. Almost immediately, however, the combined impacts of postwar growth and a sequence of dry years brought about a swift change of mood. In 1947, the San Diego County Water Authority signed with MWD. More contracts followed pell mell. Before the end of the 1950s, the agency had expanded to become the biggest wholesaler of water on earth, serving 4,000 square miles inhabited by 7.5 million people living in more than 100 cities and unincorporated districts.

To keep pace with the escalating demands, MWD spent, during the 1950s, $200 million to bring its Colorado River Aqueduct to full capacity. Meanwhile, other areas of the state — particularly the rich agricultural lands of the San Joaquin Valley — were eager to import water from the heavy rainfall areas of northern California and needed the help of southern California to make the proposal viable. But should southern California spend still more money for still more water? Some of the directors of MWD thought not. In 1952, Arizona had brought suit against California, charging that the coastal state was diverting more than its legal share of Colorado River water. As one of the principal users of that contested water, MWD feared that it might weaken its position in the bitter and protracted suit if southern California appeared to have other sources of water readily available. Accordingly, MWD at first opposed the state plan. Moods changed swiftly, however. Convinced that additional water from the north would eventually be needed to maintain the region's growth, southern

WATER FOR THE CITY: Although the St. Francis dam burst in 1928 (above), a good supply of water came to Los Angeles from the Owens Valley. Sportsmen once fished the river at the diversion point (top).

CITY ON THE MOVE: Great loops of multi-laned expressways (right) keep cars and people moving through Los Angeles, and along the Pasadena Freeway (above).

California legislators united in 1959 to help pass the Burns-Porter Act, which authorized the plan and laid the groundwork for raising part of the enormous expenses involved.

As envisioned, the complex program would cost $11 billion — far too much for even California to fund and construct in one great push. But if the legislature, following the path laid down by the Burns-Porter Act, would put on the ballot the proposal authorizing $1.7 billion in bonds, enough dams, canals and pumping stations could be built to distribute significant amounts of water throughout much of the San Joaquin Valley and carry still more over the Tehachapi Mountains to the south — *over* rather than *through* because earthquake faults inside the mountains might bring disaster to a tunnel.

Could an act authorizing the issuing of $1.7 billion in water bonds be passed? Northern California objected vehemently, fearing further erosion of its economic power. Four days before the general election of November 8, 1960, MWD signed a contract to buy 1.5 million acre-feet of water a year from the state water plan. This gave the bond issue a sound financial underpinning. Political triumph followed quickly as southern California voters, led by Los Angeles, trooped to the polls in sufficient numbers to guarantee the passage of the bonds.

The wisdom of the electorate soon became apparent. In 1963, the Supreme Court upheld Arizona's contention about water diversions and reduced the amount of water that California could take from the Colorado River. To offset the loss, the Metropolitan Water District sought and obtained an increase in its contract entitlement to state project water from 1.5 million acre-feet annually to more than two million acre-feet. Since then, work on the balance of the huge program has continued as rapidly as environmental, political and financial considerations have allowed.

But all this pertained to the Metropolitan Water District. For itself, Los Angeles still preferred water from Owens Valley. It was high quality, cheap (it did not have to be pumped *over* the mountains) and generated valuable electricity on its downhill route to the city. For these reasons, in 1963 the Los Angeles Department of Water and Power decided to build a second aqueduct from the Sierra Nevadas. Completion was scheduled for 1970 and would increase water deliveries from the mountains by about 50 percent. Thus by the end of the decade, approximately 80 percent of the city's

AUTOMOBILITY: Places to visit near Los Angeles — Capistrano and its colorful old mission (below and center), Palm Springs (right) and Big Bear skiing area (bottom) — became more accessible with the popularity of the automobile and improved roadway systems.

FIRST FREEWAY: The Arroyo Seco Parkway, later known as the Pasadena Freeway, was the first freeway created in 1938.

water supply would be imported from the eastern High Sierra watershed.

Just as vital as water — so most Angelenos believed — were freeways and the convenience of speedy routes crossing the sprawling California region. The freeway system spread rapidly after 1956 when President Eisenhower approved a $33-billion program of cooperative nationwide highway construction. California was the first western state to qualify for federal funds by drawing up a comprehensive 20-year freeway plan of its own and, in 1959, appropriating $10 billion as its share of the costs.

The national program was intended to link city to city. The Los Angeles SMSA, however — which in 1960 contained more automobiles than did 43 of America's states — decided to use the concrete veins for traffic within the metropolitan area.

Los Angeles created new patterns that broke with past traditions — freeways without excessive curves or steep grades, wide enough for safe driving, strategically built and located to facilitate both short- and long-distance driving. But there were some problems. The Santa Ana Freeway — winding northwest out of Orange County to join the massive interchange near downtown Los Angeles — was on the point of wiping out the historic plaza, heart of the old Spanish and Mexican pueblo when an upwelling of protest forced a rerouting.

Outsiders caught by the congestion when rain or accidents jammed up rush hour traffic were not always impressed with the growing freeway system. After keeping his eyes glued to nothing but shifting masses of red tail lights, Harrison Salisbury, noted reporter for the *New York Times,* exclaimed in disgust, "I have seen the future, and it doesn't work."

Angelenos — freed by their concrete escape hatches from the world's prickliest concentration of stop signs and traffic lights — took a different view. Drivers relished freeway development as it provided a faster and

safer means of travel outside the urban centers to the beaches, mountains and deserts — and there were no toll charges.

They were stubborn in defense of their new mobility. Over and over, planners told them that the city needed a municipal rapid transit system. By reducing the number of cars pouring exhaust fumes into the air, such a system would help clean up pollution. It would benefit the poor who lacked automobiles and could not accept jobs at a distance from their homes. Other major cities had alternate forms of public transportation. Why not Los Angeles?

It was a question of determining where money should be spent. Subways and elevated lines could not pay their way. Their advocates wanted to fund them with gasoline tax money. But the law stated that gas tax funds could be used only for road construction. Change the law? That might curtail freeway extensions. Most Los Angeles drivers resisted the proposal.

Angelenos admitted smog was bad; but a better understanding of its causes was opening the way to a solution that would not put limits on road developments. Consider the history of the orange-brown atmospheric soup. When it first became troublesome after World War II, Californians borrowed a word from Pittsburgh to describe it — smog, smoke plus fog — and attacked it on that basis. Recognizing that smog was a visible public concern and a major threat to community health, city and county government teamed up with industry leaders to seek solutions. Citrus growers throughout the county were ordered to cease using oil-burning, smoke-spewing orchard heaters to protect their fruit from frost. The burning of trash in backyard incinerators was interdicted on October 1, 1951. When smog persisted in spite of those measures, the Los Angeles County Air Pollution District (later expanded into the South Coast Air Quality Management District) turned its guns on factory smokestacks, particularly those of oil refineries and utilities.

GOING UNDERGROUND: A subway terminal building (top) located on Hill Street between Fourth and Fifth Streets; the underground view of the terminal (above) was full of platforms and pumps in the 1940s.

131

CITY BUILDINGS: Los Angeles' second city hall (below), which was completed in 1889 on Broadway between Second and Third Streets, was later auctioned piece by piece after a more modern structure (above) was built and opened in 1928 at Spring and First Streets. A height limitation on buildings was imposed that no structures more than 140 feet be built due to threat of earthquake; a 1928 photograph of downtown Los Angeles (right) was taken 28 years before the limitation was rescinded.

They installed expensive chimney scrubbers and other emission control devices which helped — but not enough. Whenever a normal temperature inversion occurred, the stagnant layers of warm air that lay trapped beneath higher strata of cooler atmosphere turned murky again, stinging eyes and rasping throats. Obviously smog formation was misunderstood. The answer largely came in 1952 from Professor Arie J. Haagen-Smit of Cal Tech. Haagen-Smit showed conclusively that smog was composed of neither smoke nor fog but of complex compounds that result from the photo-chemical action of sunlight on automobile exhaust gases and vapors from petroleum refining. And there was much sunlight, automobiles and refineries in the Los Angeles basin.

The Los Angeles County Air Pollution District established the nation's first motor vehicle emissions testing laboratory and campaigned for emission controls. The 1960 Legislature mandated the gradual installation of anti-smog devices on all cars sold in California. During the next 15 years, the district pioneered a series of progressively more stringent controls for commercial and industrial sources.

Would the cure work? Grumbling at costs but confident in the efficacy of technology, most Angelenos cooperated.

Cultural unities

Another phenomenon that could be blamed on automobiles was the decay of the central city. Easy mobility had led both ordinary residents and the businesses that served them to follow paths blazed by Henry E. Huntington's big red streetcars and move to the suburbs. As dispersal accelerated, the stately old Victorian homes ringing the central city (the best of them located on Bunker Hill) turned into rooming-houses for retired workers, the unemployed, minority families.

Sporadic efforts to control the trend had been stirring the community for years. During the postwar housing pinch, Los Angeles' liberal mayor, Fletcher Bowron, had obtained federal funds for developing low-cost housing on Bunker Hill, but cries of socialism defeated the program. A volunteer civic group called Greater Los Angeles Plans, Incorporated, next shifted the thrust of the renewal program toward high-income housing and sorely

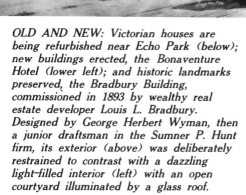

OLD AND NEW: *Victorian houses are being refurbished near Echo Park (below); new buildings erected, the Bonaventure Hotel (lower left); and historic landmarks preserved, the Bradbury Building, commissioned in 1893 by wealthy real estate developer Louis L. Bradbury. Designed by George Herbert Wyman, then a junior draftsman in the Sumner P. Hunt firm, its exterior (above) was deliberately restrained to contrast with a dazzling light-filled interior (left) with an open courtyard illuminated by a glass roof.*

133

Fort Moore Hill Memorial.

needed cultural facilities and office buildings. Land was purchased and cleared, and in 1957 the city council repealed an edict that had long limited all buildings except the City Hall to a maximum height of thirteen stories, a restriction imposed initially as an earthquake safety measure.

Not skyscrapers, however, but a striking cultural complex became Bunker Hill's first notable project. The work was the consuming love of Dorothy Buffum Chandler. Wife of Norman Chandler, publisher of the *Los Angeles Times,* "Buffie" was able, aggressive and energetic. She had served as a regent of the University of California and on the boards of several musical associations — the Hollywood Bowl, the Los Angeles Philharmonic, the Civic Light Opera. She was convinced that Los Angeles needed a cultural center second to none, and that if it were built on Bunker Hill it would serve as a magnet for drawing other enterprises into the area.

Dorothy Chandler initially raised $10 million and prevailed on the County Board of Supervisors to match the sum. Huge earthmoving machines leveled off the hilltop and construction workers swarmed in to build what became known as the Music Center, a trio of handsomely conceived auditoriums linked by mosaic pavements, reflecting pools and fountains. The largest building, designed by Welton Becket as the home of the Los Angeles Civic Light Opera and the winter home of its Philharmonic Orchestra, was completed first. Named the Dorothy Chandler Pavilion, it was opened with glittering fanfare on December 6, 1964. It was followed in 1967 by the Ahmanson Theatre and Mark Taper Forum (named for the principal donors).

The other buildings that gathered on and near Bunker Hill were, at first, governmental. The most eye catching was the headquarters of the city's Department of Water and Power. Fittingly it seemed to float on water. It was surrounded by fountains glamourized after dark by colored spotlights, and its glass facades blazed out the triumphs of hydroelectric power. From its upper stories one looked across the Music Center and down a long green mall bordered by heavily seated city, state and federal buildings to the tower of the City Hall, chunky under its pyramidal cap.

In spite of that striking building and of the Music Center across the street, private enterprise lagged behind public agencies in moving onto Bunker Hill. At the time, the slowness exasperated rather than worried. Enough other work was going on to keep spirits buoyant. The energetic stretch of Wilshire Boulevard between La Brea and Fairfax — long a strong commercial rival of the downtown area — watched proudly as its own spectacular trio of buildings designed by William Perena rose above the La Brea Tar Pits to house the permanent collections and traveling exhibits sponsored by the Los Angeles County Museum of Art. Like the Music Center, the Wilshire facilities were completed in the mid-1960s, to play its part in chorusing to the world that Los Angeles' cultural explosion was beginning.

Angelenos who were more interested in sports than in culture were also enjoying a feast. They piled up mountainous bets during horse racing season at Santa Anita and Hollywood Park. In 1946 they lured a professional football team, the Rams, from Cleveland into the 100,000-seat Coliseum. When jet aircraft made major league baseball possible in the 1950s, the city leaders set busily to work wooing the colorful Brooklyn Dodgers. Because a topnotch ballpark was considered a desirable feature of the downtown redevelopment program, Dodger owner Walter O'Malley agreed to turn Wrigley Field over to the city and spend approximately $1.7 million in the next 20 years to build and maintain a 40-acre public recreation area in Chavez Ravine. Dodger Stadium is one of the few major league ball parks in the country built by private capital.

Objections were immediate. Spanish-speaking citizens who would be ejected from the ravine howled angrily, but that subsided after relocation. In 1958 the Dodgers moved west, playing before record-breaking crowds in the Coliseum until their own stadium, one of the handsomest in America, was completed in 1962. In the meantime, the team tightened its grip on the heart of its fans by winning in 1960 the first World Series championship ever to come to Los Angeles.

Thanks to flamboyant, free-spending sports promoter Jack Kent Cooke, Los Angeles also obtained a first-class professional basketball team, the former Milwaukee Lakers and a National Hockey League team, the Kings. To house them Cooke constructed in Inglewood a $16 million neoclassical stadium called the Forum.

The amazing amusement center of Disneyland opened in 1955. There was a spreading freeway network to speed along the two or more cars that occupied nearly every middle-class garage. Gracious housing was rendered still more livable by endless gadgets and a rapidly spreading school system was crowned by several fine colleges and universities. With so much to distract the average prosperous white Angeleno, it is perhaps no wonder that in his effort to create a beautiful and widely admired region, he was short-sighted in ways that would haunt him later. That trait, too, must be taken into account when coming to grips with what is surely one of the continent's most incredible Standard Metropolitan Statistical Areas.

DOWNTOWN: The new Music Center complex with the pool and plaza area (above) and the tall building housing the Department of Water and Power (below).

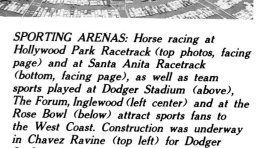

SPORTING ARENAS: Horse racing at Hollywood Park Racetrack (top photos, facing page) and at Santa Anita Racetrack (bottom, facing page), as well as team sports played at Dodger Stadium (above), The Forum, Inglewood (left center) and at the Rose Bowl (below) attract sports fans to the West Coast. Construction was underway in Chavez Ravine (top left) for Dodger Stadium in 1961.

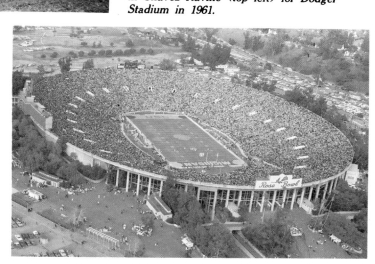

THE LAND OF DISNEY: In 1955, a wonderland opened in Anaheim for all who love the characters created by Walt Disney. A day in Disneyland (below) is often topped off with a fireworks display (left), also a trademark of the long-running "Wonderful World of Disney" television program.

137

ON THE BEACH: Long Beach (top) was already a popular site for an outing by the turn of the century. A family group (right, facing page) tents on the beach, circa 1900; G.W. James and friends (bottom left) pause after a New Year's swim. Seaside activities include riding in a glass bottom boat to Catalina Island (left center) and surfing (above), started in 1907 when George Feeth, an Anglo-Hawaiian, brought a surfboard to Redondo Beach.

BY THE BEAUTIFUL SEA: The young and old enjoy the beach at Santa Monica (left and above); sailboats await crews at Marina del Rey (below), and Balboa Pavillion (inset).

Chapter 8

Ferment

St. Paul's Episcopal Cathedral in 1971, nine years before it was demolished to make way for a downtown parking lot.

Blind spots

A sobering question arises. The 1950s and 1960s were energetic and creative times in Los Angeles. Why, then, did the trailing away of the latter decade and the onrush of the 1970s precipitate so many shocking disruptions?

National policies must take much of the blame. Soviet Russia was seen in Washington as a mortal enemy that had to be contained at all costs. One result noted earlier was a pouring of military contracts into California in general and Los Angeles in particular. These created an exciting boomtime psychology. Much money could be made by those who seized the opportunity, and because the money could be spent freely (unlike during the war), the region's affluent middle class grew.

It was remarkably homogenized and steadfastly determined to stay that way. Tens of thousands of newly prosperous residents lived with clusters of their own kind in commodious high-rise apartments, comfortable suburbs and smoothly designed mobile home "estates." They luxuriated in what came to be called in some quarters "the Los Angeles style" — sleek, high-powered cars, sleekly casual clothes, private, well-lighted tennis courts for night playing, gymnasiums for body building, sauna baths and swimming pools for smoothing away tension. (By 1962 southern California contained one-third of all the swimming pools in the nation.) The sale of luxury goods — power boats, ornamental shrubs, television sets encased in rosewood cabinets — soared high. Not everything was fluff, however. By the close of the 1950s, Los Angeles was the second busiest art and book market in the United States.

However, there were other lifestyles in the area. Of the one million people who flocked into the San Fernando Valley in the 1950s, only two percent were black — and they congregated mostly around the little manufacturing enclave of Pacoima, where others of their race had found work before the great migration had begun.

Life turned inward. Neighborly front porches disappeared. Dwellers in suburbia and its equivalents ceased walking to stores or strolling along sidewalks at night. Instead they gathered around backyard barbecue pits and on poolside patios bedecked with flowering plants. Those who had attained the good life were fiercely determined to defend it.

Red-baiting was not a new preoccupation in the nation or California. There had been the animosities that greeted allegedly radical, Bolshevik-led labor unions during the era of the first World War and the "Red-inspired" socialism of the early years of the Depression. As the 1930s drew to an end, suspicions reached such a state that both the national Congress and the California state Legislature formed Un-American Activites Committees charged with ferreting out treachery in whatever spots it might exist.

By the 1940s, the Un-American Activities Committees had gained power. Leaders of the motion picture industry who challenged the inquisitors' right to investigate their political philosophies were found guilty of treacherous thinking and denied further employment in their profession. Professors at all branches of the University of California were required to take loyalty oaths, as were state workers and employees of the city and county of Los Angeles. The county Board of Supervisors ordered that all books bearing the least taint of socialism (an elastic designation) be removed from county library shelves. Self-appointed spies listened in on church sermons and school classes to make sure all utterances were pure.

Another manifestation of the region's postwar prosperity was the move to the steep hills along the region's northern periphery. During the 1950s and 1960s, flat land suitable for home building either became unavailable or chillingly expensive. Seeking alternative sites, developers turned to the brushy canyons and the windy ridges. They found choice places. Privacy was enhanced, views were superb, and often the air was better than on the lowland since some elevations rose above the smog level. However, that area had special problems.

Small fires have always been a natural event in southern California's hill country. But no seeker of the heights wanted a fire near *his* dwelling. Even if the house escaped damage, the surroundings would be blackened and unattractive. So fires were assiduously suppressed. As a result, the chaparral, and ground litter beneath it, accumulated into denser mats than usual. By fall when Santa Ana winds were likely to roar in from the desert, the patches were so dry that a carelessly flipped cigarette, a spark from a welder's torch or a match in the hands of an arsonist was enough to turn a whole hillside into a leaping conflagration.

Every year a few homes are crisped; every decade hundreds are. In November 1961, 437 mansions in the wealthy Bel-Air district were reduced to twisted frames and gaunt chimneys; scores more were damaged. In October 1978, fourteen separate fires, many deliberately set, erupted along the metropolitan area's northern rim. The flames turned 40,000 acres of brushland into unsightly charcoal, destroyed 270 homes, killed three persons and spread havoc among uncounted wild and domestic animals. After the disaster, Los Angeles County Fire Chief Clyde A. Bagdon claimed that misuse of the mountain environment had created "a fire control problem which may be without equal in the world."

Public and private agencies involve themselves in a constant struggle to minimize such devastation. Recent building and fire codes prohibit the use

When the Beverly Hills Electric Fountain began to operate in 1931, its water jets and color effects created 60 different displays every eight minutes.

143

NATURAL DISASTERS: Forest fires
(above) and mud slides (top right) plague
the West Coast.

of highly combustible construction materials. Laws also require hillside residents to clear flammable vegetation to minimize the possibility of transmitting fire. A controversial development is prescribed burning to create a natural firebreak. City and county fire departments are also served by seasonal firefighters specially trained to fight wildland fires and equipped with the largest full-time fleet of helicopters owned by any municipal agency in the nation.

Damage does not end with the burning. Although public agencies sow grass, mustard seed and other fire-resistant plants on the denuded slopes as soon as they are cool, the growth that follows is insufficient to withstand the shock of winter rains for a year or two. Water pours unrestrained down the hillsides into the canyons. Debris basins are constructed to catch and hold mud and debris while allowing water to flow naturally through the drainage system. When unusually heavy rains fall, as happened in February and March 1980, the tortured land can do nothing but give way. The debris basins cannot be emptied fast enough and overflow. Thick streams of mud and boulders sweep through the canyons, mash garages, fill houses with goo, snap power poles and trees, tumble autos end on end and drown unwary travelers. It takes a particular kind of recklessness to persist in living in such areas, but many Angelenos have it. Said one woman whose mud-filled house lay askew in the bottom of Topanga Canyon, "I would move here again."

The big jolts

IN WATTS: Young blacks catch a snack
at a neighborhood food stand.

Still another manifestation of the era's burgeoning prosperity was the mass arrival of the black-skinned and brown-skinned minority groups who were drawn to the region by the same hope of a better life that had attracted the whites. It was a headlong movement. Between 1945 and 1965, Los Angeles' black population grew nearly tenfold to upwards of half a million persons. For many, expectation faded into frustration. Many were jammed into a district called Watts, 50 square miles of substandard housing south of the central city.

Most of the houses in Watts had been constructed as small single-family residences. The inability of black migrants to find shelter outside this area resulted in dense overcrowding in the decaying buildings. Along with high unemployment rates, this jamming together of too many people in too little space created an explosive situation, a wild outburst that shook the city's complacency.

The rioting began on the hot, smoggy evening of August 11, 1965. For five days the torrent rolled north, burning, looting, shooting. By the time

MUSEUM IN BLACK: The Dunbar Museum was founded to preserve and celebrate black history in Los Angeles. Originally the Dunbar Hotel, named for black poet Paul Laurence Dunbar, it was the site of the first national convention of the NAACP in 1928. One of the nation's first black mayors, Thomas Bradley (in large picture, far left), was elected in Los Angeles in 1973.

14,000 members of the National Guard had restored order, 34 persons were dead, 31 of them black; 1,032 had been injured badly enough to require hospital treatment; 3,952 had been arrested, 3,162 of them black; and $40 million worth of property across 46 square miles of city slums had been destroyed or damaged.

Immediately following the Watts riots, the Los Angeles Chamber of Commerce appointed a Rehabilitation Committee, headed by H. C. "Chad" McClellan, to aid recovery of the area. And in a few short months, with the help of over a hundred firms, the committee found jobs for over 2,000 blacks. Dozens of volunteer groups helped launch Head Start programs in the schools and job training among the unemployed. Streets were repaired, a fine new hospital was built, and an annual festival was inaugurated to celebrate not the riot but the community gains that the fighting brought about. There is ample room for more improvement, however. Segregation is still very much a reality, and unemployment rates among blacks, especially the young, remain well above the level of whites.

Blacks were not the only alienated people in the area. In the outlying agricultural regions, Mexican field workers led by charismatic Cesar Chavez called strikes against California's corporate farms. Within the city, the brown-skinned majority felt, as the blacks did, that they were the victims of inadequate schooling, job discrimination, police brutality and a Selective Service draft that sent undue numbers of them overseas to Vietnam.

In 1970 protests erupted in the barrios of east central Los Angeles. Although the rioting did not spread as far out of hand as it had in Watts, it drew attention because of the senseless killing of Reuben Salazar, a popular radio personality and a reporter for the Los Angeles Times. During the uproars, a white sheriff fired a tear-gas projectile into a cafe and by

19366 MAIN ST. LOOKING WEST. WATTS. CAL.

EARLY BLACKS: One of the areas black migrants settled in Los Angeles was Mud Town (above), now known as Watts. Peter "Nigger" Johnson, a preacher, politician and pork raiser (inset), was one of the approximately 2,800 blacks living in Los Angeles by the turn of the century.

Moving beyond Watts:
Los Angeles black community

Four of the 44 *pobladores* who first settled Los Angeles in 1781 were at least partially black. Pio Pico, the last Mexican governor of California and a sometime resident of Los Angeles, was a mulatto.

Despite this early black representation in Los Angeles, there were only twelve blacks recorded in the 1850 census. The failure of blacks to migrate to Los Angeles was due to the general sentiment within the entire state. Not only was Los Angeles for the most part pro-slavery, California — though officially a proponent of the Union — discriminated against blacks. The state passed a fugitive slave statute, would not accept the testimony of blacks in court until 1863 and rejected the ratification of the Fifteenth Amendment to the federal constitution. As a result, blacks did not begin to migrate to Los Angeles in great numbers until after 1880. There were 188 blacks in the county in 1880; 1,817 in 1890; 2,841 in 1900; 7,599 in 1910; 18,738 in 1920 and over 30,000 in 1930.

Most of the blacks who came to Los Angeles in the late nineteenth century worked for the railroad. Gradually they began to find employment in other fields, including fire fighting and police service. Los Angeles may have been the first American city to employ black firemen and policemen. A few local blacks became extremely wealthy in such fields as real estate, scrap iron and hog farming.

Most of the black migrants to Los Angeles from 1880 to 1940 came from the South and the Midwest. Out of a combination of choice and compulsion, they settled in Mud Town (now Watts), in a colony on Temple Street, in the Budlong district, in the First and Los Angeles Street area, along Central Avenue and in the Sugar Hill area.

In the 1910s through 1940s, Central Avenue was the hub of black life in southern California. Known as the "Lenox Avenue of the Far West," it was famous for its night clubs, particularly the Club Alabam and the Hummingbird Cafe. The Dunbar Hotel, built by Dr. John Alexander Somerville, was named for the black poet Paul Laurence Dunbar. It was a major center for cultural, business and social gatherings among blacks. (The Dunbar is now a black history museum.)

In the late '30s and early '40s, some of the wealthier blacks moved to Sugar Hill, located in the Western-Adams area. Those who lived in the area in both imposing mansions and modest residences included Cornelius Johnson, a 1932 competitor in the Berlin Olympics; Eddie Rochester Anderson, Jack Benny's sidekick; Bill Bojangles Robinson; Paul Williams, the premier architect; actresses Hatti McDaniels, Louise Beavers and Ethel Waters.

Resentment toward Anglos and the police rose over the next few decades. Blacks in Watts rioted in 1965. Since that time, government and private programs have partially alleviated the economic and social problems that led to the riots. Blacks have moved increasingly into positions of prominence and power. Thomas Bradley's 1973 election as mayor of a city whose population was only about sixteen percent black is evidence of the growing change in attitude.

chance struck Salazar in the head. Repercussions rolled as far as the Spanish language is spoken.

Racial tension was accompanied by economic shocks. During the latter part of Lyndon Johnson's presidency, defense and aerospace contracts that might have gone to California were shifted to Texas. Later, President Nixon sought to cool soaring inflation by cutting the defense budget and winding down the war in Vietnam. Meanwhile foreign manufacturers learned to flood the United States with highly competitive goods.

Suddenly a recession was stalking the land. It hit particularly hard in the Los Angeles SMSA, where a large segment of the populace depended on defense-related contracts for their livelihood. To stay alive, some aircraft firms combined. Lockheed averted bankruptcy only by going to Congress for a then-unprecedented government loan. Some high-salaried executives as well as unskilled workers found themselves hunting new jobs. It is possible that this abrupt shrinkage in everyone's expectations helped mute further violence among the blacks and Chicanos. As everyone else, they were faced not with accumulating more goods but with clinging desperately to what they had, little though it might be.

Even nature added a haymaker. At 6:01 a.m., February 9, 1971, a major earthquake, centered near the hamlet of Sylmar, rocked the northeastern part of the San Fernando Valley. Freeway bridges and several huge pillars being erected to support a high-swooping freeway interchange toppled and broke into chunks as pieces of stick candy. Close to 2,000 buildings were damaged. Sixty-four people died, nearly three-quarters of them patients in a collapsing veterans hospital. A nearby dam that stored Owens Valley water for distribution throughout the region showed severe ruptures and had to be drained into the Los Angeles River as a precaution against aftershocks.

The quake was felt for miles around. Building inspectors launched a city-wide inspection of all public edifices. So many schools were found to be in such a dangerous condition that an extensive rehabilitation program was inescapable.

There was one symbol of hope however. The new high-rise buildings that were at last being erected near Bunker Hill and along Wilshire Boulevard withstood the shock without significant damage. Call them harbingers. A new city, built to new patterns and guided in part by a new set of values, was clearly possible.

Environmental revolts

More than any other public official, Mayor Tom Bradley epitomized the shape that Los Angeles began to assume during the 1970s. The son of black sharecroppers in Texas, Bradley had served on the Los Angeles police force for 21 years and on the city council for ten. He was tall and husky, with a wispy mustache and a low-key approach to politics in an area where flamboyance was the rule. In 1969 he challenged the incumbent mayor — fiesty, folksy, conservative Sam Yorty — for the city's top job. Bradley lost by only a handful of votes.

After his defeat, Bradley told his followers to keep faith in the democratic process. "I have lived by that belief all my life," he said, "and I will not give up now." Carefully he marshalled his forces for a second try in 1973.

Los Angeles' blacks supported him, but they constituted only eighteen percent of the population. The would-be mayor had to draw support from throughout the city's voting spectrum. He accomplished this by identifying himself with an issue that concerned a steadily increasing number of citizens. How big could Los Angeles grow without severe damage to the qualities that had brought it world-wide fame in the first place? To use Bradley's own words, "There is no way our air, our streets, our soil, our energy can support so many people. We must set reasonable limits or face environmental disaster."

BOUNTY OF THE LAND: Pepper pickers
in Orange County (top, facing page), a pig
mural at Farmer John's (bottom, facing
page), an orange vendor (center, facing
page) and Farmer's Market (above)
illustrate the bountiful harvest of the Los
Angeles area.

Pollution — by then a national problem — was one of the city's most
annoying headaches. But many aspects of it could be cured, as the clean-up
of the San Pedro-Long Beach harbor showed. Sewage, garbage, ship bilge
and discharges from chemical plants and oil refineries had polluted 900
acres of the West Basin's once sparkling fish-teeming waters. But when
water quality review boards ordered improvement, industry responded with
an alacrity that surprised many doubters, and soon it was possible to hook
edible fish for supper once again.

At another harbor of sorts, the Los Angeles International Airport, jet
aircraft produced a different form of pollution — incredible noise for the
people living in those sections of Inglewood, Westchester and Playa del Rey
over which the long approach lanes extended. A program was launched in
1965 at no cost to the taxpayer. More than 2,800 parcels of property were
purchased from homeowners to clear the area. With the inauguration of
quieter, wide-bodied jets in 1970, the noisier planes are being phased out.
The airline industry and government are coordinating efforts to bring about
uniform standards and resolutions.

CHINESE COMMUNITY: Produce provided an economic stronghold for the Chinese settling in Los Angeles; they cultivated the land (below and facing page) and sold the fruits and vegetables in the city. In Chinatown, children (left, circa 1900) and young people (far left) grew up looking forward to the annual dragon parade (right, facing page) celebrating the Chinese New Year's. The Pekin Curio Store (far right, facing page) was built in 1809 by Don Juan de Dios Ballistero was a private residence and later the Washington Hotel before its development as a Chinatown landmark.

Seeking specialties for success: Los Angeles Chinese-Americans

Only two Chinese were recorded in the census as Los Angeles residents in 1850. Eleven years later, 21 Chinese men and eight Chinese women lived in the city. About 1870, the Chinese began to establish settlements in California's larger communities in Los Angeles.

Most of the early Chinese who settled in southern California arrived by way of San Francisco. Most had worked on the Southern Pacific's construction crews or in central and northern California's agricultural fields. Once in Los Angeles, they worked as cooks or domestics in private residences or hotels. Their wages often paid for the passage of relatives to America. Gradually, Los Angeles' Chinatown developed into what had previously been Sonoratown. Here, the Celestials (as they were often called) established shops and restaurants and peddled produce. By 1895, produce — particularly celery — was the Chinese economic stronghold. By that time, about 4,000 Chinese were raising and selling all the vegetables consumed in the city. They were largely responsible for the development of the citrus and the fishing industries, especially abalone fishing and the creation of abalone jewelry.

The success of the Chinese in these endeavors resulted in resentment as well as legislation that restricted their work and their legal rights. But as other racial groups moved to Los Angeles, antagonism toward the Chinese was diffused. Today, Los Angeles' Chinese-Americans are widely dispersed throughout the general population. But they continue to regard Chinatown in downtown Los Angeles as the cultural heart of their community.

152

今川焼

"IMAGAWAYAKI"
ORIGINATED IN THE AGE OF "EDO", APPROX. 150 YEARS AGO AT "EDO" (CITY OF TOKYO) KANDA
IMAGAWA-BASHI (BRIDGE OF IMA RIVER). HISTORICAL DOCUMENT INTERPRETS THIS
SPECIAL JAPANESE PANCAKE AS "A CONFECTIONERY MADE BY BAKED SMALL RED BEANS
(AZUKI) WITH BATTER OVER A COPPER SHEET METAL AND COPPER RINGS AS GUIDES.
IN "MODERN JAPAN" THIS HAS BEEN MODIFIED INTO A SERIES OF RECESSED COPPER HOLES
IN WHICH THE BATTERS ARE POURED.

FROM THE ORIENT:
Oriental people bring to Los
Angeles colorful lotus fest
dances and famous food
dishes from China (facing
page), shops with goods
from Japan (above) and a
Korean temple to celebrate
Buddha's birthday (left).

Overcoming war and relocation: Los Angeles Japanese-Americans

Only 86 Japanese resided in California in 1880. The Japanese population and their contributions have multiplied dramatically in the last 100 years. While the Japanese-Americans have greatly benefited the state, their most notable successes have been in southern California's produce, fishing, floral and nursery industries. Their progress has been made despite racial discrimination and their incarceration in relocation camps during World War II.

Until 1866, Japanese law forbade a subject to leave that country. After that legislation was rescinded, Japanese began slowly to immigrate to California to work in agriculture, to become domestics and gardeners and to establish small businesses in Japanese settlements. Though U.S. law limited Japanese immigration, those few who did settle in southern California made a significant impact on the economy. They raised strawberries, asparagus, lima beans, carrots and cauliflower and cultivated citrus trees. They also developed the fish-canning industry and the propagation and sell of decorative plants.

Their preeminence in these fields, together with racial prejudice and their strength as a world power, led to distrust between Japanese and Anglos. The bombing of Pearl Harbor and the resultant war intensified the antagonism. As a result most Japanese (who were Nisei, American-born United States citizens) were forceably sequestered in relocation centers for nearly four years. Upon their release at war's end, many resettled in the Los Angeles-Long Beach area and in San Francisco.

Since that time, the Japanese-Americans in Greater Los Angeles have assimilated into the dominant culture, settling in racially mixed areas and functioning effectively in a wide variety of jobs. In Los Angeles the cultural heart of the Japanese community remains Little Tokyo, located on East First Street beginning just east of Main Street. Restaurants, shops and celebrations characterize life in the enclave that in 1980 is undergoing expansion and renewed vitality.

JAPANESE POPULATION: In the early 1920s, Japanese vegetable stands (top) were everyday sights, while festive carousels (center) marked special occasions. In the 1940s, however, most Japanese were moved (bottom) to relocation centers for almost four years.

154

Freeways, too, fell under attack. Beverly Hills fought off a freeway that would have bisected that community. Citizen objections halted proposals to spiral one set of gray ribbons across the pastoral Santa Monica Mountains to the Ventura Freeway and another which, if it had been constructed as planned, would have walled in the coast southward from Santa Monica.

But one of the most controversial proposals has been the Century Freeway — ten lanes designed to run from Norwalk westward 17.5 miles to the International Airport. To expedite the project, the city began buying property and relocating residents along the right-of-way late in the 1960s. About 4,200 homes were scheduled for demolition. Young attorneys from the non-profit Center for Law in the Public Interest brought work to a halt by demanding a full environmental impact statement (EIS) from the city. EIS findings showed that the freeway was the most feasible solution, with no abnormal effects of smog or noise. Seven years and $5 million later, in October 1979, construction engineers were finally allowed to go ahead. Due to numerous delays, the extensive relocation program and a rapidly rising inflation factor, projected costs have doubled from $500 million to $1 billion.

Smog, unfortunately, turned out to be less amenable to frontal attack than did objectionable freeways. Even Congress proved to be a dubious ally, passing a national Air Quality Act whose standards were so mild that a special amendment had to be tacked onto the bill so that California could maintain its own more rigorous requirements. To help assure that the southland's vehicles remain in compliance with vehicle emission codes, a motor vehicle inspection and maintenance program (for "upon purchase" and "change of ownership" vehicles) was mandated for the South Coast Air Basin by the California Legislature and was implemented in 1979. Yet in spite of the special legislation, Los Angeles seemed to be running on a treadmill. Automobiles proliferated. Car manufacturers kept saying they were unable to meet West Coast specifications.

Chemists suggested that certain noxious compounds had not been adequately identified and hence were not being neutralized. And so heavy concentrations of ozone and nitrogen dioxide began having an adverse affect on vegetation in the San Bernardino Mountains and on leafy vegetables and citrus groves on the farms that still remained in the Los Angeles basin. These were creeping ills, easily overlooked. But a sharp reminder came September 24, 1979, when the city gasped under its worst smog attack in a quarter of a century — a real irony since the energy crunch was supposedly bringing about a decrease, although small, in gasoline consumption. What could be done?

Traffic congestion in the central city could be reduced by means of a Downtown People Mover (DPM); and a subway line along the Wilshire corridor (the most heavily traveled metropolitan route) seemed to offer the best hope. It was not a new idea, but it had long been blocked by a state law that limited the use of gas tax funds to road construction. Revolt was welling up, however. In 1974, voters passed Proposition 5, a constitutional amendment permitting the state, county and city to divert a portion of their road funds from gasoline taxes for "fixed guideway" transportation. The victory was doubly sweet — it not only gave direct access to state funds but opened the way to matching federal grants.

Ten years of often acrimonious discussion were needed to bring about an agreement concerning the most desirable forms and routes of transportation. In the meantime, Tom Bradley was rewarded for his support of mass transportation and other forward-looking proposals by being swept into the mayor's office in 1973 with a thumping majority over his old foe, Sam Yorty.

MASS TRANSIT: Moving masses of people to and from the International Airport (top) and during the rush hour (above) is a constant challenge in Los Angeles.

FROM ALL CULTURES: Cultural treasures are kept at the Los Angeles County Museum of Art (top left), the Norton Simon Museum (top right), the J.P. Getty Museum (center right) and at the George C. Page Museum of La Brea Discoveries (above). Artistic statements from the Chicano community are found on wall murals along Soto Street (bottom, left and right).

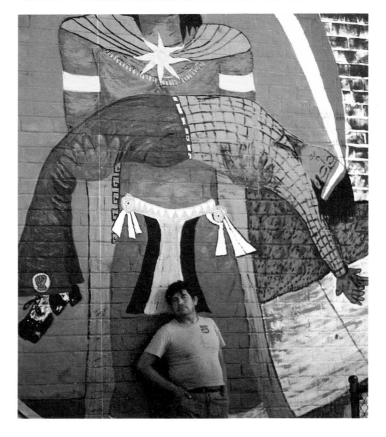

ON THE STREETS: *An eye-catching billboard on Sunset Boulevard (top), an intriguing antique store front (left) on Melrose Avenue and a luxury car in Beverly Hills color Los Angeles with variety.*

Looking toward the future

Inevitably the new administration found itself confronted with more problems than just rapid transit. A few of the difficulties were new. More — like water and race relations — were old but complicated by unexpected developments. And all were acerbated by a baffling combination of soaring inflation and, from 1972-1974, by a stubborn economic recession.

One new twist to racial problems has been the decade's astonishing influx of undocumented immigrants from Mexico and other Latin American countries to the south. Although the migration is national in scope, its impact on Los Angeles has been particularly profound. No one knows how many live in the metropolitan area, but there may be hundreds of thousands.

Has the influx seriously injured other workers, particularly Spanish-speaking American citizens? Opinions vary, even among labor unions. Some insist that the undocumented workers not only take jobs away from citizens but also place heavy burdens on the area's educational, welfare and health systems. Others retort that by doing work no one else wants, the aliens allow citizens to move up the job ladder. Furthermore, the argument continues, they contribute more to the government in the form of social security and income-tax deductions than they receive in benefits for which few apply because of their fear of deportation.

Whatever the truth, Los Angeles' Spanish-speaking population is rapidly changing the complexion of parts of the city. The east end of Broadway and the old plaza in the downtown area sound and look as fascinating as Guadalajara. Out in Sun Valley in the northeast part of the San Fernando Valley, seven Anglo precincts have become almost entirely Hispanic. The census takers of 1980 (their counterparts of 1970 admittedly underestimated the city's Spanish-speaking population by three to four percent) were careful to count everyone, citizens and noncitizens alike. As a result, Los Angeles may gain two or three more Congressional seats.

Even more disturbing is the upsurge of gang activities throughout the county's Hispanic enclaves. Police believe that there are at least 300 such gangs — composed of both citizens and non-citizens — roaming the territories to which they lay claim. Once they battled each other with fists and bicycle chains as a simple release from tension. Now they indulge in more violent acts. In 1979, the county experienced more than 250 gang-related slayings — an American record. Meanwhile social programs designed to quell the outbreaks have been reduced by fund limitations imposed by Proposition 13 and by personnel cutbacks in CETA, the national government's Comprehensive Employment and Training Act.

Equally knotty, though less violent, are the difficulties raised by a 1970 court order that the Los Angeles Board of Education eliminate school segregation. Superior Court Judge Albert Gietelson who issued the order in Los Angeles was soundly defeated at the next city election, but the edict stood. The Board of Education began studying the possibility of using busses to transport black, white and brown children among hundreds of school districts in order to achieve the racial balances demanded.

So far results have been discouraging. Inextricably mixed with the racial feelings is the reluctance of black, Chicano and Anglo parents to let small children be bussed into unknown settings far from home. So many whites have either moved into unaffected school districts or have put their children into private schools that some observers say true balances cannot now be achieved, no matter how many busses are employed. Nonetheless, Judge Paul Egly, who supervises the Los Angeles effort, keeps pushing the board for a more effective plan.

Meanwhile fresh disputes over water have arisen in the Owens Valley and in Mono Basin. During the drought of 1976-77, the city sought to increase its groundwater pumping in the valley and was challenged on the environmental grounds that it was endangering the region's still pristine

Perhaps Los Angeles' most famous intersection, Hollywood Boulevard and Vine Street.

BOOKS AND MORE: Established in 1878, the Los Angeles Public Library was housed several places until it moved to a specially designed building (top, facing page) at Fifth and Hope Streets. It was designed by Bertram G. Goodhue who patterned it on his earlier creation, the Nebraska State Capitol Building in Lincoln. For many years, the library building featured tile pools, rolling expanses of grass and many entrances; the Hope Street entrance (far left, facing page) is presided over by Herodotus, Virgil and Socrates. However, many such attractions were eliminated for parking and storage spaces. Murals by Dean Cornwall and Albert Herter enhance the rotunda (left, facing page) of the library building which was named for long-time library commissioner Rufus B. von KleinSmid in 1964. In 1967, it was designated as an historic cultural monument.

LIFESTYLES: A musician (above) and costumed strollers (right) populate Venice, while Italian fishermen (below) work the waters near San Pedro Harbor.

CITY OF ANGELS: Looking to the heavens is possible at Griffith Observatory (top) and at St. Vibiana's Cathedral (left) downtown. The Wayfarers' Chapel (above) on Palos Verdes Drive was designed by architect Frank Lloyd Wright.

MEDITERRANIA: Arthur M. Parsons, like Venice's Abbott Kinney, was captivated by the vision of canals, bridges and gondolas, and he envisioned an Italian-style resort community in southern California. In the early 1900s, he founded Naples near Long Beach, where gondolas floated on the Naples Lagoon (above). Like Venice (right), the reality did not equal its creator's dreams, but a community remains today, a testament to the romantic image of Mediterrania in California.

natural landscapes. Farther north the defenders of Mono Lake charge that the city's diversion of streams that once fed that strange, moonscape body of water is dropping its level, creating clouds of alkaline dust and opening bridges to reach islands in the lake where a major seagull rookery has existed.

An investigation of the Mono complaints by an environmental task force resulted in an order that the city reduce its water diversions by 85 percent. The Department of Water and Power is resisting. If the order is enforced, Los Angeles stands to lose fifteen to twenty percent of its vital water supply and considerable hydroelectric power that the water generates on its way through the aqueduct. (This is estimated at a total financial impact of $18 million annually.) Such a loss would seriously endanger the city's water, energy and general economic situation, as well as the entire state, since additional supplies of water and energy would have to come from other sources, which would involve electrical generating power that would consume 100,000 barrels of oil per year and a rate increase of ten percent. The quarrel is before the state Legislature with no firm conclusion in sight.

So it goes — major problems and small frustrations. One of Mayor Bradley's pet projects has been the creation of a National Urban Park in the west end of the Santa Monica Mountains where rugged ridges run parallel to a spectacular coast. Such a park would halt the development of the hills while creating an urban open-space recreational area unmatched by any other city in the world. Congress has shown a willingness to appropriate funds for land acquisition, but stubborn real estate interests and a tangle of overlapping state, county and private holdings have stalled the program. That showdown will be one of the main features of the 1980s.

Yet another project is the summer Olympic games of 1984 — won after hard bargaining with the International Olympic Committee. For sports lovers, the shock occasioned by the departure of the Rams football team for Anaheim Stadium in Orange County has been offset by the willingness of the colorful Raiders from Oakland to enrage their own fans by moving into the Coliseum vacated by the Rams — if the legal hurdles that stand in the way can be overcome.

ON THE WATERFRONT: Coastal waters mean maritime commerce at the Port of Los Angeles.

Constant clashes of interest are common in Los Angeles — and yet the very heat they engender is a sign of vitality rather than of decay. A sharp rise in orders for aircraft from commercial operators enabled Los Angeles to help lead the nation's economy back toward healthy indexes. The revitalization made clear what the newly modernized harbor and the giant new skyscrapers rising near Bunker Hill were already proclaiming — the Los Angeles metropolitan area has replaced San Francisco as the financial center of the West and as America's gateway to the entire Pacific Rim.

The innovativeness that Angelenos have long insisted was a fundamental characteristic of their city is widely evident. To keep pace with the demands of overwhelming growth, Los Angeles International Airport plans to invest $250 million for improvements over the next four years. The annual passenger traffic volume is expected to push the 40 million mark in the 1980s. Construction of the People Mover — more than 50 fully automated cars moving at 90-second intervals along elevated guiderails — is on the point of being launched. With the business community financing a large portion of the operating costs, the unique, highly experimental system will follow an S-shaped curve from the reawakened, refurbished Union Station through the Bunker Hill area to the cavernous Convention Center. Enormous parking buildings near either end of the people mover will absorb automobiles fed into them from the freeways so that no commuter will thereafter need to take his car into the once-congested downtown area.

After endless discussion, subway planners have also settled on a route to drastically reduce automobile traffic while at the same time bringing in enough people to add vitality not just to Bunker Hill but also to the mid-Wilshire and Hollywood districts. This system will also be anchored on the Union Station. From there it will strike out along Wilshire Boulevard and bend north over Cahuenga Pass into the densely populated San Fernando Valley.

Striking architectural expressions of the new energy and of a new concern for people rather than for automobiles runs throughout the vaulting glass towers — some cubical, some round, some multifaceted — of Bunker Hill. Open space is emphasized. In the plazas (many of them elevated well above street level), water drops in carefully contrived falls, leaps in fountains, pulls the sky down into reflecting pools bordered by cool greenery. Benches are scattered close to monumental modern statuary or beside huge Spanish- or Mexican-style pots filled with flowering trees. Less noticeable but essential to the pervading sense of well-being is the placing of new structures in such a way that every neighboring area receives sunlight at least part of each day.

Through traffic has been confined in part to double-decker roadways. High pedestrian crosswalks are beginning to link plaza to plaza. In other places, escalators drop underground to malls lined with exciting shops and restaurants. It is just a beginning. If current plans for the redevelopment area — and it is only one of the many sections of the city feeling the new stir — are fully realized, downtown Los Angeles will contain at least 28 ultramodern living and working centers, each different in its ambience, each containing parking space for cars on its lower levels, recreation centers atop and green spaces in between.

Inevitably, as in any megalopolis, problems and frustrations will continue. But no city — least of all Los Angeles — ever grew great without facing challenges head-on. Los Angeles has done just that — with surprising success. Now, moreover, the region is again remembering that one of the chief reasons people wanted to live here in earlier times was the relaxed beauty that surrounded them. Planners vow that the same inducements can be made as persuasive today as they ever were. They are probably right. Just looking at the new shape of the 200-year-old city is enough to convince one that, here indeed, at the continent's sunniest edge, is a land where — in spite of all odds — dreams have a way of being realized over and over again.

THE WATTS TOWERS: Constructed from broken tiles, bottles and other assorted discards, the towers of Simor Rodia are considered the folk sculptor's masterpiece. In 1963, the Watts Towers were declared an historical cultural monument by the Los Angeles cultural heritage board.

MOVING PICTURES: Old sets at Zoetrope Studios (top) being refurbished by Francis Ford Coppola, the main entrance at Paramount Pictures (left) and street scene "props" at Universal Studios are tangible evidence of the motion picture business in Los Angeles.

IN CONTRAST: The sleek lines of the Arco Tower and Public Library (above) and the modern sculpture in the Arco Tower Plaza (inset) provide a contrast to a quaint storefront in Venice (right), all part of the spectrum of the Los Angeles cityscape.

*The city's first automobile toots down
Spring Street, circa 1905.*

166

Chronology

Cahuilla Indians, weavers of yucca mats.

1533 Fortún Jiménez discovers Baja California.
1542 Juan Rodríguez Cabrillo discovers San Diego Bay, Catalina Island, the Channel Islands, San Pedro Bay and Santa Monica Bay.
1579 Sir Francis Drake explores the California coast and claims California for England.
1602 Sebastián Vizcaíno visits San Diego, San Pedro and Monterey bays.
1767 Gaspar de Portolá appointed the first Spanish governor of the Californias.
1768 The Spanish undertake four expeditions to colonize Alta California.
1769 The fourth colonizing expedition, led by Portolá, arrives in what is now Los Angeles, thus becoming the first white group to visit the area. The area is inhabited solely by Indians, known as Garieliños and Fernardiños. Portola names the site of Los Angeles "El Pueblo de los Angeles de la Reyna."
1771 Franciscan Father Junipero Serra, who had accompanied Portolá, establishes Mission San Gabriel, the fourth of the California missions.
1775 Felipe de Neve appointed governor of the Californias. His goal is to establish more settlements in Alta California and to make it agriculturally self-sustaining.
1777 De Neve decides to establish a pueblo at Los Angeles to produce food for the garrisons.
1777 Monterey is made the capital of the Californias by Felipe de Neve.
1777 300 Indians are baptized at Mission San Gabriel.
1779 De Neve issues *Reglamento,* the first laws for California.
1779 De Neve sends Lieutenant Governor Rivera y Moncada to Mexico to recruit soldiers for the Los Angeles settlement.
1781 The first settlers, led by Lieutenant José Zuniga, arrive at Mission San Gabriel.
1781 On September 4, in accordance with de Neve's orders, a colonizing expedition leaves Mission San Gabriel to settle in Los Angeles. The 44 *pobladores* are all Indian, Spanish, Negro or of mixed blood.
1782 De Neve becomes *comandante general* of the *Provincias Internas* which includes Mexico, Texas and the Californias.
1784 Governor Pedro Fages grants the first three ranchos in California in what will become Los Angeles County. The recipients, all soldiers, include Juan José Dominguez, Manuel Nieto and José María Verdugo.

1785 Governor Fages has the pueblo land surveyed and gives settlers official title to the property.
1787 Vicente Féliz is placed in charge of the pueblo as *comisionado,* superior to the civilian mayor and the two councilmen.
1788 Fages appoints an Indian, José Vanegas, *alcalde.*
1790 The pueblo's population is 139.
1795-98 Governor Diego de Borica introduces the planting of grapevines and olive orchards to Los Angeles.
1797 Mission San Fernando is founded on Francisco Reyes' rancho.
1800 The pueblo's population is 315.
1804 California is divided into Alta California and Baja California.
1805 Captain José Shaler, the first American to visit the pueblo, passes through Los Angeles on his return trip from Hawaii to New England. His visit inaugurates trade between New England and California.
1806 Los Angeles' artillery militia formed.
1809-10 A subsidy leads Angelenos to raise hemp.
1809 (circa) Brandy production begins.
1809 Mission San Fernando is expanded by absorbing Mariano Verdugo's rancho at Cahuenga.
1810-11 During the winter, an Indian revolt takes place at Mission San Gabriel. Mission Indians are aided by those from around Riverside and San Bernardino.
1815 Plaza Church under construction and plaza laid out.
1815 Boris Tarakanof, a Russian trader, becomes the first foreigner to be imprisoned in the city.
1815 Portuguese-born José Antonio Rocha becomes the first foreigner to settle in Los Angeles.
1817 The first school in the pueblo is established with retired soldier Maximo Pina as schoolmaster.
1818 Joseph Chapman, the first English-speaking person to settle in the pueblo, arrives.
1818 Francisco Ávila constructs the Ávila Adobe (later Olivera Street).
1820 The population of the pueblo is 770.
1822 The pueblo learns of the Mexican Revolution and the end of Spanish rule.
1822 Foreigners are allowed to settle in California.
1822 The Plaza Church is completed and dedicated.
1826 Jedediah Smith and a crew of trappers visit Los Angeles and are thrown out. Smith and several others return to settle.
1826 A priest is sent to reside permanently in the pueblo.
1827 Joseph Pryor, the second American to settle in the pueblo, arrives from Santa Fe.
1828 John Groningen moves to Los Angeles and purchases the Indian village of Yang-na. After expelling the Indian residents, he abolishes the village as a public nuisance.
1830 The population of the pueblo is 1,200.
1831 Governor Manuel Victoria attempts to become a dictator and banishes or imprisons those with whom he disagrees, including Los Angeles' prominent Abel Stearns. Revolutionists who had fled to San Diego later liberate the political prisoners in Los Angeles. The governor subsequently resigns.
1834 Secularization of the missions begins.
1835 The Mexican Congress decrees Los Angeles a "city" and designates it the territory's capital, replacing Monterey.
1836 John Bautista Alvarado unseats Mexican governor Carrillo and declares California an independent republic. Southern Californians refuse to recognize his government.
1837-38 Revolution continues; northerners captured.
1838 The first vigilante committee in California is formed in Los Angeles.
1839 The first official census of Los Angeles and environs shows a population of 2,228 including 603 men, 421 women, 651 children and 553 "domesticated" Indians.
1839 After Mexico's government is reorganized, Los Angeles becomes the seat of the prefecture of California's southern district.
1839 Governor Alvarado exiles all foreigners in California who are

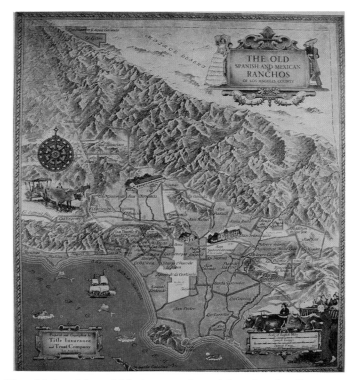

The old Spanish and Mexican ranchos of Los Angeles County.

not naturalized, married to native women or gainfully employed in respectable occupations.

by 1840 There are at least 35 ranchos in the Los Angeles area.

1842 Francisco Lopez discovers gold in Placerita Canyon near Los Angeles.

1842 Governor Manuel Micheltorena carries out orders to restore Mexican rule to Los Angeles and expels all Americans.

1845 Los Angeles is made the capital of Alta California.

1846 Juan Bautista Alvarado and Jose Castro defeat Governor Manuel Micheltorena at Cahuenga Pass. This leads to Micheltorena's expulsion.

1846 The United States and Mexico are at war. (July 7, 1846 — January 13, 1847).

1846 Robert F. Stockton and John C. Fremont seize Los Angeles.

1846 Governor Pico grants Catalina Island to Tomas Robbins. The land subsequently is sold to a series of owners.

1847 Stockton appoints Fremont military governor of California.

1847 The Articles of Capitulation are signed between the Californians and Fremont at the Cahuenga ranch house outside Los Angeles.

1848 California is ceded to the United States by the Treaty of Guadalupe Hidalgo.

1848 Peonage is abolished.

1848 Los Angeles' first English-speaking theater opens in an addition to Don Antonio Coronel's residence.

1849 Lieutenant E.O.C. Ord completes the city's first survey.

1849 Peter Burnett becomes California's first civil governor.

1849 San Jose is made the capital.

1849 The first state constitution is ratified.

1849 Abel Stearns is elected *alcalde*.

1850 The state Legislature establishes Los Angeles County as one of the 27 counties and incorporates Los Angeles as a city.

1850 The city council is established.

1850 Alpheus P. Hodges becomes mayor of Los Angeles.

1850 Reverend J. W. Brier, a Methodist, conducts the first Protestant services in Los Angeles.

1850 Peter Biggs, a barber, becomes the city's first known black resident.

1850 A volunteer police force is organized.

1850 Two young Chinese men are listed on the census for Los Angeles.

1850 The first Protestant services are held by Methodist minister J. W. Brier in a private residence.

1850 The city population is 1,610.

1850 A statute is passed in California excluding the testimony of blacks and Indians in courts of law.

1850 California is admitted to the Union.

1851 The first edition of the bi-lingual newspaper *The Star (La Estrella)* is published.

1851 The City Council organizes the city's first police force.

1851 Phineas Banning establishes the first stage line to cover most of southern California.

1851 The state capital moves to Vallejo.

1851 The United States Congress passes the Land Law of 1851 which establishes a Board of Commissioners, who from 1852 to 1856, judge claims resulting from old Spanish land grants.

1851 Benjamin D. Wilson becomes mayor.

1852 A public school system is established.

1852 John G. Nichols becomes mayor.

1853 John Schumacher sells the first lager beer in Los Angeles which he purchased from San Francisco.

1853 Don Matteo Keller plants the state's first orange trees in Los Angeles.

1853 The first Protestant church is established in a former saloon, El Dorado. The church was later razed for the Merced Theater.

1853 San Bernardino County is established.

1853 Benicia becomes the state capital.

1853 Antonio F. Coronel becomes mayor.

1853 The Sisters of Charity establish their first hospital in Los Angeles on upper Main Street.

1854 Gambling and crime rampant in Los Angeles. A murder a day is the norm.

1854 The first Jewish services are held in Los Angeles by Rabbi A. W. Edelman.

1854 The Hebrew Benevolent Society is established.

1854 The first brewery opens in Los Angeles.

1854 The newspaper, *Southern Californian,* begins publication.

1854 The first tannery in Los Angeles is established.

1854 Stephen C. Foster, physician and interpreter, becomes mayor.

1854 Sacramento becomes the state capital.

1855 The first Spanish language weekly, *El Clamor Publico,* begins publication.

1855 The first school house, School No. 1, opens at Spring and Second streets.

1855 A major earthquake causes considerable damage.

1856 The United States Land Commission confirms Los Angeles' title to four square leagues of land derived under Spanish laws governing pueblos.

1856 John G. Nichols becomes mayor.

1857 Wells Fargo opens an office in Los Angeles.

1857 Anaheim is founded.

1857 Phineas Banning founds Wilmington.

1857 William Dryden gives the first franchise for a water company.

1857 Collapse of the boom in southern California that has been the result of the gold miners' huge demand for beef.

1858 Protestant ministers close churches and leave the city due to an apparent disinterest in their respective faiths. They return the following year to establish a joint church.

1858 The first library association opens a reading room at Court and Spring streets.

1859 Senator Andrés Pico put through both houses of the state Legislature a resolution separating southern California into a new territory. In a local plebiscite, the measure is supported three to one.

1859 Damien Marchessault becomes mayor.

During 1850s The Democratic party is dominant.

Late 1850s Depression hits.

1860 Telegraph service is established between San Francisco and Los Angeles, thereby connecting the latter city with the rest of the country.

1860 Presidential elections show Los Angeles' pro-slavery bias: Breckenridge-267; Douglas-264; Lincoln-197.
1860 Bull and bear fights (popular during Spanish rule) are outlawed.
1860 Ten-day stage service is established between Los Angeles and the Mississippi River.
1860 The French Benevolent Society is organized.
1860 Los Angeles County mines produce $12,000 worth of gold a month.
1860 Henry Mellus is elected mayor.
1861 The first freight schooner arrives at San Pedro inaugurating that harbor's future as a cargo port.
1861 Hesperian College is founded in Woodland; in 1934 it moves to Orange and becomes Chapman College.
1861 Damien Marchessault re-elected mayor.
1862-64 Drought endangers the already faltering cattle industry.
1863 A board of health is established.
1863 The Fourth of July is not celebrated in Los Angeles due to Civil War tensions.
1864 The Fourth of July is again not celebrated.
1864 The first Protestant church in Los Angeles is built.
1864 Flood, smallpox and currency problems along with the persisting drought continues to plague the cattle industry.
1865 Saint Vincent's College is founded, later known as Loyola University. Originally located on the Plaza, in 1867 it moves to Sixth and Broadway.
1865 Comptonville, the first dry community in Los Angeles County, is established and named for its founder, G. E. Compton.
1865 José Mascarel is elected mayor.
1866 Cristobal Aguilar is elected mayor.
1866 Kern County is established.
1866 Mayor Aguilar approves an ordinance providing for a public square. It is known over the years by a variety of names: Central Park, Sixth Street Park, Public Square. In 1918 it is renamed Pershing Square in honor of Gen. John J. Pershing.
1867 The city council passes an ordinance prohibiting all but officers and travelers from carrying weapons. It is commonly violated.
1867 Under the direction of W. H. Perry, the Los Angeles City Gas Company contracts to light the principal city crossings with gas.
1867 Damien Marchessault re-elected mayor.
1868 The first artesian well in Los Angeles County is sunk near Wilmington.
1868 Cristobal Aguilar is elected mayor.
1868 The University of California is chartered.
1868 The first bank in Los Angeles, Hayward and Company, is established.
1868 The Los Angeles water system begins to use iron pipes.
1868 The Los Angeles-Wilmington Railway begins.
1869 Joel H. Turner becomes mayor.
1869 The Los Angeles Board of Education is established.
1869 The first city fire company is organized.
1869 Hacks and omnibuses come into use.
1869 The transcontinental railroad is completed at Promontory Point.
1869 The first known tryout of a bicycle in Los Angeles occurs.
1869 The Los Angeles and San Pedro Railroad begins operation.
1869 Pio Pico, California's last Mexican governor, builds the elegant Pico House. Now part of El Pueblo de los Angeles State Historic Park, the Pico House is being restored.
1869 Depression hits.
Until 1870 Hispanics, including neophyte Indians, outnumber Yankees.
By 1870 Disease kills nearly all the Indians in the area.
1870 Houses are numbered to prepare for a city directory which is published in 1871.
1870 Los Angeles' population is 5,728.
1870 The last recorded lynching by a vigilance committee in Los Angeles takes place when Michael Lachenias is killed for Jacob Bell's murder.

1870 William Abbot's Merced Theater opens.
1870 The Los Angeles County Medical Society is organized.
1871 The United States government begins improvements on the Wilmington harbor.
1871 The death of an Anglo policeman who had been trying to break up a disturbance among Chinese, prompts the Chinese Massacre during which a mob of 1,000 Anglos kill nineteen Chinese.
1871 An ice cream parlor opens on Spring Street in the Temple block, the first in the city.
1871 The Southern District Agricultural Society opens its first fair at Agricultural Park, now known as Exposition Park.
1871 A roller skating rink opens at Teutonia Hall.
1871 The first book and periodical store opens by Brodrick & Reilly, adjoining the Spring Street post office.
1871 Cristobal Aguilar becomes mayor.
1871 The Board of Public Works is established.
1872 Ventura County is formed.
1872 Charles Nordhoff's *California for Health, Wealth, and Residence* is published.
1872 The city votes to give the Southern Pacific Railroad a subsidy as encouragement to build a branch through Los Angeles.
1872 Asians and American Indians are first allowed to testify in court against Anglos.
1872 A public library is founded.
1873 James R. Toberman becomes mayor.
1873 The *Herald* begins publication.
1873 The first synagogue is built on the east side of Fort Street, now Broadway, between Second and Third.
1873 The first high school is constructed on a hill at Temple and Broadway. Later it moves across the street, and in 1917 it moves to Olympic Blvd.
1874 The Irish Literary and Social Club is established.
1874 Bandit Tiburcio Vasquez is captured.
1874 Los Angeles outlaws prostitution.
1874 Los Angeles' first city railroad — the Spring and Sixth Street streetcar line — is built.
1874 Compulsory grammar school attendance begins in Los Angeles.
1874 The city requires all saloons to be licensed.
1875 Prudent Beaudry becomes mayor.
1875 Wine is a chief product of the region.
1875 The Spanish American Benevolent Society is established.
1875 The Los Angeles and Independence Railroad begins operation.
1875 The *Mirror* begins publication.
1875 The *Santa Monica Outlook* begins publication.
1875 The first German newspaper, *Sued Californische,* begins publication.
1875 Elias J. (Lucky) Baldwin purchases Rancho Santa Anita, now known as the Los Ang   state and County Arboretum.
1876 The Southern Pacific cor   es its line between Los Angeles and San Francisco.
1876 The golden spike is driven at Lang's Station at Soledad Pass, marking the completion of the Southern Pacific transcontinental railway.
1876 The Cathedral of St. Vibiana, at South Main and Second streets, formally opens.
1877 The Southern California Horticultural Society is organized.
1877 The Italian Mutual Benevolence Society is organized.
1877 J. F. Gerkins is appointed the first chief of police.
1877 The first oranges from the Los Angeles area are shipped to eastern markets.
1877 Frederick A. MacDougall becomes mayor.
1877 Caroline M. Severence starts the city's first kindergarten.
1877 Nigger Alley, known in earlier times as *Calle de los Negroes,* is renamed Los Angeles Street.
1878 The Los Angeles Bar Association is founded.
1878 Southern Pacific purchases rail and wharf improvements at Santa Monica and closes the port, thereby compelling all

The Slauson Tower and Watts trolley, on the four-track Long Beach Line.

to use Wilmington Harbor.

1879 James R. Toberman becomes mayor.
1879 California's Second Constitutional Convention.
1879 The Los Angeles Athletic Club is founded.
1879 William Young, an Englishman who had moved to Santa Monica, introduces tennis to California.
1879 The subdivision of land grants leads to settlement of communities in the area.
1880 The Santa Fe Railway breaks the Southern Pacific's monopoly when it announces that Los Angeles rather than San Diego will be its terminus.
1880 The University of Southern California is founded.
1880 Los Angeles' first cement and asphalt are laid on Main Street north of First.
1880 Los Angeles' population is 11,183.
1881 The Los Angeles *Times* begins publication.
1881 The State Normal School is founded at Fifth and Grand. (In 1914 it moves to Vermont Ave.) The school is the forerunner of UCLA.
1881 Helen Hunt Jackson publishes *A Century of Dishonor.*
1881 Snow falls in Los Angeles.
1882 Electric lighting is introduced to Los Angeles.
1882 Citywide blue laws are repealed after Democrats win a statewide victory.
1882 Brush Electric Lighting Company installs the city's first electric street lights.
1882 Further Chinese immigration is barred.
1883 Cameron Thom becomes mayor.
1883 Southern Pacific's southern route to the East opens.
1883 The Historical Society of Southern California is established.
1884 For the first time in its history, the city votes overwhelmingly Republican.
1884 Helen Hunt Jackson's *Ramona* is published.
1884 Southern California's oranges beat those of Florida at the International Exposition in New Orleans.
1884 Childs' Opera House, a professional theater, opens on Main near First Street.
1884 Charles Fletcher Lummis arrives in Los Angeles after having hiked from Ohio.
1885 The Atchison, Topeka and Santa Fe Railroad is completed to Los Angeles and thus breaks Southern Pacific's monopoly. A rate war ensues with prices dropping from $125 for a ticket from the Missouri River to Los Angeles to $1. For a time, the population and economy booms.
1885 The old *zanja* system is abolished.
1885 Caroline Severance organizes the Los Angeles Free Kindergarten.
1885 Firemen become city employees.

1886 The United States Congress agrees to allocate funds for a harbor near Los Angeles. The site is not determined.
1886 Los Angeles received 32.15 acres of land for what becomes Westlake Park. In 1942 it is renamed MacArthur Park in honor of Gen. Douglas MacArthur.
1886 Major real estate boom occurs.
1886 Pasadena is incorporated.
1886 Santa Monica is incorporated.
1887 The Orange Growers' Protective Union of Southern California is founded.
1887 Pomona is incorporated.
1887 Clearwater is incorporated
1887 Burbank is incorporated.
1887 The first public high school opens.
1887 Monrovia is incorporated.
1887 The Los Angeles School of Art is founded.
1887 William H. Workman becomes mayor.
1887 Pomona College is founded.
1887 The California Club is founded.
1888 Occidental College is founded.
1888 The Los Angeles Chamber of Commerce is founded.
1888 Long Beach is incorporated.
1888 San Pedro is incorporated.
1888 The city consolidates all its street car systems.
1888 Pomona is incorporated.
1888 South Pasadena is incorporated.
1888 Compton is incorporated.
1888 Land boom collapses.
1888 Charles Fletcher Lummis leads in founding the Association for the Preservation of the Missions, later known as the Landmark Club.
1889 An ordinance is passed calling for the closing of all gambling houses.
1889 Orange County is founded.
1889 The first college football game is played in Los Angeles (Saint Vincent's College, now Loyola, versus USC).
1890 The first Tournament of Roses is held.
1890 William Workman and Mrs. J. E. Hollenbeck present Hollenbeck Park to the city.
1890 Charles Dudley Warner's promotional book on southern California, *Our Italy,* is published (financed by the Santa Fe Railroad).
1890 Edwin T. Earl invents the ventilated refrigerator car which allows oranges to reach the east with optimum freshness.
1890 Frank Wiggins of the Chamber of Commerce inaugurates the practice of promoting Los Angeles by sending farm exhibits to the midwest, particularly to fairs.
1891 Whittier College is founded.
1891 Throop Polytechnic Institute (later California Institute of Technology) is founded.
1891 Henry E. Huntington and Isias W. Hellman establish the Pacific Electric Railway.
1891 The state's first golf course opens at Riverside.
1892 Edward L. Doheny and C. A. Canfield strike oil near Second Street and Glendale Boulevard.
1892 Phineas Banning, Judge Joseph Brant Banning and Hancock Banning establish the Santa Catalina Island Company.
1892 Abbot Kinney and F. G. Ryan begin to develop Ocean Park as a resort.
1892 Redondo Beach is incorporated.
1892 Angeles National Forest, the first such forest in the state, is established.
1893 T. E. Rowan becomes mayor.
1893 Poor economic conditions nationwide prompts four Los Angeles banks to close.
1893 The Mount Lowe Railroad, named for Thaddeus S. C. Lowe, opens.
1893 A dispute ensues between the city and the Southern Pacific Railroad as to whether San Pedro or Santa Monica will be the harbor site.
1893 The brand name Sunkist is adopted by the Southern California Fruit Exchange for all California oranges.

1893 Riverside County is founded.

1893 The Greene brothers begin their architectural practice in Pasadena.

1894 *Land of Sunshine* begins publication; in 1902, the name is changed to *Out West*.

1894 The first Fiesta de los Angeles is held as a means of drawing tourists from San Francisco's Midwinter Fair to Los Angeles.

1895 Frank Rader becomes mayor.

1895 Highland park is annexed.

1895 Clara R. Shatto gives the city Layafette Park.

1895 William Denton is the first known individual to find a fossil at the La Brea Tar Pits. It is a sabre-toothed cat's tooth.

1895 Wilshire Boulevard is named.

1895 By this year, approximately 4,000 Chinese produce almost all the city's vegetables.

1896 The United States appropriates $3.9 million to build a harbor at San Pedro.

1896 Colonel Griffith J. Griffith presents the city with 3,015 acres for a park (Griffith Park).

1897 Long Beach is incorporated.

1897 M. P. Snyder becomes mayor.

1897 Charles Fletcher Lummis founds the Landmarks Club.

1897 The Landmarks Club restores Mission San Fernando.

1897 J. Philip Erie maneuvers an automobile that he and S. D. Sturgis had built on Los Angeles' streets; it is the first known auto in Los Angeles.

1898 The Spanish American War begins.

1898 Los Angeles begins to support a symphony orchestra.

1898 Southern Pacific founds *Sunset Magazine,* known at first as *Touring Tropics.*

1898 The Los Angeles Country Club is incorporated.

1898 Azuza is incorporated.

1899 An elevated bicycle path is constructed between Los Angeles and Pasadena.

1899 The Southern California Golf Association is created.

1899 Garvanza is annexed to Los Angeles.

1899 University is annexed to Los Angeles.

1899 The Los Angeles Stock Exchange is founded.

1899 Fred Eaton becomes mayor.

1900 Los Angeles' population is 102,479.

By 1900 Los Angeles experiences its first oil boom.

1900 Meredith P. Snyder is mayor.

1900 The Los Angeles Stock Exchange is organized.

1900 The Automobile Club of Southern California is founded.

1901 Twelve Japanese fishermen start a Japanese settlement in the Los Angeles area.

1901 Petroleum geologist William W. Orcutt discovers more fossils at the La Brea Tar Pits. Excavations are conducted from 1906 to 1913.

1901 The Pacific Electric Railway is incorporated.

1901 Angels Flight is constructed.

1902 Los Angeles begins to operate its own water company.

1903 William Randolph Hearst founds the Los Angeles *Examiner.*

1903 Los Angeles joins in the formation of the Pacific Coast Baseball League.

1903 Alhambra is incorporated.

1903 Arcadia is incorporated.

1903 Hollywood is incorporated.

1904 Owen C. McAleer becomes mayor.

1904 The El Camino Real Association of California is formed.

1904 Ocean Park is incorporated.

1904 Venice is incorporated.

1904 The Board of Water Commissioners begins to investigate the possibility of piping water to Los Angeles from the Owens Valley.

1904 A ten-year fight begins, led by W. M. Brown, to save Agricultural Park (later known as Exposition Park) from subdivision.

1904 The Carnegie Institute founds the Mt. Wilson Observatory.

1905 The Philharmonic Auditorium is constructed.

1905 The Los Angeles school system begins to offer classes for the deaf and blind.

1905 Vernon is incorporated.

1905 Voters approve a bond issue of $1.5 million for the Owens River Valley project.

1905 The San Pedro, Los Angeles and Salt Lake Railroad is completed.

1905 Wilmington is incorporated.

1906 The first Los Angeles-Honolulu Transpacific Yacht Race is held.

1906 The first motion picture studio in Los Angeles is established.

1906 Sawtelle is incorporated.

1906 Sarah Bernhardt performs in Los Angeles.

1906 Lordsburg is incorporated.

1906 Glendale is incorporated.

1906 Immaculate Heart College is founded.

1906 Huntington Park is incorporated.

1906 La Verne is incorporated.

1906 The "shoestring strip" area contiguous to Wilmington is annexed to Los Angeles.

1907 Arthur C. Harpe becomes mayor.

1907 Watts is incorporated.

1907 Hermosa Beach is incorporated.

1907 Sierra Madre is incorporated.

1907 Claremont is incorporated.

1907 George Feeth, an Anglo-Hawaiian, brings his surf board to Redondo Beach and thereby introduces surfing to California.

1907-13 The Los Angeles Aqueduct is constructed.

1908 Inglewood is incorporated.

1908 The first taxi cab drives through the streets of Los Angeles.

1908 Belmont Heights is incorporated.

1908 The building height is limited to 150 feet.

1909 Belmont Heights is annexed to Long Beach.

1909 Southern California Edison is founded.

1909 Redlands University is founded.

1909 Colegrove is annexed to Los Angeles.

1909 Wilmington is annexed to Los Angeles.

1909 San Pedro is annexed to Los Angeles.

1909 William D. Stephens becomes mayor but serves only a few days.

1909 George Alexander becomes mayor.

1909 Los Angeles schools begin to offer physical education.

1910 The first air meet in the United States is held at Dominguez Field.

1910 Hollywood is annexed to Los Angeles.

1910 The breakwater is completed at Los Angeles harbor.

1911 Tropico is incorporated.

1911 Burbank is incorporated.

1911 San Fernando is incorporated.

1911 Glendora is incorporated.

1911 Eagle Rock is incorporated.

1911 Ocean Park's name is changed to Venice.

1911 Los Angeles' street and inter-urban railroad lines consolidate with the Pacific Electric.

1912 Arroyo Seco is annexed to Los Angeles.

1912 The Museum of History, Science and Art opens at Exposition Park.

1912 El Monte is incorporated.

1912 Manhattan Beach is incorporated.

1912 The Red Squad is established to fight social and economic unrest.

1912 John Steven McGroarty's mission play premieres at the Mission Inn in Riverside.

1912 Earle Anthony opens the United States' first gasoline station at Grand Avenue and Washington Street.

1913 San Gabriel is incorporated.

1913 The Los Angeles aqueduct opens.

1913 San Marino is incorporated.

1913 Avalon is incorporated.

1913 Henry Rose becomes mayor.

1914 The steamship *Missourian* is the first ship to arrive at Los

Home of the National Orange Show in San Bernardino in the early 1900s.

Angeles harbor via the Panama Canal.
1914 The Southwest Museum opens.
1915 The city annexes the San Fernando Valley.
1915 Los Angeles annexes Palms.
1915 Los Angeles annexes Bairdstown.
1915 Charles E. Sebastian becomes mayor.
1915 The Universal Film Company founds Universal City.
1915 The Panama-California Exposition is held in San Diego.
1916 Westgate is annexed to Los Angeles.
1916 Occidental is annexed to Los Angeles.
1916 Harris Newmark's *Sixty Years in Southern California* is published.
1916 Los Angeles harbor is fortified and the National Guard sent to the Mexican border.
1916 Los Angeles experiences a war scare as a result of the publication of the Zimmerman note.
1916 Large numbers of Southern blacks settle in Los Angeles.
1916 Monterey Park is incorporated.
1916 The Bureau of Power and Light erects the first overhead power lines at the corner of Pasadena Avenue and Piedmont in northeast Los Angeles.
1916 Captain G. Allan Hancock donates Hancock Park, including the La Brea Tar Pits, to Los Angeles County.
1916 Fredrick T. Woodman becomes mayor.
1917 The Otis Art Institute is founded.
1917 The Tournament of Roses abandons chariot racing in favor of football games.
1917 El Segundo is incorporated.
1917 Culver City is incorporated.
1917 Lordsburg's name is changed to La Verned.
1917 Forest Lawn in Glendale is established.
1917-23 Frank Lloyd Wright constructs five houses in the Los Angeles area.
1918 Tropico is annexed to Glendale.

1919 The Henry E. Huntington Library and Art Gallery is founded.
1919 UCLA is established as the University of California's southern branch.
1919 A syndicate that includes William Wrigley Jr. buys Catalina Island from the Bannings.
1919 Meredith P. Snyder becomes mayor.
1920 The All Year Club of Southern California is formed to popularize California as a year-round vacation spot.
1920 Montebello is incorporated.
1920 The Los Angeles Planning Commission is created.
1920 The first performance of the pilgrimage play at Hemet is given.
1920 The Huntington Beach oil fields are discovered.
1921 George E. Cryer becomes mayor.
1921 Pacific Palisades is founded.
1921 Lynwood is incorporated.
1921 Torrance is incorporated.
1921 Hyde Park is incorporated.
1921 Simon Rodia begins to build Watts Towers.
1922 The Hollywood Bowl opens.
1922 Sawtelle is annexed to Los Angeles.
1922 KHJ and KFI begin radio broadcasting.
1922 The Rose Bowl is completed.
1922 The Torrance oil fields are discovered.
1922 Rudolph M. Schindler establishes his architectural practice in Los Angeles.
1922 Hawthorne is incorporated.
1922 Angelus Temple is dedicated.
1923 Memorial Coliseum at Exposition Park opens.
1923 The Hollywood sign is erected.
1923 Hyde Park is annexed to Los Angeles.
1923 South Gate is annexed to Los Angeles.
1923 South Gate is incorporated.
1923 West Covina is incorporated.

1923 Boulevard stop signs first appear at dangerous intersections.
1924 Signal Hill is incorporated.
1924 Maywood is incorporated.
1924 Los Angeles founds an opera company.
1924-27 Los Angeles aqueduct is repeatedly dynamited by angry Owens Valley residents.
1925 Tujunga is incorporated.
1925 Venice is annexed to Los Angeles.
1925 Claremont Graduate School is founded.
1926 The current Los Angeles Public Library at 630 West Fifth Street is dedicated.
1926 Barnes City is incorporated.
1926 Watts is annexed to Los Angeles.
1926 UCLA is dedicated.
1926 La *Opinion* is founded.
1926 Architect and city planner, Richard Neutra, begins his practice in Los Angeles.
1926 Santa Monica purchases Clover Field for a municipal airport.
1926 Scripps College in Claremont is founded.
1926 Bell is incorporated.
1927 Alice Barnsdall deeds eleven acres to Los Angeles for Barnsdall Park.
1927 The Los Angeles Open Golf Tournament is founded.
1927 Barnes City is annexed to Los Angeles.
1928 The present Los Angeles City Hall at 200 North Spring Street is completed.
1928 The Henry E. Huntington Library and Art Gallery opens to the public.
1928 Daily passenger airline flights begin between San Francisco and Los Angeles.
1928 The Zamorano Club — a Los Angeles bibliophile society — is established.
1928 St. Francis Dam at San Francisquito Canyon collapses.
1928 Union Air Terminal is established at Burbank.
1928 The Metropolitan Water District is formed.
1928 The Dunbar Hotel, now a museum of black history, opens. The Dunbar hosts the first national convention of the NAACP in 1928 and is a popular home-away-from-home for leading black entertainers.
1929 The Academy of Motion Pictures, Arts and Sciences gives its first awards.
1929 The Graf Zeppelin, a dirigible, lands at Mines Field.
1929 The first transcontinental air service begins between Los Angeles and San Francisco.
1929 Los Angeles County produces 1.76 million barrels of oil.
1919-1929 Automobile registrations increase 5.5 times in Los Angeles.
1920-1930 Southern California experiences a large increase in Mexican immigration.
1930 Gardena is incorporated.
1930 Olvera Street opens.
1931 Work begins on Boulder Dam.
1931 The *Los Angeles Herald* and *Los Angeles Express* merge to form the *Los Angeles Evening Herald Express.*
1932 The Tenth Olympiad opens at the Los Angeles Coliseum.
1932 Tujunga is annexed to Los Angeles.
1932 The County Relief Budget Committee demands a $12 million bond issue for unemployment relief.
1933 The *Los Angeles Sentinal,* a black newspaper, is founded.
1933 The Long Beach earthquake causes extensive damage.
1933 "Singing John" Steven McGroarty is made poet laureate of California.
1933 Frank L. Shaw becomes mayor.
1933 *Westways* is founded.
1934 The Santa Anita Park Race Track opens.
1934 Farmers Market opens.
1934 Clark Library is added to UCLA.
1935 The Griffith Park Planetarium is dedicated.
1936 Power from Boulder Dam's electrical generators is brought to Los Angeles.
1936 Los Angeles policemen — 136 of them — are stationed on highways and railroads leading to the city to prevent unemployed individuals from entering.
1937 Pepperdine University is founded.
1937 Los Angeles purchases Mines Field for a municipal airport.
1937 Los Angeles ranks fifth among the industrial counties in the United States.
1937 Los Angeles ranks first in the nation in oil refining, movie production, airplane manufacturing and secondary automobile assembly.
1938 The Red Squad is abolished.
1938 Fletcher Bowron is mayor.
1938 A new state law creates the non-stop parkways that become known as freeways.
1939 Palos Verdes Estates is incorporated.
1939 Union Passenger Terminal opens.
1939 The first semi-commercial television station in Los Angeles opens.
1939 Los Angeles County becomes fourth in the manufacture of women's apparel and furniture and second in tires in the United States.
Late 1930s Supermarkets become popular in the area.
1940 Los Angeles city's population is 1,504,277; the county's population is 2,785,643.
1940 The Arroyo Seco Parkway opens (later known as the Pasadena Freeway). It is the first segment of the freeway system.
1940s Illustrious German emigrés live in the area, including Thomas Mann, Lion Fechtwanger, Bruno Walter, Franz Werfel, Arnold Schoenberg and Igor Stravinsky.
1941 The Japanese bomb Pearl Harbor, thus prompting an invasion scare along the West coast.
1941 Business booms as a result of war contracts.
1941 The Colorado River aqueduct begins delivering water to the area.
1942 Japanese Americans are sequestered in relocation camps.
1942 The Sleepy Lagoon murder takes over headlines.
1942 Camp Pendleton is founded.
1943 Los Angeles experiences the first major smog attack; visibility is reduced to three blocks.
1944 The board of supervisors establishes the County Commission on Human Relations in response to the Zoot Suit riots.
1945 The city approves a master development plan.
1946 The Comprehensive Zoning Ordinance for the city goes into effect.
1946 Claremont Men's College in Claremont is founded.
1946 Carey McWilliams' *Southern California Country* is published.
1947 The Rams comes to Los Angeles from Cleveland.
1947 The trial of the "Hollywood Ten " takes place.
1948 The city fires seventeen employees who refuse to sign loyalty pledges.
1949 The Los Angeles Chamber of Commerce forms Los Angeles Beautiful to promote the beautification of the urban environment.
1950 Los Angeles city's population is 1,970,358; the county's population is 4,151,687.
1950 Los Angeles is the first city in the U.S. to remove wartime rent controls, thus spurring post-war construction.
1951 The bracero program is introduced.
1951 "I love You California" becomes California's official song — lyrics by F. B. Silverwood; music by A. F. Frakenstein.
1952 The Hollywood Freeway is completed.
1953 The development of El Pueblo State Historical Park begins.
1953 The Fowler Museum, named for Francis E. Fowler Jr., is opened.
1953 Morris Poulson becomes mayor.
1954 The University of California establishes the Riverside campus.
1954 Lakewood is incorporated.
1954 The J. Paul Getty Museum opens; the present museum is completed in 1974.
1955 Disneyland opens.
1955 Harvey Mudd College is founded.

Pipe line bringing water to Los Angeles across the desert from Owens Valley, circa 1950.

1956 The City Council repeals a law limiting buildings to 140 feet in height.
1956 The Beat Movement becomes prevalent throughout the U.S.
1956 Baldwin Park is incorporated.
1956 Dairy Valley is incorporated.
1956 La Puente is incorporated.
1956 Downey is incorporated.
1957 Backyard incinerators are banned in an effort to hinder the creation of smog. .
1957 Rolling Hills Estates is incorporated.
1957 Paramount is incorporated.
1957 Santa Fe Springs is incorporated.
1957 Bradbury is incorporated.
1957 Industry is incorporated.
1957 Irwindale is incorporated.
1957 Duarte is incorporated.
1957 Norwalk is incorporated.
1957 Bellflower is incorporated.
1958 Pico Rivera is incorporated.
1958 The Los Angeles Dodgers and the San Francisco Giants bring major league baseball to California.
1958 Vandenberg Air Force Base is established.
1958 Rosemead is incorporated.
1958 Lawndale is incorporated.
1959 Walnut is incorporated.
1959 Artesia is incorporated.
1959 Los Angeles Memorial Sports Arena opens.
1959 The University of California establishes a campus at San Diego.
1959 The Los Angeles Dodgers win the world series.
1960 Commerce is incorporated.
1960 Mirada Hills is incorporated. (Later in the same year, the name is changed to La Mirada.)
1960 Temple City is incorporated.
1960 San Dimas is incorporated.
1960 Cudahy is incorporated.
1960 The Lakers basektball team moves from Minneapolis.

1960 The Dodgers become the first California team to win the World Series.
1961 Bell Gardens is incorporated.
1961 Hidden Hills is incorporated.
1961 Century City is created.
1961 Samuel Yorty becomes mayor.
1962 The *Examiner* is absorbed by the *Herald*.
1962 Palmdale is incorporated.
1962 The city establishes a Cultural Heritage Board to designate historic-cultural landmarks.
1963 Pitzer College is established in Claremont.
1963 Aerospace becomes Los Angeles County's leading industry.
1963 Three blacks are elected to the Los Angeles City Council; they are the first blacks to serve in this capacity in the city.
1963 The Los Angeles Dodgers win the world series.
1963 Leslie N. Shaw, a black, becomes postmaster general of Los Angeles. He is the first black man to be appointed to that position in any major American city.
1963 The United States Post Office authorizes CA as California's abbreviation and introduces the zip code system.
1964 Hawaiian Gardens is incorporated.
1964 Lomita is incorporated.
1964 The bracero program ends.
1964 The Los Angeles Music Center opens.
1965 The Watts Riots take place.
1965 The University of California establishes the Irvine campus in Orange County.
1965 The Los Angeles County Museum of Art is established.
1965 The Los Angeles Dodgers win the world series.
1965 Los Angeles County is second to New York in international trade.
1967 Dairy Valley's name is changed to Cerritos.
1967 The Los Angeles Kings, a hockey team, is founded.
1967 The Queen Mary is docked at Long Beach.
1967 The Forum is built in Inglewood.
1968 Carson is incorporated.
1968 The San Onofre nuclear generating station opens.
1969 The Plaza de la Raza Cultural Center is established in Lincoln Park.
1971 The San Fernando Valley earthquake takes place.
1973 Rancho Palos Verdes is incorporated.
1973 Councilman Thomas Bradley becomes Los Angeles' first black mayor.
1974 John Clifford establishes the Los Angeles Ballet.
1974 The City Council abolishes "sexist" titles from city jobs.
1974 The Oakland Athletics defeat the Los Angeles Dodgers in the first All-California world series.
1975 A forest fire sweeps through Tujunga.
1975 The Norton Simon Museum opens.
1977 The George C. Page Museum of La Brea Discoveries opens.
1978 Floods and landslides plague Los Angeles.
1979 The Los Angeles Children's Museum opens.
1980 Immaculate Heart College closes.

Los Angeles mayors

1850-1851	Alpheus P. Hodges	1889-1892	Henry T. Hazard
1851-1852	Benjamin D. Wilson	1892-1894	Thomas E. Rowan
1852-1853	John G. Nichols	1894-1895	Frank Rader
1853-1854	Antonio F. Coronel	1896-1898	Meredith P. Snyder
1854-1855	Stephen C. Foster	1898-1900	Fred Eaton
1855-1856	Thomas Foster	1900-1904	Meredith P. Snyder
1856-1859	John G. Nichols	1904-1906	Owen C. McAleer
1859-1860	Damien Marchesseault	1906-1909	Arthur C. Harper
1860	Henry Mellus	1909	William D. Stephens
1861-1865	Damien Marchesseault	1909-1913	George Alexander
1865-1866	José Mascarel	1913-1915	Henry R. Rose
1866-1868	Cristobal Aguilar	1915-1916	Charles E. Sebastian
1868-1870	Joel H. Turner	1917-1919	Frederick T. Woodman
1871-1872	Cristobal Aguilar	1919-1921	Meredith P. Snyder
1872-1874	James R. Toberman	1921-1929	George E. Cryer
1874-1876	Prudent Beaudry	1929-1933	John C. Porter
1876-1878	Frederick A. MacDougall	1933-1938	Frank L. Shaw
1878-1882	James R. Toberman	1938-1953	Fletcher Bowron
1882-1884	Cameron E. Thom	1953-1961	Norris Poulson
1884-1886	Edward F. Spence	1961-1973	Samuel Yorty
1886-1888	William H. Workman	1973-present	Thomas Bradley
1888-1889	John Bryson		

Partners in economic progress

The Walnut Elephant

It was larger than life, completely covered with extra-large California walnuts and had a belt of lemons strapped around its stomach.

The "Walnut Elephant" was the idea of Frank Wiggins, who was something of an early-day publicity genius. Wiggins served for many years as the Los Angeles Chamber of Commerce's superintendent of exhibits. The "California on Wheels" display was also his idea.

"California on Wheels" was a railroad car outfitted with area agricultural products. It rolled through major Midwest and Southern towns displaying the state's bounty. During its two-year tour, more than a million people passed through its doors.

The "Walnut Elephant" was built for the Los Angeles exhibit at the Chicago World's Fair in 1893. A strong wire framework was covered with the walnuts and a howdah of corn, wheat, barley and moss was strapped around the stomach by the lemon belt. It proved such a popular exhibit that the original was placed on permanent display at the Chamber's Los Angeles headquarters, and a mate was constructed to travel around the country to fairs.

Such promotions widely publicized the area's advantages. And while the circulation of printed matter was valuable, the visual presentation of farm produce was largely responsible for bringing settlers to the region.

The Los Angeles Chamber of Commerce

As Los Angeles celebrates its Bicentennial and looks back on its heritage of the past, a clear line of demarcation emerges between its two centuries of existence. From 1781 to 1881, the sleepy pueblo grew slowly into a small town with no perceptible impact on the outside world. The action was all up north — the discovery of gold in 1849 made boom towns of San Francisco and Sacramento.

The phenomenal growth of Los Angeles in its second century is concurrent with the formation and growth of the Los Angeles Area Chamber of Commerce, now nearing the end of its first century.

In 1888, the city of Los Angeles was in deep trouble. The bubble had burst on get-rich-quick land speculations. These had increased the city's population from 11,000 to 70,000, and now people were moving out at the rate of 1,000 per month. The developers had failed to recognize that geographic isolation, an inadequate water supply and a weak industrial base were problems that had to be solved before more growth could be handled.

A small group of concerned businessmen knew that the time for an action plan had come, and they decided to form an organization to represent all segments of the community. They rallied the business and professional leaders of the city for the formal establishment of a Los Angeles Chamber of Commerce. Fifty-seven men joined at a charter membership rate of $5 per year. Their purpose was to gain access to the resources of the area, take steps toward their development and establish agricultural and industrial interests.

Organizational meetings were held in an assembly room over a livery stable at First and Broadway, now the site of the Los Angeles County Law Library.

These men had vision and foresight, but they were also practical. They realized that their objectives would be impossible to achieve without a deep-water harbor and an adequate and assured water supply — no easy matter in the arid, semi-desert topography of Los Angeles.

The action plans they developed to meet these needs took years of hard work and effort by dedicated Chamber members. The plan for the harbor involved battling an apathetic Congress 3,000 miles away for federal participation, local squabbles over site selection and hundreds of other difficulties. But the efforts paid off, and in ten years San Pedro's deep-water port was underway.

Water was equally hard to come by, and many years of Chamber effort finally resulted in the opening of the Los Angeles Aqueduct, which brought water from the Owens Valley and opened the door to population and industrial growth beyond the wildest dreams of the earliest Chamber directors.

The Los Angeles Area Chamber of Commerce today represents the interests of business in the five counties of Los Angeles, Orange, Riverside, San Bernardino and Ventura. It has occupied five homes since the original livery stable and in 1956 moved to its own headquarters at

A livery stable at the corner of First and Broadway served as the original home of the Los Angeles Chamber of Commerce when it was founded October 15, 1888; today the Los Angeles County Law Library stands on the site.

404 South Bixel Street. It currently employs some 60 professionals working with hundreds of volunteers to serve 3,500 member firms.

The Chamber provides over 100 services to its members, ranging from coping with red tape to solving environmental problems. It maintains a legislative advocacy program which positions staff professionals in direct contact with lawmakers and a Growing Companies Program designed to handle the special needs of a company with less than 50 employees. The Chamber daily provides all types of business information from its library of source material and a buyer's service detailing more than 40,000 products, local distributors and manufacturer's representatives. It also conducts meetings and seminars to keep members informed and updated.

Today's Action Plan still has concerns for adequate water supply and harbor improvements, but at a vastly different level. The Chamber has a leadership role in the plans to build a Peripheral Canal to bring much needed water from the Sacramento Delta to southern California and is in the forefront of the efforts to improve the harbor to accommodate a growing volume of international trade.

Over the years, certain themes have been recurrent. In the recession of 1907, the Chamber sponsored a Prosperity Week, which was highly successful in turning the tide of the city's economy. More recently, in the recessionary period of the early '70s, the Chamber led in the creation of jobs and stimulation of the economy.

In 1932, the Chamber was largely responsible for having brought the Olympic Games to Los Angeles, with lasting physical improvements and financial gains in another depression era. The Chamber has again played a leading role in securing the 1984 Games for Los Angeles. Members will be working to assure financial success and to restore the prestige lost in the unfortunate events surrounding the 1980 Olympiad in Moscow.

A large portion of the Chamber's efforts today includes developing affordable housing and new sources of energy, as well as working to eliminate excessive government regulations and restrictive taxes. The Chamber has also been instrumental in developing a freeway system to serve the vastly expanded southern California area. It is now engaged in a four-point mass transportation program which includes improved bus service on surface streets and freeways, a Downtown People Mover to relieve downtown traffic congestion and a subway starter line on Wilshire Boulevard as the first step in a high-speed mass transportation system.

As Los Angeles celebrates its Bicentennial in 1981, there is much to be proud of and much yet to be done to make the community a more ideal place in which to live and do business. The Los Angeles Area Chamber of Commerce has been one of the important factors in the heritage of the past, and it remains the dynamic leader in facing the challenges of the area's second century.

American Honda Motor Co., Inc.

From motorcycles to automobiles — always an industry leader

Its beginnings were indeed humble back in 1959: 12 employees working out of a one-room building in Los Angeles.

But American Honda Motor Co., Inc. did quite well that first year, everything considered: more than 2,500 motorcycles sold, primarily because they were reliable, quiet, easy to maintain and inexpensive.

Honda had already established a reputation for quality and reliability in Japan and on the race tracks of Europe where the company campaigned extensively trying to learn more about its product.

What those engineers discovered in the late 1950s is still at Honda today and this benchmark attention to detail and performance has taken the company out of that one-room building into the forefront of America's motorcycle industry.

Today Honda remains the largest-selling motorcycle line in the United States with sales capacities augmented by the construction of a motorcycle assembly plant in Marysville, Ohio.

Motorcycles have only been part of Honda's business, however. In the late 1960s, Honda turned its two-wheel technology to design of an automobile that would retain the same reliability and ease of maintenance characteristics of its motorcycles. After limited success in marketing a tiny sports car and two-door sedan, incorporating many of the components found in its motorcycles in 1970, Honda introduced the much heralded Civic in 1972.

The Civic is regarded as one of the best-engineered automobiles to ever be mass-produced, and this single model soon made Honda and its U.S. distribution network an enviable competitor in the import auto business.

By 1979 Honda sales had grown to a point where it ranked third out of all import cars sold in the U.S. Quite an achievement for a company still regarded as "small" in Japan by such industry giants as Toyota, Nissan and Mitsubishi.

The extent of Honda's growth is further emphasized in the fact that its sales grew an amazing 134 percent in the three-year period of 1976-1979 while imports in the U.S. as a whole blossomed a more conservative 43 percent during the same period.

Honda first opened its doors to America in 1959 in this small building in Los Angeles. The corporate offices are now located in a 6,969,600 square feet facility in Gardena, California.

Mr. K. Yoshizawa, President of American Honda Motor Co., Inc., is being presented the Motor Trend 1980 Import Car of the Year Award by Mr. Robert Brown, Vice President of Petersen Publishing Co.

Though now firmly established as the number one motorcycle in America, Honda's desire to continue as a viable force in the automotive marketplace led the company to announce in 1980 that it would establish a $200 million auto assembly facility near its motorcycle plant in Ohio. The move was a Japanese auto industry first.

The growth of Honda's U.S. marketing operations can be seen by the fact that when Honda sold its first car in the United States, it had a network of 50 dealers, most of whom were motorcycle dealers handling cars on the side. By 1980, however, the picture had changed drastically: there are more than 700 Honda automobile and some 1,800 motorcycle dealers nationwide.

A key factor for Honda's success in the automotive and motorcycle industry is the far-reaching vision and energy of Soichiro Honda, who founded the parent company in 1948. Instrumental in the early design decisions that led to the wide acceptance of Honda motorcycles, Mr. Honda also worked side by side with factory engineers during the development of the CVCC® advanced stratified-charge engine that has maintained Honda's reputation for leadership in the automotive field.

Honda has successfully entered other markets as well. In 1965 it introduced a compact gasoline-powered generating system that has become an industry standard. The Honda Power Products Division now offers such diverse products as outboard motors, garden tillers, lawnmowers, general purpose engines and irrigation water pumps through a network of nearly 3,000 dealers nationwide.

Today, American Honda Motor Co., Inc. is firmly established in the U.S. marketplace, dedicating its efforts to fulfill the needs of the American consumer with products that are economical, well-engineered and in harmony with the environment.

Honda has come a long way from that one-room building in 1959.

177

American Medical International

Pioneer hospital company is international health care leader

In two decades, the hospital management industry has grown from one Los Angeles man's idea to a $14 billion industry.

The company he founded, now called American Medical International (AMI), has progressed from a local firm with one hospital and a medical reference laboratory to a $700 million international health care company with 65 hospitals, numerous medical service subsidiaries, and more than 16,000 employees.

AMI today is the international leader in providing acute hospital care, and also delivers specialized health care services to government and private sector clients in 500 communities on six continents.

In 1960, though, American Laboratories, Inc., founded by Uranus J. Appel three years earlier, was a modest enterprise. It had the backing of a small group of Los Angeles businessmen and a net worth of about $142,000. To finance the purchase of its second hospital — the 99-bed Westside Hospital in the Wilshire district — the company made a public offering of common stock. The $180,000 underwriting provided the capital for expansion.

By 1964, the company had acquired a new name — American Medical Enterprises — owned three hospitals, and had a net worth of more than one million dollars.

The time was right for Bob Appel's concept that modern management techniques should be applied to hospitals. There had been a large growth in the suburban population of Los Angeles following World War II, creating a need for outlying health care facilities. In many cases physicians met that need by opening their own hospitals. Many doctors soon found that they lacked the time and knowledge to manage a hospital properly while trying to keep up their practice of medicine.

For many such groups, turning over the management to Appel's company demonstrated that quality in hospital care could be delivered in a businesslike, efficient manner.

Since that time, AMI's growth has been a result of practicing the philosophy that quality health care can be achieved cost-effectively.

AMI milestones include several major events which led the company to its current prominence.

In 1968, the company began to expand from a relatively small, exclusively California-based firm to one of both national and international scope. Appel brought Royce Diener on board as an outside director. Diener, who became president of AMI in 1973 and is today chairman and chief executive officer, brought additional financial and management experience to the company and together, Appel and Diener steered the firm on its new broader course. Within two years the company had acquired hospitals in Miami and Houston, and its first non-U.S. hospital, the prestigious Harley Street Clinic in London. By 1970 the company had also moved from the American Stock Exchange to an NYSE listing.

In 1972 the company doubled its size by acquiring another hospital management company with 22 hospitals — Chanco Medical Industries. The new American Medical changed its name, becoming American Medical International. Thanks to that acquisition, AMI gained another asset — a Chanco executive who is today president and chief operating officer of AMI, Walter L. Weisman.

The acquisition of Chanco expanded AMI's operations to nine states and amplified AMI's regional structure. AMI today has four regional offices — in Atlanta, Houston, Anaheim, and London, England — in addition to its corporate headquarters in Beverly Hills.

Included in the company's international activities are hospitals in Great Britain, France, Spain, Switzerland, Egypt, Australia, and Singapore; and extensive health care development services in South America.

As AMI expands its hospital operations, it continues to develop the business concept of providing individual health care services to clients other than AMI hospitals. The company offers services through ten divisions: Among them, Inhalation Therapy Services provides diagnostic and therapeutic cardiopulmonary services to more than 250 hospitals worldwide; and STAT Medical Records is a leading consultant in regulatory compliance.

Other AMI subsidiaries include Professional Hospital Services (PHS), offering computerized financial and management control systems; Stewart Design Group, specializing in computer-aided hospital planning and architectural design; and Mobile Computerized Tomographic Services. This division pioneered the concept of placing costly CT scanners on wheels to serve a number of hospitals, and its fleet is unique in the U.S.

American Medical International continues to grow as private health care flourishes here and abroad. In the United States, many tax-exempt, county, and religious order hospitals are turning to the investor-owned sector for help in dealing with the costly and complex issues American hospitals face today. Internationally, demand for American style private hospital care, even in countries with nationalized health care, is growing along with the recognition that American health care is the finest in the world.

AMI headquarters at 414 North Camden Drive, Beverly Hills.

Ameron

Seven decades of service to utilities, construction and industry

In the '70s, Ameron furnished its own pipe movers, including the remarkable Pipemobile Mark IV, right, a giant step from moving pipe in the '20s, below.

In 1907, a concrete pipe company of modest size began production in Los Angeles. Over the next quarter century, through mergers with similar pipe companies, it became a substantial supplier of concrete pipe for water and waste-water systems in the western United States. Eventually, it selected the name of American Pipe and Construction Co., a name that was abandoned in 1970 for Ameron.

As western population grew, along with the need to move large volumes of water, so did the company's ability to produce concrete pressure pipe more sophisticated in design and in larger diameters. This reached record proportions in the 1970s with a series of terrestrial and submarine pipelines that are the largest in the world, with pipe diameters ranging upward to 21 feet. Along the way, permanent and project pipe plants have been located throughout the western U.S. and in South America.

An extension of the company's pipe technology occurred in 1940 when a special service began to clean and cement-mortar line old waterlines in place.

At the same time the company was advancing its concrete and steel pipe capabilities, it ventured into other product lines. In 1938, the company began a search for materials that would protect concrete pipelines from sewage gas. So intensive was the basic research that the company discovered corrosion control systems of value to many industries. Today, its products include an ever-increasing variety of high-performance protective coatings, surfacers and cements. Manufactured worldwide, they protect steel and concrete industrial structures, deep hull vessels, offshore platforms, and power plants. Subsequently, Ameron extended its interest to industrial coatings, finishes and to enhance and protect business aircraft, fire engines and farm equipment, construction, oil field and other industrial equipment.

Based upon the knowledge acquired through research into the chemistry of corrosion, the company in 1953 began fabricating a new kind of pipe and fitting system. Known as reinforced thermosetting resin piping, these products contain and transport corrosive liquids and withstand highly corrosive industrial and marine environments.

In 1957, to provide a source of steel rod to reinforce concrete pipe, the company built a mini-steel mill at Etiwanda, California. When production exceeded internal needs, the company found outside customers for its steel in the construction industry. In the mid-1970s, the old melt shop and billet caster were abandoned for a new melt shop and steel billet facility, both of larger capacity and both housed in a pollution-proof plant. Quality of product improved along with the kinds of carbon-alloy steel produced. Today, wire products manufacturers as well as construction steel customers are served.

Ameron acquired HC&D, Ltd. of Hawaii in 1967. The company, now an Ameron division, is a principal supplier of concrete products in the Islands. Backed by substantial quarry holdings, the division's sand manufacturing operation is an essential supplier to Hawaii's construction industry.

In 1969, the company acquired a steel lighting pole manufacturer in Oakland, California. Shortly thereafter, Ameron built a second pole plant in Southern California to manufacture prestressed concrete lighting poles. Poles from Ameron now are in use in most western states.

As Ameron enters the 1980s, its concrete and resin-based pipe and corrosion control operations are multinational. Besides serving the western United States, concrete pipe operations are under way in Columbia, S.A. where the company has been for a quarter century, in Ecuador, and in Saudi Arabia through a joint-ownership company whose plants serve the Kingdom. The cement-mortar lining of pipelines in place also is international in scope. Corrosion control products are manufactured throughout the United States, at a wholly owned subsidiary in Europe and by affiliates and licensees around the world.

Lawrence R. Tollenaere has been president of Ameron since 1965. The company employs 3,900 and its stock has been traded on the New York Stock Exchange since 1970.

Atchison, Topeka and Santa Fe Railway Company

Santa Fe and L. A. — partners in progress for nearly a century

February 12 has been recognized as the day Americans everywhere celebrate the birth of our 16th President, Abraham Lincoln. On that day in 1859, two years prior to Lincoln becoming President, Cyrus K. Holliday, a young Philadelphia lawyer, found reason to hold his own celebration in Atchison, Kansas. The Kansas Territorial Legislature had granted approval of his charter for the Atchison and Topeka Railroad Company the day before. With that legislative action the Atchison, Topeka and Santa Fe Railway Company was launched.

As a visionary, Holliday dreamed of a railroad stretching from Chicago to both the eastern and western seaboards and eventually extending to the Gulf of Mexico. More than a few of his acquaintances labeled him "an old fool" or a "lunatic." But time has proven him neither!

That humble beginning served as a catalyst for a series of events that would eventually lead to the construction of a 13,000-mile rail network operating in a dozen midwestern, southwestern and western states. Although ground was not broken until 1868, once the first spade of earth had been turned, construction of the railway progressed rapidly. The company was renamed the Atchison, Topeka and Santa Fe Railroad Company as work commenced towards Santa Fe, New Mexico. Santa Fe tracks spread out in several directions and one aimed at the Pacific Coast.

After absorbing the Atlantic and Pacific Railroad and expanding through New Mexico and Arizona to the California border, Santa Fe signed a trackage lease agreement with competitor Southern Pacific, and gained entry into "The Golden State" itself — California! The next step was to gain control of trackage between Needles and Barstow (known as Waterman then), where the Santa Fe joined the California Southern Railroad Company. The acquisition of the California Southern gave Santa Fe trackage all the way into San Diego; the route, however, did not gain access to Los Angeles.

In order to achieve entry into the City of Angels, Santa Fe formed the Los Angeles and San Gabriel Valley Railroad Company and the San Bernardino and Los Angeles Railway Company, which

Hobart yard, Los Angeles, California.

built track between Los Angeles and San Bernardino via Pasadena. At last, Santa Fe had track into Los Angeles, beginning May 31, 1887. A second route into Los Angeles, via Orange County, was completed August 12, 1888, linking the Riverside, Santa Ana and Los Angeles Railway Company and the California Southern. With Los Angeles as their terminal, trains like the California Limited, Super Chief, Grand Canyon and El Capitan became household names, while promoting development of Los Angeles and surrounding areas throughout Southern California.

It was soon apparent that Los Angeles would become a major point on the Santa Fe, offering a West Coast location that lent itself to transcontinental rail transportation. West Coast headquarters were established downtown at Sixth and Main Streets in 1908. In 1915, Santa Fe leased the building it occupied at that location and annexed one next door, at Sixth and Los Angeles Streets. The buildings, fused together with hallways, were

purchased in 1945 and served as West Coast headquarters until 1979. A modern office complex with a campus-like atmosphere and quality, appropriately named Santa Fe Plaza, became the new headquarters in May, 1979. Located at 5200 East Sheila Street, on the east side of the city, Santa Fe Plaza is near the railway's busy Hobart Yard and Piggyback terminal.

Hobart Yard is especially important to Santa Fe because of its proximity to both the Ports of Los Angeles and Long Beach. Thousands of containers arrive and depart the ports, many of them traveling via rail car to and from various points throughout the United States.

Today, Hobart Yard itself is undergoing extensive revitalization to better accommodate the demands and challenges of future freight operations in Los Angeles. The yard has facilities capable of accommodating 271 87-foot flatcars for intermodal loading and a storage area for up to 2,100 containers and trailers.

Despite the growth of intermodal traffic, the importance of every type of rail freight shipment cannot be minimized, especially during these fuel-conscious times. Utilizing its inherent fuel efficiencies, Santa Fe anticipates a bright future in the city. The railway has re-invested $10 billion for improvements and maintenance since World War II, a portion of which has had a positive influence on Southern California and, in particular, the City of the Angels.

Today's Santa Fe Railway provides employment to more than 32,000 Americans and operates 12,300 miles of railroad. The railway's 1,800 locomotives and 70,000 freight cars keep shipments moving along trackage that consistently exceeds industry standards. As a part of parent company Santa Fe Industries, the Atchison, Topeka and Santa Fe Railway looks forward to continued growth and cooperation in Los Angeles during the next 200 years.

Atlantic Richfield Company

The second century of developing global resources for global needs

In the early 1850s, there was no American — or worldwide — oil industry. The first commercial oil well would not be drilled until 1859 at Titusville, Pennsylvania. That well, in popular legend, marked the dawn of the petroleum age.

But seven years earlier in Pittsburgh, an immigrant Scot named Charles Lockhart was already building a tiny petroleum business. Nearly 130 years later, that business — now headquartered in Los Angeles — is the 15th largest industrial company in the world: Atlantic Richfield Company.

Charles Lockhart's venture was in "rock" oil — an annoying substance that seeped into brine wells. By the time a well was actually drilled to produce oil, Lockhart and others were already marketing petroleum as an illuminating fuel.

Lockhart and his partners became oil producers and refiners, and were the first to ship oil to markets in Europe. Their endeavors led to the founding, in Philadelphia in 1870, of The Atlantic Refining Company.

In 1874, Atlantic became part of John D. Rockefeller's Standard Oil empire. In 1912, after the dissolution of the Standard Oil trust by the U. S. Supreme Court, Atlantic set forth again as an independent company. For the next 50 years, under the leadership in turn of J. W. Van Dyke, Robert H. Colley, and Henderson Supplee, Jr., Atlantic grew slowly as an integrated oil company in the U. S. and abroad.

Its most dramatic growth, however, still lay ahead.

ARCO has been led since the mid-1960s by Robert O. Anderson, chairman of the board and chief executive, and Thornton F. Bradshaw, president. In 1965, the two executives sketched out, in Anderson's words, "a determined program of balanced growth." The goals: new emphasis on crude production; streamlining of refining, marketing, and transportation activities; expansion into petrochemicals; more attention to alterna-

Completed in 1929, the black and gold Richfield Building was a Los Angeles landmark for many years.

tive energy sources; more selectivity in international ventures; and development of other natural resources.

In the 12 short years which followed, three mergers raised ARCO to the financial scale required of a modern resource-based corporation.

The Atlantic Refining Company and Richfield Oil Corporation merged in 1966. Starting in 1902, Richfield had grown piecemeal from smaller oil enterprises of the western United States. By 1965, under the guidance of Charles S. Jones, Richfield's standing in the west was not unlike Atlantic's in the east. Richfield had

In 1972, Atlantic Richfield Company moved its corporate headquarters from New York to the ARCO tower (left) in Los Angeles.

pioneered the first commercial oil production in Alaska. Most importantly, it held the North Slope acreage that made possible Atlantic Richfield's discovery in 1968 of the ten-billion-barrel Prudhoe Bay oil field — the largest oil and gas deposit yet found in the United States.

ARCO merged next, in 1969, with Sinclair Oil Corporation. Harry F. Sinclair had begun trading oil leases in Kansas in 1903. The company he left to his successors had its production, refining, and marketing centered in the U. S. midcontinent, and was a natural fit with ARCO's east and west coast balance. Moreover, Sinclair brought to the merger substantial chemical and pipeline assets.

The third merger, in 1977, was with The Anaconda Company. Anaconda's beginnings were on the copper-rich hillsides near Butte, Montana, in 1875. By the late 1960s, it led the copper industry in sales and assets. Anaconda brought to ARCO its large U. S. copper operations and major activities as well, in aluminum, other metals and minerals, and industrial products.

ARCO today is structured as nine autonomous operating companies. Its businesses include U.S. oil and gas exploration and production; marketing of petroleum products; transportation of crude oil and products; exploration and production of oil and gas and other resources overseas; production of basic, intermediate and specialty chemicals; mining and marketing of copper, aluminum and other metals and minerals; metals manufacturing; coal mining and marketing; and development of new ventures in solar energy and other advanced technologies.

From Alaska to Indonesia, from the Gulf of Mexico to the North Sea, from China and Australia to Somalia and Chile, ARCO is active on every continent except Antarctica. With revenues of $16.7 billion, assets of $13 billion, and a 1980 capital budget three times as large as the company's entire asset base in 1965, Atlantic Richfield Company is committed to a future of developing global resources for global needs.

Beckman Instruments, Inc.

Lemon juice launched a high-technology pioneer

It began with a better way to measure the sourness of lemon juice. It's come a long way since.

In 1934, Dr. Arnold O. Beckman, then an assistant chemistry professor at Caltech, made a small electro-chemical instrument to measure the acidity of lemon juice for a Southern California citrus processor. The instrument, a pH meter, did its job — and then some.

Because it performed so well, the citrus processor soon came back for another. Because it simplified precise acidity and alkalinity measurements, it quickly found applications in many other fields. Because it applied innovative technology to real customer needs, it launched a company toward world leadership in modern scientific instrumentation and a pioneering role in southern California's evolution as a major high-technology center.

Today, Beckman Instruments, Inc. produces more than 6,000 instruments,

Dr. Arnold O. Beckman (left), founder and chairman, and Dr. William F. Ballhaus, president, with new automated blood analyzers at Beckman's Clinical Instruments Division in Brea, California, 1979. The instruments perform glucose and other blood tests in seconds.

systems, fine chemicals and precision electronic components. They are used throughout the world in medicine, science, industry, environmental technology, energy research and management, and many other fields. The company employs some 13,000 people worldwide. Sales in the last fiscal year exceeded $500 million.

The pH meter led to the creation in 1940 of two more products that set the young company's course. One was the helical potentiometer, or Helipot®, a precision variable resistance device similar to a radio volume control that was developed originally for the pH meter. That put Beckman into the field of electronic components. The other was the Beckman DU® Spectrophotomer, an optical instrument that dramatically increased the speed and precision of chemical analyses. Its impact on chemical technology was comparable to that of the DC-3 on commercial aviation.

Beckman began operations in rented quarters in East Pasadena and spent its first two decades expanding in the Pasadena area. In 1954, the company consolidated its principal operations in Fullerton and since then has established additional facilities in La Habra, Brea, Irvine and other Orange County communities.

In 1953, the company's first overseas manufacturing facility was opened in Munich, Germany. Today, Beckman serves customers in more than 120 countries through three business groups — Analytical Instruments, Process Instruments and Controls, and Electro-Products — which, in turn, consist of 47 divisions, operations and subsidiaries.

Dr. Beckman served as president of the company until 1965, when he was named chairman of the board. On January 1 of that year, Dr. William F. Ballhaus joined Beckman as president and a director after a distinguished aerospace career. He has played a key role in the firm's continuing growth and expansion into new markets, including the development of a leading position in the health care field and the creation of new consumable chemicals businesses that complement Beckman's traditional instrument businesses.

Throughout its history, Beckman has placed strong emphasis on creative, market-oriented research and development, augmented by selective acquisitions of complementary businesses. The result has been a broadening array of advanced products that have contributed significantly to the company's growth.

Beckman has produced many highly important products for science and man, some with formidable names — analytical ultracentrifuges, synthetic enkaphalins, bilaterial impedance rheographs, RIA phase thyroid batteries, rate nephelometry systems, and planar gas discharge displays, to name just a few. Their uses and benefits are much easier to grasp. In biomedical research laboratories, Beckman instruments and chemicals speed studies of fundamental life processes and defenses against disease. In clinical laboratories, Beckman health care products simplify and reduce the cost of blood analyses and other diagnostic tests. In industry, Beckman systems and components increase the efficiency of petroleum refineries and chemical plants, and improve the performance and cost-effectiveness of electronic products. In environmental management, Beckman instruments monitor air and water quality and help control pollutants released by plants, factories

The pH Meter, developed in 1935 by Dr. Arnold O. Beckman to measure the acidity of lemon juice, launched the pioneering high-technology company.

and motor vehicles.

Building on its past achievements, Beckman will continue to expand its technical and business strengths and enter promising new fields that research and advancing technology inevitably will produce. "Whatever these fields may be," Dr. Beckman observes, "the company will be governed by the same policies it has followed since the beginning — strong emphasis on creative research, no compromise on quality or integrity, and the pursuit of leadership in whatever we do. In our judgment, there is no satisfactory substitute for excellence.

"The past 45 years have been rewarding in many ways. Perhaps the greatest reward is the knowledge that Beckman products are contributing to the progress of mankind. The expansion of such contributions is Beckman's commitment to the future."

The Bekins Company

Always a move ahead

It seems appropriate that Bekins — a name that means moving — moved here during one of the largest western migrations in U.S. history. Established in 1895, Bekins is one of Los Angeles' oldest and most respected companies.

Actually, John and Martin Bekins, sons of Dutch immigrants, established their moving and storage business in 1891 in Sioux City, Iowa. But recognizing the increasing westward movement, they headed for the West Coast.

After investigating the burgeoning cities of Sacramento, San Francisco and Los Angeles, Martin chose Los Angeles as the place to open his own business in 1895. Named simply "The Van and Storage Company," Martin's first office was an old van with the wheels removed.

The Bekins brothers were the first to specialize in the handling of household goods and pioneered new concepts in moving and storage. Martin brought the first covered moving vans to California,

and in 1903, he introduced the first motor trucks into the West Coast moving industry. At a time when there were only 700 motor trucks in the entire nation, Martin was operating two air-cooled, two-cylinder trucks, one in Los Angeles and one in San Francisco.

In the early 1900s, Martin established The Bekins Household Shipping Company in Chicago so that household goods bound for California could be pooled into carloads and shipped at a lower rate.

The first Bekins warehouse, at Fourth and Alameda Streets in Los Angeles, this brick building had stalls for the horses as well as space for storing furniture. The entrance led to a ramp so that the horses and vans — the only covered vans in the industry — could be driven right into the building for loading and unloading. There were six teams and vans, and twelve employees at that time (1900).

Martin purchased the property for the first Bekins warehouse at Fourth and Alameda in Los Angeles, and in 1896, a two-story brick building was constructed. A wooden ramp, running from the rear of the building to the second floor, was used so that the horse-drawn vans could drive up to unload the furniture. By 1900, there were six teams and vans and 12 employees working for Bekins.

Many of his brick warehouses became casualties in the San Francisco earthquake, so Martin constructed his first steel and concrete warehouse in Los Angeles in 1906. The six-story structure, at 1335 South Figueroa Street, is still in

Martin (left) and John Bekins, founders of The Bekins Company, 1902.

full service as a Bekins Moving & Storage facility.

In the 1920s, The Bekins Company, then under the direction of Martin's children, pioneered an off-shoot of the pool car — containerization. Bekins developed specially constructed shipping boxes of plymetal and steel to contain household goods which moved via boat and rail between points on the West Coast and the Atlantic seaboard.

Bekins made the first transcontinental motor van move from Sioux City to Los Angeles in 1928. During the '30s, motor van operations extended into the Northwest and the East, and culminated in the formation of Bekins Van Lines Company, which now operates throughout the United States.

Shortly after World War II, The Bekins Company began a suburban warehouse program, an innovation in the industry. Prior to that time warehouse construction was confined to centers of key cities. This innovation was designed to meet the needs of the growing number of families moving away from the central city.

In recent years, Bekins has applied its expertise to businesses in related industries. One of the fastest growing of these is the Bekins Building Services Group. Launched in 1969, it provides complete operational maintenance and guard services for office buildings, industrial plants, hospitals and other public facilities through Bekins Building Maintenance and Bekins Protection Services. With further expansion, Ace Termite and Pest Control was acquired.

Other Bekins subsidiaries include DATA Transportation Company, DATA Air, Bekins International Group, Adams, Clay Insurance Brokerage Company, U-Rent Furniture Company, Bekins Distribution Services Company and Bekins Record Storage Company.

From a humble, one-van beginning, The Bekins Company has become the world's largest moving and storage company and the nation's fifth largest national van lines company, traversing the globe with trucks, ships and airplanes and transporting everything from grandmother's fine china to IBM's largest computers to the household effects of the Russian ambassador to the United States.

The Bekins Company is proud that Martin chose Los Angeles in which to grow and diversify, and 96 years later, looks forward to another century of excellence.

Beneficial Standard Corporation

Innovation set the pace for growth

Although the word *innovate* dates from the 13th century French, it has become a uniquely American phrase. Perhaps no other word more incisively describes that singular quality which has

distinguished Americans for more than two centuries. More than settlers, builders and designers — even more than consumers, profiteers and imperialists — Americans are known throughout the

world as innovators.

From the nation's inception, America's citizens have somehow possessed an ability not only to invent, but to innovate — not only to introduce new ideas into

Beneficial Plaza, head-quarters for Beneficial Standard Corporation, occupies an entire square city block on Wilshire Boulevard. The building sits 135 feet back from the busy artery, and is fronted by a park of grass, flowers and evergreen trees.

the world, but to improve on concepts already discovered, to find a better way, to build that proverbial better mousetrap. America itself is an innovation.

Consider, for example, Edward D. Mitchell, Beneficial Standard Corporation's founder. One of the great "rags-to-riches" stories in the classical Horatio Alger tradition, his entire life has been marked by innovation. And innovation has been Beneficial Standard Corporation's hallmark since its first subsidiary was founded 40 years ago.

Born in Poland in 1889, Edward D. Mitchell immigrated to America with his parents when he was two and grew up on New York City's lower east side. He spent his early youth selling newspapers and shoelaces and running concessions at carnivals. Although he would later characterize formal education as one of life's most important assets, his own education has been derived from his voracious reading and from a vast store of experience.

While still in his teens, Mitchell moved to Alberta, Canada, where he helped to attract settlers from Europe to Western Canada. Later, he helped found the town of Edson, which still stands at the heart of the Peach River country. He also organized a farm cooperative, The Grain Growers Grain Company. But at age 39, his businesses were wiped out in the stock market crash of 1929.

During the Great Depression, Mitchell moved to California and started over. Throughout those dark years, he learned the value of life insurance. "I found out," he once recalled, "that the only things

One of Beneficial Plaza's artifacts, an exact replica of the Liberty Bell cast by the same English foundry which made the original, was shipped to America on the final voyage of the Queen Mary ocean liner.

that had real value in a crisis were my life insurance policies. And yet, I placed no importance to it when I bought them. But when times were hardest, I found I could borrow money on those policies and if I hadn't had them, I would have lost what other little money I had left. All would have been gone."

Acting upon that realization, Mitchell founded Beneficial Standard Life Insurance Company in Los Angeles in 1940. It was a fortuitous time to begin, for the city was on the brink of a massive population explosion. Thousands of people migrating to southern California each week needed many goods and services, including insurance.

From its original headquarters at 2505 Wilshire Boulevard, Beneficial Standard

Life quickly built a reputation for offering affordable life and accident and health insurance, and for innovatively marketing those policies. The company was one of the first to make significant use of direct mail as a marketing tool; today, its mass-marketing reputation is well known throughout the insurance industry.

During the 1950s and 1960s, new subsidiaries in life insurance (Fidelity Interstate Life Insurance Company), property-casualty insurance (Transit Casualty Company), mass marketing (Direct Marketing Company of America), real estate development and management (Beneficial Standard Mortgage Company), and investment management (Beneficial Standard Investment Management Corporation), were either formed or acquired.

In 1967, Beneficial Standard Corporation was formed in response to the growth and sophistication of both its subsidiaries and their increasingly competitive markets. Later that year, Beneficial Standard Corporation and its subsidiaries moved into their new headquarters, Beneficial Plaza, at 3700 Wilshire Boulevard.

Throughout its history, each of the corporation's subsidiaries has responded to Edward D. Mitchell's creed: *Do something better than your competitor. Improve. That is what our aim is. We're aiming, we're thinking, we're dreaming to bring out something which is always better than what we or anyone else has had before. The day is not here when there isn't room for improvement.*

The Biltmore Hotel

Style and grace of its past became its measure for the future

In March 1921 some 40 of Los Angeles' most influential financial individuals gathered to consider whether the time had come for Los Angeles to fill a need for a hotel worthy of the civic pride of this leading community. Their decision was an affirmative one.

One year later, on March 27, 1922, ground was broken at 5th and Olive. The Central Investment Corporation was formed to construct and build the hotel; the architectural firm of Schultze & Weaver was selected to design the hotel; and John McEntee Bowman was named to manage The Biltmore, leasing it from Central Investment Corporation.

October 1, 1923, marked the opening of a new era for the City of Los Angeles. One hundred distinguished hoteliers rode The Biltmore Special on its 10-day run from Penn Station in New York to Los Angeles for the opening of the $7.8 million, 1,000-room Biltmore Hotel. They were among the 3,000 opening-night guests representing the social and business community of Los Angeles. They marveled at the Spanish-Italian Renaissance architecture and hand-painted ceilings highlighting the artistry of Giovanni Smeraldi, which told the story of early California and underlined its heritage and traditions.

The elegant interiors, the high standards of service, the utmost attention to detail were to make The Biltmore *the* place to be seen and the proudest of all of the hotels in The Biltmore circle. So, it was not surprising when, in 1928, the hotel underwent a $4 million expansion which brought the total number of guest rooms to 1,500 and introduced America's largest ballroom — Sala de Oro, later to be known as The Biltmore Bowl.

The Biltmore frequently hosted guests from around the world including heads of state, royalty and celebrities. It was only natural, therefore, that on May 11, 1927, some of the most prominent names in the film industry — including Mary Pickford, Douglas Fairbanks, Sr., Cecil B. DeMille — gathered in the Crystal Ballroom of The Biltmore for an elaborate dinner marking the formation of a new association. On one of the hotel's linen napkins a dinner guest scrawled a sketch of a statue which is known today throughout the world as Oscar.

Large living rooms with high ceilings, wet bars, live plants and original work of contemporary American artist Jim Dine are features of the stylish suites of The Biltmore Hotel. Decorated in warm earth tones, each suite provides an atmosphere for relaxing, entertaining or conducting small business meetings and luncheons.

Restoration of The Biltmore Hotel's famed Main Galeria highlights hand-painted ceilings and sculpture of Italian Giovanni B. Smeraldi.

It was the birth of the Academy of Motion Picture Arts and Sciences.

The scene was to be repeated 50 years later on May 11, 1977, again in the Crystal Ballroom, with Bob Hope, Charleton Heston and Gregory Peck in attendance to pay tribute to Oscar on his golden anniversary. During those 50 memorable years, several of the Academy Awards ceremonies were held in The Biltmore, including the year when "It Happened One Night" made a sweep of the awards.

The Biltmore became a focal point for major social events and gatherings. Names like former Presidents Harry Truman and John F. Kennedy, Eleanor Roosevelt, J. Paul Getty, Howard Hughes, Douglas Fairbanks, Casey Stengel and John Wayne appeared on the guest list. And, on July 2, 1969, The Biltmore was declared a Historical Cultural Monument by the Los Angeles Cultural Heritage Board.

But a shift away from the central city caused a general decline in the 1960s. And, it was obvious in the 1970s that the famous hotel was in need of a major revitalization if it were to play a leading role in the redevelopment of downtown Los Angeles.

On March 1, 1976, The Biltmore was purchased by architects Phyllis Lambert and Gene A. Summers, who immediately embarked on a $35 million restoration/renovation program dedicated to the preservation of the aesthetic and architectural beauty of the hostelry. The results were impressive: 1,027 luxurious suites and guest rooms featuring the artistry of Jim Dine, with live trees and plants; a French restaurant, Bernards; restoration of the magnificent banquet and meeting rooms.

Once again, The Biltmore's guest list is most impressive: President Carter, Princess Margaret, the Duke of Kent, Liza Minnelli, Robert De Niro.

And once again, The Biltmore stands proud in its tradition of elegance and distinction and its continuing contribution to the growth of downtown Los Angeles.

Bixby Ranch Company

"A mainstay in southern California's growth for over 100 years"

Bixby Ranch Company is a family company that dates back to the arrival of John W. Bixby in California more than 100 years ago. Bixby, who came across the continent from Maine, settled in 1878 on the Spanish land grant known as Rancho Los Alamitos. That land is located in what is now the east Long Beach-Seal Beach-Garden Grove area. He moved his wife Susan and baby son Fred into the dilapidated old adobe ranch house — one of California's oldest, dating back to 1806 — and proceeded to repair and add to the house, build barns and corrals and gradually pull the ranch into shape. This was the start of a cattle and real estate business that has been carried on continuously since that time, a business in which Rancho Los Alamitos has been and still is the tap root.

In 1906 Fred H. Bixby, son of John, moved into the old adobe with his wife Florence and baby daughters Katharine, Elizabeth and Deborah, and took over the reins of Rancho Los Alamitos. During the 46 years that he ran the business, Fred expanded the cattle operations to other ranch properties in Santa Barbara and Los Angeles counties, northern California and Arizona. In the late 1920s, oil was discovered on a portion of the Rancho Los Alamitos property. It was Fred who was responsible for incorporating the business and giving birth to the large, diversified company which exists today.

At about the time Fred died in 1952, the post World War II real estate boom in southern California was just starting. For a time his daughters carried on the company's business. Then Preston Hotchkis (1953-1966), followed by his son, Preston B. Hotchkis (1966 on), directed the company's business. During this period, the company began to gear itself to deal with the gradual urbanization occurring on its Los Angeles and Orange County ranch properties.

Today, in addition to its historical cattle business, Bixby Ranch Company carries on an extensive and diversified real estate development and property management business. Its developments include commercial, industrial, office, recreational, multi-family, single-family and community projects. Its headquarters are in Los Angeles and its development and property management offices in east

Fred H. Bixby branding cattle in 1907.

Long Beach. Approximately 200 persons are employed throughout its operations.

The individuals who have led the company, as well as its major shareholders, have contributed greatly to the civic and cultural advancement of southern California and have been leaders in the state and their professions. John Bixby served on the Long Beach City Council and Long Beach's first Board of School Trustees. He also was instrumental in the donation of the land for Bixby Park. Fred Bixby started and endowed the practical farming program at the University of California (Davis campus) and was president of the American and California Cattlemen's Association and the California State Fair. Preston Hotchkis was a leader in bringing Colorado River water to southern California, served as president of the California State Chamber of Commerce and as the U.S. representative on the Economic and Social Council of the United Nations. Florence Bixby, Fred's

wife, founded and headed for years the Long Beach Day Nursery, a facility for low-income working mothers and the first licensed social welfare agency in California. Katharine Bixby Hotchkis was a statewide leader in California history and historical preservation. She, along with her sisters, Elizabeth Bixby Janeway and Deborah Bixby Green, was instrumental in the donation and establishment of the Rancho Los Alamitos ranch house, barns and gardens — a much visited Long Beach historical site (depicting ranch life of the 1800s and early 1900s).

Bixby Ranch Company today is a pleasing blend of the old and the new. The bulk of the shareholders are descendants of John and Fred Bixby and the firm is steeped in history and tradition. At the same time, the company has had to cope with change that occurs at an ever increasing pace, change which already has resulted in the urbanization of its Los Angeles and Orange County ranch holdings and the conversion of its employee base from rural to largely urban personnel. Despite this development, the basic purpose of the company, its management and its owners remains the same — to be responsible, to take the long-term view and to continue to contribute all they can to the community around them and to the general growth of Southern California.

187

The Broadway Department Stores

From "Don't worry — watch us grow" to "Your neighborhood store"

The first Broadway, inset, opened in 1896 at Fourth and Broadway. Later, in 1915, Broadway trucks were photographed before new nine-story Broadway at same site.

There are usually two key ingredients to the making of a successful business: a workable idea which meets a need and the appropriate timing for acting on that idea. For Arthur Letts, a young emigrant from England, the timing was right for his first Broadway department store — opened at Broadway and Fourth Streets in the growing metropolis of Los Angeles in 1896.

So right, in fact, that ten years later when E. T. Earl, a Los Angeles builder, began construction on a seven-story building at Broadway and Seventh Streets, Letts signed a 50-year lease on the structure to save the location for the Broadway. Letts gave John Gillespie Bullock, a Canadian who had been with the store almost since its inception, $250,000 with which to stock the new store. Bullock later acquired the store from Letts.

The Broadway prospered until it became necessary to plan for a larger building that could accommodate the expanding business and reflect its growing prestige in the community. In 1915, a new nine-story Broadway opened at Fourth and Broadway, fulfilling Letts' motto: "Don't Worry, Watch Us Grow."

Arthur Letts, Jr., son of the founder, took over the operation of the Broadway upon his father's death in May 1923 and served the company until 1926. At that time, Malcolm McNaghten, former financial vice president, was appointed president.

The Broadway grew and prospered through the years. In 1931, it acquired a second store in Hollywood, an 18-story building at Hollywood and Vine which became a familiar landmark to the millions of tourists who thronged to the cinema capital of the world.

The Broadway continued to expand and, in 1940, built a new store in Pasadena. Strikingly different in architecture from the usual department store of the era, it was regarded as one of the most beautiful buildings erected on the Pacific Coast.

The mid-'40s brought more growth and with it, a change in leadership. James Lamb was elected president in 1945, succeeding McNaghten who became chairman of the board of directors.

In 1946, a man who would have significant impact on the growth of the Broadway department stores, Edward W. Carter, was appointed executive vice president by Blyth and Company, investment brokers who had purchased the controlling interest from the Letts family. Carter was appointed president in 1947.

One of Carter's first moves was to halt construction on the Broadway Crenshaw and enlarge the plans for that store. Carter was convinced the company's course lay in rapid suburbanization with relatively large stores. The regional chain concept, then revolutionary, is now considered one of his most significant accomplishments.

In 1951, Hale Brothers Stores purchased controlling interest in the Broadway. Carter continued to forge new links in the Broadway chain and, with Prentis Hale, sought to speed Broadway-Hale Stores' growth by acquisition.

By 1969, the Broadway had a new president and chief executive officer, Philip Hawley; Carter had become president and Prentis Hale chairman. Hawley was elected chairman in 1970.

Under the leadership of J. Hart Lyon, who was named chairman in 1972, the Broadway's growth picked up momentum. With the opening of the $75 million Broadway Plaza in November 1973, the Broadway had come full circle — pioneering the move to the suburbs and then, in the vanguard of urban redevelopment, building Los Angeles' first downtown department store in 50 years. The first downtown Broadway had closed in 1966.

The growth-oriented Broadway had increased to 38 stores by February 1974, and Broadway-Hale Stores, Inc. changed the corporate name to Carter Hawley Hale Stores, Inc. to identify the company with the executives instrumental in its development: Edward W. Carter, chairman of the board, Philip M. Hawley, president, and Prentis C. Hale, chairman of the executive committee.

The year 1979 saw the creation of a new division, the Broadway-Southwest, with nine stores in Arizona, Nevada and New Mexico. J. Hart Lyon moved to Carter Hawley Hale as executive vice president and Francis H. Arnone added the responsibilities of chief executive officer to those of president, which he assumed in 1978.

Today the Broadway stores number 40, with a new store replacing the Pasadena facility and a new store recently opened in Santa Monica.

Planning and building for progress, always keeping in mind the primary goal of serving the customer, has made the Broadway the largest department store group in Los Angeles and Southern California and the third largest in the United States.

Arthur Letts' idea was a good one.

California Federal Savings and Loan Association

America's largest federal dedicated to serving Los Angeles since 1926

For most Los Angelenos, 1926 was a comparatively uneventful year. Prohibition was in its seventh year, and local headlines were filled with lurid reports about the mysterious disappearance of evangelist Aimee Semple McPherson, who purportedly drowned in the ocean at the height of her preaching career.

Los Angeles was exploding with excitement, opportunity — and nearly a million people. It was against this backdrop that a small "building and loan association" was formed in a three-person office downtown on the second floor of the Pacific Electric Building at 6th and Main Streets.

The Railway Mutual Building and Loan Association was created on October 20, 1926, to serve the financial and home finance needs of employees of the Pacific Electric and other railways serving Los Angeles. The PE's old "Red Cars" crisscrossed the city in one of the most efficient rapid transit systems of the day.

In its first report to the California Building and Local Commissioner, in 1927, Railway Mutual reported assets of $262,000. The association offered 6 percent savings certificates and charged a low four percent for home loans. The fledgling association would continue to

prosper for two more years — until the economy screeched to a halt during the Great Depression.

Following the bank holiday of 1933 and New Deal legislation that created the Federal Home Loan Bank system and the Federal Savings and Loan Insurance Corporation, Railway Mutual became one of the first applicants to become a federally chartered, federally insured *savings* and loan.

In 1936, the association's name was changed to Railway Federal and a year later, in 1937, the name California Federal was adopted. This coincided with the association's move from downtown to the newly developed Miracle Mile district — a former Mid-Wilshire bean patch.

From assets of $1 million, the association grew rapidly during World War II and the postwar building boom, reaching $100 million in 1954. It was in that year that Cal Fed's first branch was opened in Reseda. Others quickly followed in Rancho Park, Lakewood, Hollywood, Granada Hills and Inglewood — all to serve the growing suburbs.

California Federal became America's largest federal in 1959, when it merged

The downtown office of California Federal's forerunner, Railway Mutual, as it appeared circa 1934.

with Standard Federal Savings and Loan, a downtown financial institution established in 1925. Their combined assets of $500 million doubled in just four years, surpassing the $1 billion mark in 1963. Cal Fed then was one of only four businesses in the city that had reached that milestone.

With completion in 1965 of its 28-story Plaza headquarters on the association's original Wilshire Boulevard site, California Federal embarked on a new period of growth.

In the early 1970s operations were expanded outside Los Angeles for the first time — into San Diego, the San Joaquin Valley and Northern California. This process was accompanied by the acquisition of several smaller associations. The largest was the 22-office Pacific Savings and Loan Association, acquired in 1975. New subsidiaries were also created to provide ancillary services in the areas of real estate development, building, mortgage banking, insurance and pension plan administration.

Today, California Federal, with assets over $6 billion, is a statewide financial institution serving more than half a million savings customers through 100 offices from Sacramento to the Mexican border.

The association's Miracle Mile headquarters, completed in 1965.

Carnation Company

An eighty year tradition of quality that began with "contented cows"

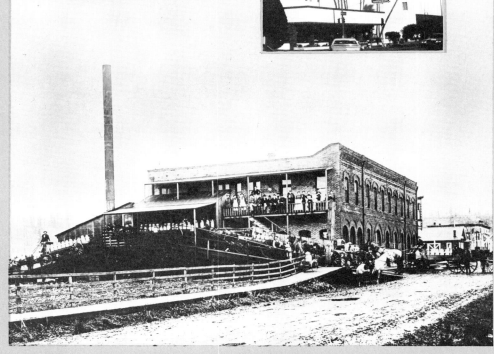

Carnation Company's World Headquarters, Los Angeles.

E. A. Stuart's unshakable faith in the quality of his product saved the Pacific Coast Condensed Milk Company when his partner was forced to sell out due to heavy losses in the company's first year.

It was this same faith, along with a good measure of pragmatic determination and ingenuity, that shaped the re-christened Carnation Company into a highly diversified international foods corporation with more than 2.7 billion dollars in sales annually. Today, Carnation's Los Angeles World Headquarters is the administrative center for the more than 20,000 people who work at 216 major locations, to produce some 258 Carnation products.

Back in 1901, Stuart was able to overcome the difficulties of canning and spoilage that plagued his evaporated milk company as he strived to produce a premium quality product safe for every use — from making baby formulas to quenching the thirsts of gold miners in the Klondike. His original red and white cans of evaporated milk quickly found wide spread acceptance along the adventurous Western coastline, where poor refrigeration and pasturization made fresh milk a rarity. However, the former Los Angeles grocer wasn't satisfied with limited distribution and set out to convince grocers nationwide of the merits of his milk.

Stuart's continuing demand for a better product resulted in the introduction of one of the first homogenizers in the United States and the purchase of the Carnation Farm, not far from the site of his original condensery near Seattle, Washington.

The farm's herd of pure bred Holsteins, affectionately termed "contented cows," delighted Stuart by consistently producing the finest quality milk and butterfat in record-breaking amounts.

The modern Carnation Farm is world renowned for its research and contributions in the areas of livestock breeding, feeding and management.

By the time Carnation entered the fresh milk and ice cream business in 1926, the company had 30 evaporated milk plants, including condenseries in Canada and Europe.

Carnation, in 1929, acquired Albers Milling Company, which included a Los

Employees gathered on the balcony of the original Carnation condensery in Kent, Washington, to watch farmers delivering milk on opening day, September 6, 1899.

Angeles mill, and in 1931, a fresh milk and ice cream plant in this city.

In 1947 Los Angeles was selected as the location for Carnation's new World Headquarters. Completed two years later, the Carnation building became a prominent landmark in the Wilshire district.

As Carnation continued to expand so did its interests in the Los Angeles area. The Carnation Research Laboratories in Van Nuys were built in 1952. In 1954, the company acquired McGraw Colorgraph, a Burbank manufacturer of photographic and art products. The following year saw the opening of Carnation's ice cream parlor at Disneyland.

By 1956 the company's new products included Instant Nonfat Dry Milk, Friskies dry dog and cat foods, and the forerunner of its modern Hot Cocoa Mix.

Under the guidance of Chairman and Chief Executive Officer H. E. Olson and

President Dwight L. Stuart, the company has followed a carefully planned course of growth and diversification while maintaining E. A. Stuart's original devotion to the highest quality products.

In accordance with this managerial philosophy, Carnation introduced a number of new products during the 1960s and '70s, including Coffee-mate non-dairy creamer, Instant Breakfast, Slender diet foods, Chef-mate line of canned entrees, soups, salads and sauces, Mighty Dog canned dog food, Friskies Buffet canned cat food, Spreadable sandwich spreads and Carnation potato products. Acquisitions during this period were Contadina Foods, a California processor and distributor of tomato products; Trenton Foods, a major meat processor; Dayton Reliable Tool and Manufacturing Company in Ohio; and Herff Jones, an Indianapolis company which produces school-related products.

Today, with a history of quality products and services that goes back to 1899, Carnation is working to help meet future world food needs through continued research and product development.

190

Coast Federal Savings and Loan Association

Helping communities prosper and progress

When Coast Federal Savings opened its doors for business in 1935 at Eighth and Broadway in downtown Los Angeles, it began with an office, one employee, and $49,000 in assets. Today, Coast, with corporate location at Ninth and Hill, has more than 50 branch offices, 900-plus employees, and assets of nearly $3 billion.

The real key to this financial institution's dynamic growth has been its philosophy of helping communities prosper and progress. Yet Coast's responsibility does not stop with financial services. The Association continually supports and places major emphasis upon programs aimed at the betterment of the communities it serves.

Ross M. Blakely, Coast's chairman and president, is a director of the Federal Home Loan Bank of San Francisco and an active participant in numerous other community organizations. He sets the example for his senior officers, department heads and managers for leadership in civic affairs.

To Coast's branch offices, which regularly sponsor community activities, civic involvement takes many interesting forms. Coast employees coach Little League teams, serve in municipal government and contribute many volunteer hours to nonprofit agencies. Coast Federal actively sponsors the Bill of Rights Commemorative events, a program which encourages greater awareness of our national heritage and responsibilities among high school students.

In addition to its active involvement in community-oriented affairs, Coast Federal has, through the years, been a leader in business and professional activities and policies of the industry. Since the post-World War II period it has played a major role in the fulfillment of housing credit needs. The Association was one of the first lenders to invest in tract homes and in government guaranteed loans for returning servicemen, and in loans insured by the Federal Housing Administration.

Coast has financed housing and commercial property for low and moderate income groups and has assisted minority communities. More than $4 million has been loaned by the firm to finance low-cost housing for senior citizens and it has

This building of Coast Federal Savings, located at 9th and Hill Streets in downtown Los Angeles, was purchased in 1936. It is Coast's current corporate headquarters/main branch office and stands as a dramatic contrast to today's modern architecture of Los Angeles office buildings.

invested substantial amounts in construction and permanent financing of convalescent health care facilities.

Coast's emphasis on leadership is further exemplified by its participation in the Community Investment Fund to help stimulate home financing in mature communities. It has supported Los Angeles Mayor Tom Bradley's Homeownership Opportunity Programming Effort (HOPE), offering mortgage counseling and information on financial contracts, taxes and interest.

Coast assists with housing information services in other California communities and has been instrumental in the establishment of facilities and programs to aid urban reinvestment and housing rehabilitation.

The association is continually increasing its available services to customers, and was among the organizers of the statewide Home Loan Counseling Center formed to educate the public about personal finances. Coast was one of the first savings and loan institutions to install IBM computers, 24-hour automated teller machines, and computerized Cash

Flow Service. Travel and entertainment service for customers is available through its Insiders Club.

Coast Federal has been helping communities prosper and progress from the time it was chartered; its growth record shows the results of these efforts all over the State of California. With its philosophy of looking ahead with vision, and its willingness to adapt to new demands in the years ahead, Coast has weathered periods of national economic upheaval and has come out a leader in the California financial community — for today and for tomorrow.

Coca-Cola Bottling Company of Los Angeles

World's most widely known soft drink

Seventy-eight years ago, all that marked the modest beginning of Coca-Cola in Los Angeles were a two-man staff, a one-room "bottling works," a virtually unknown product and a growing community.

Coke came to Los Angeles in 1902, just 16 years after a Georgia pharmacist first blended cocoa leaves and cola nuts into a "Delicious and Refreshing" soft drink named Coca-Cola. Conceived, some say, as a medicinal tonic, the new soft drink — with its distinctive taste and flowingly-scribed trademark— soon was selling for a nickel a drink at soda fountains across the country.

A local bottler, A. T. Gantt, obtained the Los Angeles franchise, which extended 50 miles in all directions from City Hall. The first year, from the basement of a small brick building on East Third Street, he bottled 720 gallons of Coke, using a single foot-powered machine that was said to break more bottles than it filled. Driving a horse-drawn wagon, his salesman sold 92,000 bottles of Coca-Cola that first year — the equivalent of about 15 minutes' production on one of today's high-speed bottling machines.

Mechanization had its impact on Coke during the 1911-1920 decade, as outlying dealers ordered by mail and cases of Coke were often delivered by the "Big Red Cars" of the Pacific Electric Railway that knit the city together. The company's two horse-drawn wagons were replaced by a single Hartcraft truck — a far cry from the giant and colorful diesels in today's CCLA fleet, which now includes more than 2,000 vehicles of all types.

Russell and Arthur Pratt purchased the "bottling works" in 1915, later relocating in a new and larger factory on 14th and Central Avenue. The site would eventually become the company's headquarters and principal manufacturing plant and 56 years later — with its unique natural facade — CCLA's "Flagship" would be honored as a Los Angeles

historic-cultural monument.

In 1923, the Barbee brothers — Stanley, A. K., and Cecil — purchased the Los Angeles bottling rights, a year later renaming the operation the Coca-Cola Bottling Company of Los Angeles and offering the first public sale of stock.

Throughout the '20s and '30s the company continued to expand as new merchandising techniques were developed. The first 12-pack carton was introduced in Los Angeles as well as the first "ice-powered" cooler.

Following the War years and throughout the '50s, CCLA continued to add new products and develop new markets. However, it wasn't until 1961, when A. D. MacDonald became CCLA's third president (and later its board chairman), that the company developed long-range programs which have made it one of the largest beverage bottling companies in the world.

CCLA has expanded its soft drink operations to include most of Southern California, Nevada and Hawaii. The acquisition of the Coca-Cola Bottling Company of Mid-America in 1976, with headquarters in Kansas City, Kansas and serving parts of six Midwestern states,

CCLA's famous "Flagship" headquarters with its unique facade was declared a Los Angeles historic-cultural monument in 1976.

added more than five million people to CCLA's marketing territory.

In addition, bottling rights for other leading beverages increased CCLA's product line to encompass more than 20 brands of beverages in 133 different sizes, shapes and containers, with Coca-Cola continuing to be by far the dominant market brand.

With the purchase of Arrowhead and Puritas Waters Inc. and its subsidiary, Ozarka-Houston, in 1969, CCLA entered into a new field — bottled and industrial water. Throughout the years, CCLA has actively participated in community projects and programs. Focusing particular attention on young people, CCLA sponsors educational programs, career planning seminars and a variety of athletic events, including the Handicapped Olympics, Watts Junior Olympics and GO WITH SOCCER, a skills contest involving over 100,000 children in California and Nevada. In addition, CCLA actively participates in local community programs benefiting civic, cultural and charitable causes.

And today, with more than 3,500 employees, a marketing area covering thousands of square miles and serving over 20 million people, the Coca-Cola Bottling Company of Los Angeles under the leadership of its current president Thomas P. Kemp is proud to be identified with the world's most widely known soft drinks and one of the world's truly great cities.

Collins Foods International, Inc.

A saga of a fast food pioneer

The friendship that has always existed between Colonel Harland Sanders and Jim Collins was reaffirmed at the Colonel's 80th birthday celebration in Los Angeles.

Collins Foods International began with a talented entrepreneur and his determination to build a company. James A. Collins trained as a different kind of builder at UCLA where he earned an engineering degree. For two years after graduation, he worked as a civil engineer, then decided to go into business for himself.

At age 25, Collins opened his first "Hamburger Handout" self-service drive-in in Culver City, California, and recorded sales of $421,000 for that first year. By 1959, he was operating four self-service restaurants, and early in 1960, he obtained a franchise for Kentucky Fried Chicken. This relatively unknown brand of fried chicken was added to the menu.

In the next few years, Collins opened three additional franchised Kentucky Fried Chicken stores in Southern California. In 1963, he entered into a contract with Colonel Sanders to be the exclusive agent for Kentucky Fried Chicken stores in Southern California. In this position, he had the responsibility to develop, organize and grant franchises for others and for himself.

In 1965, Collins formed several companies to engage in wholesale operations for his own stores and others in the area. Two years later, he and two associates acquired the Sizzler Family Steak House chain. By this time he had established 33 KFC kitchens of his own. With the sale of 300,000 shares, Collins took his company public in November 1968 as Collins Foods International.

Over the next 10 years, CFI grew rapidly. Revenues went from $9 million in fiscal 1968 to $213 million by fiscal 1979. Growth has been both internal and external, through the acquisition of Kentucky Fried Chicken stores and further development of the Sizzler and Collins Foodservice concept.

Collins Foods proved to be an innovative franchisee, having been the first to develop a standard image take-out store throughout a major marketing area. Today, Collins Foods is the largest franchise operator of Kentucky Fried Chicken Corporation with 232 KFC stores. About half are located in Southern California with

Sizzler offers its customers an attractive menu and decor that represents an excellent price/value relationship, with many of its entrees at half the regular menu prices of the full-service dinner houses.

other units located in Florida, Oregon, Texas, Illinois and Queensland, Australia.

Sizzler Family Steak Houses began business in the West when Del Johnson opened his first unit in January 1958. When Collins acquired the Sizzler chain in 1967, there were 156 franchises in 20 states. Although the original concept relied on price alone to succeed, emphasis changed from price to that of high value and of being a "marketer" desirous of meeting the changing needs of the consumer and his lifestyle. Sizzler quickly became a leader among the popular priced steak houses. It was the first chain to abandon the budget steak house position and broaden its appeal by offering prime rib, salad bars, beer and wine, combination plates such as steak and lobster, "semi-service," and an upgraded decor.

The results were outstanding. Today there are more than 400 Sizzlers in 39 states and franchise operations in Japan, Guam and Saudi Arabia.

Rounding out the company is the distribution operation, carried out through the Collins Foodservice Division. With sales in 1979 in excess of $100 million, this division operates from six strategically located distribution centers — Los Angeles, Santa Clara, Phoenix, Portland, San Diego and Tampa. The primary purpose of Collins Foodservice is to serve its own retail units. However, Collins Foodservice is also the authorized distributor for all Kentucky Fried Chicken stores in nine western states and is a major KFC distributor in Florida.

The development of Collins Foods International is rather unusual because it is the saga of how a successful franchisee of one fast food operation has become, in addition, a successful franchisor of another. Its dedication to the healthy economic growth of the southern California area is witnessed by the more than 400 Kentucky Fried Chicken and Sizzler restaurants in the Los Angeles area.

This is the story of a company that has grown, changed and become increasingly seasoned and responsive to the needs of the quick service restaurant industry — both "eat-in" and "take-out." As the nation's technology continues to advance, the leisure time of Americans will also increase, and with this growth in freedom will come accelerating demands for quality foods prepared away from home. Collins Foods International is a professionally well-managed company — positioned to meet the foodservice industry's demanding needs today and in the future.

Continental Airlines

The airline that pride built

On July 15, 1934, one of three single-engined, four-passenger Lockheed Vegas owned by the Southwest Division of Varney Speed Lines lifted off the runway at El Paso, Texas, on a 520-mile flight to Albuquerque, New Mexico, and Pueblo, Colorado.

The plane carried 100 letters, but no passengers, and in the next 15 days, the little airline flew only nine cash customers. Since there were eight employees on the payroll, it seems fair to say that things were off to a less than soaring start. In fact, only 600 passengers were carried during the first year of operation.

Today, those eight employees have become 12,000; the three Lockheed Vegas have become a fleet of 67 jets; the 600 annual passengers have become eight million, and the company's name has been changed to Continental Airlines.

Robert F. Six, who joined the company as operations manager July 5, 1936, and who replaced Avery Black as president February 3, 1938, remains as chairman of Continental's board of directors. The company still flies between El Paso and Albuquerque but its routes cover the Mainland U.S. and extend south to Mexico and west to Hawaii and beyond to Fiji, American Samoa, New Zealand and Australia, and to Micronesia, Guam and Japan.

Continental's growth from its small beginning into a regional carrier, then into a major trunkline, was slow but sure.

In 1936, the little airline purchased the Denver-Pueblo route of Wyoming Air Service and moved the company's headquarters from El Paso to Denver. Later the same year, the company's name was changed to Continental Airlines.

Through a series of awards from the Civil Aeronautics Board beginning in 1939 and covering more than a dozen years, Continental's basic Denver-El Paso route was extended throughout the Southwest and Rocky Mountains.

This was Continental Airlines City Ticket Office in Chicago 23 years ago, in 1957.

In 1955, absorption of the routes and operations of Pioneer Air Lines added cities in Texas and New Mexico, and Continental began service between Chicago

Unlike today's modern jet transports that use specially designed containers which hold a large number of bags (and are then put in the belly of the aircraft), loading bags in yesteryear was quite different. This picture (taken in 1941) shows a Continental Airlines Lockheed Lodestar being loaded with individual suitcases by white uniformed baggage handlers. The forward (nose) baggage pit, was one of four on the airplane.

and Los Angeles via Denver and Kansas City, turning the company into a major trunk carrier. With annual sales of just $16 million and assets of only $14 million, Continental ordered $64 million worth of DC-7Bs, jet powered Viscount IIs and pure jet Boeing 707s to operate over the new routes.

Continental continued to grow in the

1960s, adding service throughout the western two thirds of the Mainland U.S., and to Hawaii in 1969 and in 1971, Continental and its affiliate, Air Micronesia, were certified for a route from Hawaii through Micronesia to Guam and Okinawa.

In the last few years, Continental has become an international airline with routes to Japan, Australia, New Zealand, Fiji, American Samoa, and Mexico's west coast resort cities of Cabo San Lucas, La Paz, Puerto Vallarta, Manzanillo and Acapulco. During the same period, east coast service was added bringing Miami, Washington, D.C. and Newark/New York on-line.

In May of 1975, at Six' recommendation, the airline's board of directors named Alexander Damm president and chief operating officer of Continental. Six was elected chief executive officer and chairman of the board.

In December of 1979, Six announced that on February 1, 1980, after 43 years at the helm of Continental, he was turning the reins over to A. L. Feldman as president and chief executive officer. Prior to that, Feldman had been president and chief executive officer of Frontier Airlines. Six will remain as chairman of the board of directors until July 1982, when he retires.

Ducommun Incorporated

A tradition of anticipating needs — and meeting them

In 1849, as gold seekers by the thousands rushed to California, a solitary Swiss immigrant watchmaker set out on foot for Los Angeles from Fort Smith, Arkansas. Following him was a mule carrying everything he owned.

He arrived nine months later in a strange land without friends or relatives. Beyond his few possessions, the 29-year-old pioneer had only high hopes.

The man was Charles Louis Ducommun, one of that early breed of settlers who found in Los Angeles not the riches of gold but the challenges of business opportunity.

Young Charles set out to serve the little frontier cattle town with a small watch repair shop in a one-story adobe. The pueblo's scant population was not a promising prospect but cattlemen and prospectors by the thousands were passing through and Ducommun was soon catering to their needs for clocks, jewelry and books. He learned to anticipate and meet their needs — saddles and rope for cattlemen, tools for miners, shears for sheepmen. The business prospered and Charles Ducommun moved to larger quarters with his company.

Through boom and bust, his rise was steady. Ducommun phased out his watches and stocked more hardware. He became an early supplier to local farmers, to the first telephone company, to the infant petroleum industry. Before the turn of the century, his business had become a virtual department store to industry.

As California's oldest continuing industrial company passed from father to sons, it first specialized in wholesaling equipment, tools, brass and copper. Next it began to represent eastern metals

Founder Charles L. Ducommun, second from right, with fellow employees before one of the first stores — at Main and Commercial — circa 1874.

suppliers, and the distribution of metals sparked a new era of Ducommun growth. The firm became a key link between eastern metals producers and western users, buying in large quantities and processing sizes and shapes to order. It was the beginning of the Ducommun "metals service center" concept.

With World War I, the metals business increased. When Donald W. Douglas pioneered the local aviation industry early in the '20s, credit from Ducommun helped him enter commercial production. As construction, oil drilling and re-

195

fining, and motion pictures boomed, Ducommun was on the scene with its supplies and services. In 1923, the company bought an unheard-of amount of carbon steel from Bethlehem Steel — a shipload of 5,000 tons.

That shipload of steel was a turning point for Ducommun. From it stemmed the company's deeper involvement with the aircraft industry and essential service to the space age industries of electronics, missiles and scientific instruments.

With the west on the move and industry diversifying throughout the '50s and '60s, Ducommun moved with it. Metals and supply centers were established from San Diego to Seattle, from Tulsa to Hawaii. And it didn't stop there. Ducommun acquired Kierulff Electronics, Inc. in 1961 and developed it into a national distribution network for electronic components. In 1962 the company became Ducommun Incorporated. And in 1967 it acquired Digital Machines International with capabilities for manufacturing reinforcing bar fabricating equipment for the heavy construction industry.

Today Kierulff Electronics, Inc. is the fifth largest electronics distributor in the industry. Digital Machines International is the acknowledged leader in reinforcing bar fabricating techniques. And Ducommun Metals Company, largest of the three Ducommun operating companies — backed by 130 years of experience and now expanded into Georgia and Florida — is among the nation's five largest independent distributors of metals.

In all, these firms achieved sales of well over $300 million in 1979 with profits after taxes in excess of $5 million.

Charles Louis Ducommun might not recognize his company today with its more than 2,000 employees and plants and branches throughout the U.S. and in Europe. But he undoubtedly would share with its nearly 3,000 stockholders the pride they take in Ducommun's ability as a metals distributor — to provide service that is at once timely, reliable and inexpensive — and its vast electronics warehousing and distribution capabilities.

After all, ever since its establishment in a little tar-roofed adobe on Commercial Street in the pueblo called Los Angeles, Ducommun has been anticipating needs — and meeting them.

Ernst & Whinney

Continuing professional excellence through disciplined creativity

In 1903 the first flight of a heavier-than-air machine took place (it lasted 12 seconds), the United States was crossed by an automobile for the first time (it took 70 days), and Alwin and Theodore Ernst established an accounting firm in Cleveland, Ohio.

At that point, it would have been difficult to conceive of today's jumbo jets and superhighways that attest to the drastic changes which have swept over the world during the past 77 years. Likewise, it is doubtful that even A. C. Ernst, visionary though he was, could have foreseen the size, scope, and complexity of the 1980 firm when he and his older brother set up shop in 1903.

Three years later, in 1906, Theodore withdrew, leaving 25-year old A. C. to carry on the business alone. And so he did, for the next 42 years, while providing the industrious and imaginative leadership needed to make his firm one of the largest and most progressive accounting organizations in the world.

In the early years of the century, accounting was considered to be little more than routine bookkeeping. A. C. Ernst had little tolerance for that viewpoint. Quality of service was his watchword. The accountant, he believed, should use his intimate knowledge of a client's affairs to advance those affairs by drawing attention to weaknesses and

Young A. C. Ernst at the beginning of his career.

making constructive suggestions. In 1908, this concept led to the formation of the precursor of the firm's present management consulting services. Like its tax services, which came into being shortly after the 1913 introduction of the federal income tax, these many and varied management consulting services today are recognized for their depth and quality.

In 1908 an office was opened in Chicago. New York followed in 1909 and, in quick succession, so did other cities. When the Los Angeles office was opened in 1923, there were 39 Ernst & Ernst offices from coast to coast. By that time, the acquisition of some clients with foreign operations had made apparent the necessity for an international affilia-

Seen with a map identifying the 300 Ernst & Whinney offices throughout the world is Walter F. Beran, partner in charge of the firm's Western region.

tion. Accordingly, A. C. Ernst got in touch with Lord Palmour, managing partner of the prestigious British accounting firm of Whinney, Smith, and Whinney. A working agreement was drawn up between the two firms which proved so mutually satisfactory that it evolved into the entity of Whinny Murray Ernst & Ernst in continental Europe.

For the next 25 years, under the inspired leadership of A. C. Ernst, the firm continued to expand both its domestic and its international operations. New United States offices were opened seemingly every year. International affiliations were established on every continent except Antarctica.

A. C. Ernst died in 1948. He left behind not only a vigorous and growing accounting firm, but also a world facing a host of new problems, among them postwar economic adjustments, changing tax laws, and further expansion of American business to foreign countries. In adapting to the rapid and sometimes frantic transactions in the business world, Ernst's once-small firm has been in the front ranks of accountancy, and frequently a pioneer.

The fact that over the first 74 years the firm had only three managing partners says much for its character and stability. Under the fourth, Ray Groves, the seven worldwide affiliated partnerships have been brought together into one organization called Ernst & Whinney. This new partnership comprises more than 16,000 professionals, operating 300 offices in 70 countries on six continents. It is carrying on the firm's long-standing tradition of searching tirelessly for better and more efficient auditing and consulting techniques, and of speaking out forthrightly in support of any cause that will further the profession, the clients, and the society it serves. Los Angeles is the Ernst & Whinney headquarters for the Pacific basin and the city of the future.

First Gray Line Corporation

Helping travelers enjoy Los Angeles for more than seven decades

First Gray Line Corporation traces its local roots to a Pasadena livery stable in 1906. It was there in that year, with the automobile barely more than a modern curiosity, that horse-drawn buggy tour operations began, serving the stylish local hotels and providing a popular pastime for vacationers to the area. It could barely have been imagined then that motor transportation would soon transform the American way of life and become one of the major elements of the culture and character of the city of Los Angeles.

Encouraged by the initial success of his tour enterprises, Charles Tanner, who had come to the city from Texas in 1905 to begin the operations, proceeded to expand the business and began replacing the buggies with "horseless carriages" in 1909. The livery stable evolved to a "car barn" and the service of liveried chauffeurs driving automobiles became available to local citizens and tourists alike requiring personal transport. Early customer experiences were mixed, however, and more than a few patrons who had departed in elegant style from their hotels found themselves assisting in the repair of a tire or other problem shortly thereafter.

While motoring became less of an ad-

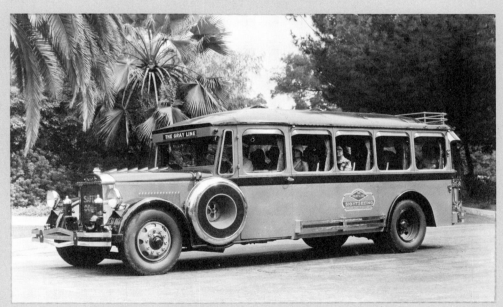

Sightseeing at the Alligator and Ostrich Farms, 1931.

venture, transportation needs and horizons expanded as the city grew. Taxi operations were initiated in 1917, and in 1921 motorcoach sightseeing tours were begun. By 1931 the touring fleet had grown to 33 motorcoaches and 200 limousines and taxis, and most significantly, Tanner operations joined that year with an association of eastern sightseeing companies and offered Gray Line Tours for the first time to such now forgotten attractions as the Mt. Lowe Observatory and the Alligator and Ostrich Farms.

During the war, services were oriented to the transport needs of servicemen, defense workers, USO troops and the Red Cross. In 1946, rebuilding of the tour business began and by 1948, the fleet

Limousines parked at the Pasadena livery stable, 1914.

consisted of 55 motorcoaches, 190 taxis and 150 limousines. Expanding most rapidly after the war, however, was the need and use of the automobile, and Gray Line "Drive Ur-Self" operations, as they were known, had built to a fleet of 255 vehicles in Los Angeles by 1948 and were soon to become associated with Warren Avis and his idea of building a new, nationwide car rental system.

Shortly after the war, Avis had become interested in the problem of dependable ground transportation from U.S. airports, where car rental services were non-existent, and formed the Avis Airlines Rent-A-Car System. In 1946 his first airport car rental counter opened at Willow Run Airport near Detroit, and Avis set out to develop a nationwide car rental network. To accomplish this, he enlisted independent u-drive operators in large cities throughout the country, selling them exclusive licenses to operate as Avis Rent-A-Car in return for instant recognition of his system. In 1952, for the initial sum of $1, the system was joined and U-Drive Services as Avis were provided for the first time in Southern California.

In 1965 the company's operations were acquired by First Gray Line Corporation, founded by another pioneering Gray Line operator, Henry Burroughs of Washington, D.C. Fascinated by Los Angeles and its opportunities as one of the most exciting tour and travel destinations in the world, Burroughs brought his family and his First Gray Line Corporation to California in that year and restructured and revitalized the operations to provide the best in tour and travel oriented ground transportation for Los Angeles and Southern California's millions of annual visitors. Upon his death in 1968, Burroughs' leadership was followed by that of his wife, Marguerita, who died in 1975, whereupon the second generation of the Burroughs family succeeded to the traditions of service in the city's travel industry, begun more than 70 years ago.

Today, First Gray Line Corporation is one of the state's largest ground transportation service organizations, with subsidiaries providing sightseeing and charter services throughout Southern California and Las Vegas, Nevada, as well as operation of the Las Vegas Transit System. Avis Car Rental Services are provided in these same areas, and comprise the largest independent licensee operation in the worldwide Avis System. The one thing unchanged since the beginning, however, is the commitment to helping visitors enjoy our great city.

Fluor Corporation

More than half a century meeting the challenges of the future

In 1977, Fluor Corporation moved its headquarters from East Los Angeles to Irvine, California, marking a homecoming to the area near the company's birthplace 65 years earlier. The fledgling Fluor Construction Company sired by Simon Fluor Sr. in 1912 bore little resemblance to the mammoth construction and process engineering firm and related subsidiaries that in 1980 held contracts totaling more than $12 billion.

Si Fluor Sr. was a perfectionist who demanded the utmost from his employees, but he was quick to reward those who produced. A Swiss immigrant

Fluor's first Los Angeles headquarters, at 909 East 59th Street, in the early 1930s.

and carpenter by trade, Fluor was practical, with marked talents as a designer and craftsman. In its early days before California's oil boom, the Fluor Construction Company was a general contracting firm. But the future of Si's small company would soon become tied to America's developing energy industry.

Fluor received its first contract from the oil and gas industry in 1915 when the Southern California Gas Company hired the firm to build meter shops and an office. The company's breakthrough into process construction came in 1922 with a 10,000 gallons-per-day natural gasoline plant for the Richfield Oil Company at Signal Hill. By 1925, Fluor was virtually out of the general contracting business.

Until 1930, the company's work had been limited to California. That year, its services were used to construct compressor stations on a pipeline between Texas and Indiana. The venture marked the company's entry into a national market and it soon opened a Kansas City office to handle mid-continent contracts.

In 1946, Fluor received one of its most significant contracts — the engineering and construction of a grass-roots refinery for Carter Oil Company at Billings, Montana. This job established Fluor as a refinery engineering firm, adding to its reputation as a constructor. The following year, the company obtained its first major overseas assignment, an expansion of Aramco facilities in Saudi Arabia.

In the mid 1950s, Fluor branched out, designing and building plants for the burgeoning petrochemical industry. The decade ushered in an expansion program that continues worldwide today. Fluor opened a London office in 1957. Two years later, the company expanded its overseas operation by buying a 75 percent interest in a small engineering firm in Haarlem, The Netherlands. Four years later, Fluor purchased the remaining 25 percent of what is today Fluor Nederland.

New Fluor Corporation International Headquarters building in Irvine, California.

Fluor Corporation continued to diversify as it entered the '60s. Early in 1967, a group of five offshore and land drilling companies merged into Fluor, giving the company its first contract drilling organization — Coral Drilling, Inc. The acquisition of Pike Corporation of America in 1969 brought Western Offshore Drilling and Exploration Company, Republic Supply Company of California, and Kilsby Tube Supply into Fluor. Western Offshore and Coral Drilling became the operating units of Fluor Drilling Services. In 1968, Fluor Ocean Services, Inc. was formed to concentrate on specialized engineering and construction management projects within the offshore industry.

A year later Fluor acquired the construction division of Utah Construction and Mining Company. This operation is now Fluor Mining & Metals, Inc., headquartered in San Mateo, California, and Fluor Australia, based in Melbourne.

Expansion of Fluor's services to the natural-resource industries was the company's main thrust as it entered the 1970s. The firm reorganized engineering and construction activities in 1971, forming Fluor Engineers and Constructors, Inc. A Fluor-pioneered task force concept was employed to keep pace with remarkable changes in the size and scope of projects. Jobs had evolved from the early straightforward gas plants in Texas to multibillion dollar projects with all supporting infrastructure.

Fluor began to serve the utility industry with the purchase in 1974 of Pioneer Service & Engineering Company of Chicago, one of the first firms involved in the development of nuclear power plants. It is now known as Fluor Power Services, Inc.

In 1977, Fluor made its largest acquisition — Daniel International Corporation, an industrial contractor with revenues of about one billion dollars a year.

Today, Fluor holds contracts all over the world ranging from several in excess of $250 million to the largest — Esso Resources' Cold Lake, Canada oil sands recovery facility, which will total more than $6 billion. Fluor leads in synthetic fuels experience, with construction of the huge Sasol Two coal-into-fuels plant in South Africa completed in 1980 on schedule and within budget. A duplicate, Sasol Three, is scheduled for completion by Fluor in 1982. Several million dollars of other types of synthetic fuels studies and projects are now in progress.

Fluor's assets have increased to $1.2 billion and its employee population now crests at more than 23,000. Although the most intense change in Fluor has occurred over the past 17 years, the company's most dramatic growth probably lies ahead. The basic reason can be summed up in a few words — the worldwide quest for more energy. The world's developing need for energy from every possible, practical source has become today's most urgent concern. The company started 65 years go by the creative carpenter is prepared to meet that challenge.

Golden State Mutual Life Insurance Company

The cause that became a company

William Nickerson Jr., arrived in Los Angeles in the late spring of 1921 hoping to establish new marketing inroads for the Texas-based life insurance company he represented.

A black man in his early '40s, Nickerson found the need for life insurance among the nearly 40,000 blacks who lived in California to be far greater than he had imagined. With few exceptions, existing insurance companies doing business in the state regarded black people as uninsurable or, at best, extraordinary risks. So, blacks were either denied life insurance coverage altogether or were accepted only at exorbitant premium rates.

What started out as a challenge to his business acumen became for Nickerson a challenge to his sense of social justice as well. They were challenges that be-

199

Present home office of Golden State Mutual Life, 1999 West Adams Boulevard, Los Angeles, California.

came even more pronounced when, three years later, the Texas company decided to withdraw from California. But Nickerson remained and, along with two associates in his Los Angeles office, decided to organize a new company.

Norman O. Houston and George A. Beavers, Jr. were practical men with intelligence, drive and more than a dash of self-confidence. They shared Nickerson's dissatisfaction with the system that excluded blacks generally from life insurance ownership, as well as his enthusiasm for doing something about it. Together, in 1924, these three set in motion the organizing machinery that would produce the Golden State Guarantee Fund Insurance Company.

George A. Beavers, Jr., Wm. Nickerson, Jr., and Norman O. Houston (left to right).

With the backing of an inspired black community in Los Angeles, the organizers succeeded in getting the 500 paid applications for life insurance required by California law, as well as in raising the $15,000 required as a guarantee fund. On

July 23, 1925, the Golden State Guarantee Fund Insurance Company received its license to operate.

With $17,800 in capital assets and a handful of agents, the organizers set up shop in a cubicle-sized office over a Central Avenue store. Nickerson was chosen president of the new company, Beavers, vice president and agency director, and Houston, secretary-treasurer. By the end of 1925, Golden State had paid its first death claim and established its first branch office. In 1928, the company built its own home office building at 42nd Street and Central Avenue, not far from the site of its first office.

Changing its name to Golden State Mutual Life Insurance Company in 1931, the company succeeded in converting to the more secure status of an old line legal reserve insurer in 1942.

Nickerson's death in 1945 preceded by four years the dedication of the company's present home office, a five-story structure on the corner of Western Avenue and Adams Boulevard. By late 1945 Houston had succeeded Nickerson as president, and Beavers had been elected chairman of the board. Beavers retired from active management in 1962 and Houston in 1970.

In 1972, the company's insurance in force surpassed the $1 billion milestone. Five years later, it recorded its second billion dollars' worth of insurance in force.

Today, more than a half-century since its founding, Golden State Mutual Life Insurance Company stands as a giant among minority-owned businesses and a symbol of loyal service to many. In 55 years of competitive existence, it has established a solid reputation as a well-managed financial institution, with assets in excess of $81 million and insurance in force of more than $2.5 billion, making it the second largest black-owned insurance company in the United States.

Licensed to operate in 22 states and the District of Columbia, the company maintains district offices and service centers in key communities across the country and employs more than 700 people.

Golden State takes pride in the cause which was the foundation for its inception: the creation of a black economic unit which could serve the economic needs of the black community; a cause which earned it that extra measure of zeal in the support it received from the Los Angeles community.

Golden State takes pride in still being a highly visible and respected symbol of that cause.

Golden West Broadcasters

Imagination and planning: successful formula for company's dynamic growth...

In 1927, Al Jolson made movie history. He spoke a line of dialogue on film and for the first time audiences were able to hear his words. The film was "The Jazz Singer," Hollywood's first talking picture. His prophetic line: "You ain't seen nothing yet."

A satellite receiver dish now stands on the site where Jolson spoke, indicative of how far the industry has progressed. Today, the old Warner Brothers Studio on Sunset Boulevard, which has since been named a Los Angeles cultural landmark, is the home of Gene Autry's Golden West Broadcasters, one of the most diverse and fastest growing independent entertainment companies in the country.

Golden West Broadcasters is the parent company of Los Angeles television station KTLA and radio station KMPC, which share the 10.2 acre studio complex with the other divisions and subsidiaries of the burgeoning company.

Since 1952, Golden West Broadcasters, with Chairman of the Board Gene Autry at the helm, has grown from one radio station to a group of eight AM and FM stations in five cities; a television station, KTLA; a videotape production center; a program development unit; a subscription television division and the California Angels baseball team.

Both KMPC and KTLA (Channel 5) are pioneer broadcasters in Los Angeles and both are known and respected for their community involvement and service. Together they represent more than 90 years of broadcasting service to the local community.

KMPC actually began operations in 1927 under the call letters KRLO. Autry and two partners acquired KMPC in 1952, with Autry the principal owner. In 1968, The Signal Companies, Inc., a multi-industry California based company, bought a minority interest and currently holds 49.9 percent of Golden West Broadcasters.

KMPC is the flagship station for the Golden West Broadcasters radio group, which also includes: KSFO, San Francisco; KVI and KPLZ-FM, Seattle; KEX and KQFM, Portland and WCXI and WTWR-FM, Detroit. Subsidiaries of the radio division are Major Market Radio, a national sales representative company; Market-Buy-Market, a syndicated media re-

"OPERATION BIG SHOT" — KTLA distinguished itself in 1952 with the first live telecast of an Atom Bomb blast from Yucca Flat, Nevada. KTLA's picture was relayed nationwide and the historic event was witnessed by more than 35 million people.

KMPC's pilot and helicopter support fire fighters and provide emergency assistance.

search and planning service; and Golden West Radio Productions, a complete production service for the radio industry.

KTLA was established by Paramount Pictures in 1941 as experimental televi-

sion station W6XYZ. In 1947, W6XYZ became KTLA and the first commercially licensed television station in the western United States. Golden West Broadcasters acquired KTLA and the Sunset Boulevard studio from Paramount in 1964.

As a pioneer in the industry, KTLA helped set the pace for television in many areas. In its first years, under the guidance of television genius Klaus Landsberg, KTLA introduced musical and variety shows and names to television, including Spade Cooley, Lawrence Welk and Ina Ray Hutton and Her All Girl Band. KTLA was also the first to televise wrestling, boxing, "Hopalong Cassidy," "Cecil and Beany" and the Rose Parade.

KTLA set the pace for television news coverage, as well, by televising news live from the scene. Some of KTLA's history-making coverage included the 17-1/2 hour uninterrupted telecast of the Kathy Fiscus well tragedy in 1949, the first telecast of an atom bomb test in 1952 and the unparalleled coverage of the 1965 Watts riots and the 1971 Sylmar earthquake.

Golden West Videotape Division, which also shares the entertainment complex, is one of the busiest television production facilities in Hollywood. With eight sound stages and sophisticated technical capabilities, Golden West Videotape Division is the production home of many network and syndicated series, pilots, specials and commercials.

Several years ago in a desire to further utilize the company's excellent facilities, combined with a personal and industry need for more quality programming, Golden West Broadcasters spawned Golden West Television, the production arm of the company. Golden West Television develops and produces television programs for syndication, network sales and subscription television.

In mid-1979, the company joined a few other industry pioneers in the new arena of subscription television. Golden West Subscription Television Division markets its pay TV service under the banner of Golden West Entertainment Network.

Golden West Broadcasters is an important part of Los Angeles' dynamic entertainment industry and offers a success story proving the link between imagination, planning and growth.

Hughes Aircraft Company

Local firm made 'electronics' before word was widely-known

Hughes Aircraft Company was in the electronics business before the word "electronics" had worked its way into the average person's vocabulary.

The company's origins were humble. In 1936 at the Union Air Terminal in Burbank, Howard Hughes set up an organization of only 24 engineers and craftsmen, and named it Hughes Aircraft Company, established as an operating division of Hughes Tool Company.

By 1938, when Hughes was preparing for his round-the-world flight, this group of men designed and built special radio communication equipment, including an emergency transmitter that was waterproof, unsinkable and self-contained.

During the record global flight of 14,672 miles, the flight crew maintained complete radio contact with ground stations except for the final leg.

By meeting requirements that were beyond the state-of-the-art, the company had, at the same time, entered the field of electronics and also demonstrated the reliability of radio communications as a safety factor for future worldwide commercial air travel.

As winds of war whispered in 1940, Hughes purchased land in Culver City near Lincoln and Jefferson amid celery fields farmed by Japanese-Americans — a site which would become the fledgling company's headquarters until the 1980s.

Over the July 4th weekend in 1941, the company, which had grown to nearly 500 people, moved into the newly constructed plant to find itself knee-deep in mud on land that was below sea level — moist enough to grow celery.

Dirt was hauled from canyons to elevate the sod runway by 10 feet. The runway later was paved for 9,000 feet — still probably the longest privately owned runway — to handle swift military jets approaching over old celery sheds that still exist as carpenter and paint shops.

On that Independence Day exodus from Burbank, "hacksawed" in half to make the trek through lazy pre-war streets, came a tiny, one-story frame structure which still stands at 11940 West Jefferson Boulevard, wearing a sign reading "Hughes Employment" and bearing the diffident name of Building 40. Through its portals have passed many

Hughes Aircraft Company headquarters and labs in Culver City, California in 1954. The 9,000-foot runway is the longest privately owned landing strip in the world (inset). Hughes Aircraft Company's Building 40, in recent years an employment office.

thousands of new employees, from engineers to clerks, who now help form a company of 53,000.

But earlier the little building was to have an even more exalted role. It became perhaps the industry's first "think tank." In 1946, when the government cancelled airplane contracts and switched emphasis to guided missiles, the company was faced with finding new directions. A small number of scientists and engineers gathered in the building to figure out "Where do we go from here?"

There they literally conceived the first air-to-air radar-guided missile (the Falcon) and its companion fire control system, a concept that has been called one of the boldest decisions in the aerospace industry. The concept permitted jet pilots to "seek, find and kill" without seeing their foe, making white-scarf dogfighters relics of the past.

On December 17, 1953, Hughes Tool Company caused to be formed what is now the Howard Hughes Medical Institute, a non-profit charitable institution. It was established for the stated purpose of "the promotion of human knowledge within the field of the basic sciences (principally the field of medical research and medical education) and the effective

application thereof for the benefit of mankind."

To support the Institute, Hughes Tool Company donated its electronic business represented by the contracts and good will of its division, Hughes Aircraft Company, and made available the initial plant and facilities in which to operate that business.

In 1954, Lawrence A. Hyland joined the company as vice president and general manager. Following the death of Hughes in April 1976, Hyland became president and later chairman of the board. He was followed in those positions by Dr. Allen E. Puckett, now chairman and chief executive officer. John H. Richardson is now president.

By mid-1980, the company had grown to 53,000 employees, a $1-billion yearly payroll, annual sales of $2.2 billion, 100 product lines, thirteen facilities, 25 U.S. regional and district offices, and thirteen overseas offices.

Company "firsts" include the first operating laser, the first 3-D radar, the first synchronous-orbiting communications satellite, and the first soft-moon-landing spacecraft — the Surveyors.

Hughes also pioneered a hire-the-handicapped program and has funded thousands of scholarships and fellowships leading to B.S., M.S. and Ph.D. degrees.

For the future, the company is expanding its facilities, including new construction on 143 acres in El Segundo scheduled for completion in 1981.

Johnson & Higgins

From clipper ships to computers

In many ways, the history of Johnson & Higgins is the history of business insurance and the brokerage function in America, for Johnson & Higgins is the country's oldest insurance broker, dating from the clipper ship days of 1845.

Many of the vessels that plied the California coast for trade — as well as the flotilla that carried the human cargo of the California gold rush — hoisted sail after seeking advice from Johnson & Higgins.

The company was founded by a pair of 24-year-olds who started in business as marine average adjusters and insurance brokers on Wall Street. Because American underwriting firms of that day preferred to deal directly, however, brokerage business was slim.

Evidently, the young partners were exceptional adjusters. (These specialists are called upon to decide how loss is to be shared whenever more than one party is involved in a marine incident, such as when a collision occurs, cargo has to be jettisoned or piracy takes place.)

As the partners' reputation for arranging equitable financial settlements spread, shippers began using them as brokers to negotiate the insurance terms as well.

By the turn of the century, Johnson & Higgins had established branch offices across the country so that its network stretched from the Atlantic to the Pacific. At that time, it also formed an international connection with the leading English firm — Willis Faber & Co., Ltd. (now Willis Faber & Dumas, Ltd.)

After 1900, J&H evolved from a firm primarily engaged in marine matters, to a leadership role in every aspect of corporate risk coverage and employee benefit planning throughout the world.

Today, the global network of Johnson & Higgins consists of 28 offices in major cities in the U.S., seven offices across Canada, 34 J&H offices overseas, and a 71-office worldwide network of exclusive correspondents in principal business and financial centers in 20 countries — a total of 140 offices around the world.

J&H opened its Los Angeles office in the spring of 1923 and, until the end of World War II, its staff numbered between 25 and 30.

The Pacific Financial Building was headquarters. Shortly after the War, the population explosion and industrial

J&H has built a tradition of service from clipper ships to computers.

growth of Los Angeles caused an increase in business which necessitated a series of moves by the company. In 1959, offices were relocated to Wilshire Boulevard and, in 1978, to Century City.

Dickinson C. Ross and E. Eric Johnson are the managing directors of the Los Angeles office which employs almost 400, at 2029 Century Park East. J&H Los Angeles is the largest of four J&H offices in California (San Francisco, San Diego and Orange County are the others) and is the second largest office in the J&H worldwide system.

Today, Johnson & Higgins stands not only as America's oldest broker but also as one of the largest in the world. Significantly enhancing its unique position and capabilities is the fact that J&H is the only privately-owned firm among the major American brokers.

With more experience than anyone else in the field, the company has developed unparalleled resources to identify, analyze and solve the unique problems of each of its clients. It offers the steady hand that helps minimize risks and costs in an uncertain world, with the utmost professionalism in all its dealings.

Specialized departments utilize a team approach and provide more than adequate services for all clients in: Property, Casualty, Employee Benefits, Marine & Aviation, International, Mass Coverages, Commercial Accounts and Special Projects.

Because clients have needs in many separate fields, the firm places the full resources of all its departments at their disposal. A client of the Los Angeles office is a client of all J&H offices. And that can make all the difference when the right answers are needed as quickly as possible.

J&H is proud of its history in the California business community; and of the contributions of its people to the civic, cultural and charitable life of Los Angeles.

From clipper ships to computers, J&H has built a tradition of service to California; a tradition which will become even more glowing as the 21st Century approaches.

Knudsen Corporation

A monument to a man with a vision

Knudsen's Laboratory, founded in 1914, was the forerunner of Knudsen Creamery Co. of California. During the "Roaring Twenties" it boasted its own fleet of "modern" milk trucks.

When that ship pulled into New York harbor on May 31, 1910, and disembarked a 19-year-old emigrant from Denmark by the name of Thorkild Rostgaard Knudsen, little did anyone realize that the first sentence in a long chapter of California's dairy industry story was being written.

This young man, known in later years as "Tom" Knudsen, had a burning desire to rise in the world, coupled with ambition and an acquaintance with hard work. But above all, he was imbued with integrity. He had a vision.

His vision began to materialize in the early summer of 1919 when Knudsen started manufacturing cottage cheese, cream cheese, and buttermilk in Los Angeles, his newly-adopted city. Thus the Knudsen Creamery Co. was begun—with three employees, a secondhand delivery truck, a few hundred dollars in borrowed capital, some used machinery, and Tom Knudsen's personal philosophy of high quality and fair dealings as the guiding policy. Out of his zeal for excellence Knudsen began fashioning superior products; out of his consideration for others, outstanding people began arriving to join the company. And from it all, a slogan evolved: "The Very Best."

Knudsen was less than optimistic about the prospects for his fledgling company's newest product...yogurt. Introduced in late 1919, he was fond of reminding people that most customers for his peculiar and tart item were referred by doctors. "The patient either got well (and stopped eating the product) or died. In either case we lost a customer!" Today, more than 60 years later, yogurt has become a phenomenal industry success story and Knudsen is clearly the market leader in California.

During the first 15 years the company was in business, it dealt exclusively in milk by-products. In 1934 it entered the wholesale milk business. Ice cream production began in 1955. And, by the time the company celebrated its golden anniversary in 1969, 13 Knudsen plants dotted Southern California, from Visalia to San Diego. With the purchase of Borden, Inc.'s California fresh milk division in 1970, Knudsen's operations expanded statewide.

The pioneering spirit that led to the

The main Los Angeles dairy products processing plant along with an expanded truck fleet indicates steady growth in the mid-1940s.

first turning of the key in the lock at 1965 Santee Street marked the whole development of the company.

First, Knudsen patented a special process for making cottage cheese from skim milk. This created a shelf-stable product of consistent high quality, prompting dairy product manufacturers throughout the nation to scramble for the Knudsen license. But the war came in 1917 and Knudsen gave the government the patented process as a contribution to the "Food Will Win The War" campaign. In so doing, Tom, not yet an American citizen, gave away his most important — and lucrative — asset. He relinquished security to help gain freedom and sustain opportunity.

Later, the company was the first to pioneer in the development of "half 'n' half", and originated the name to go with the new product. Knudsen Creamery is also credited with popularizing buttermilk and sour cream in California.

Packaging, too, has played an impor-

tant part in the Knudsen story. Knudsen was among the first to pioneer in the use of paper containers. The company provided technological expertise in the development of homogenizing machines.

Other Knudsen "firsts" of major importance to the industry include the invention of a method of blending fruit into yogurt, patented in 1966, and, 10 years later, introducing Sweet Acidophilus™ milk to the Western United States.

Today, Knudsen is much more than a dairy company. Its diversified nature is evidenced by two wholly-owned subsidiaries: Knudsen Agricultural Management Company, which develops and finances dairy farms and provides management services; and, National Fast Foods, Inc., which operates a chain of deli/convenience grocery stores in the Western states.

Since its inception, the company has genuinely earned a reputation among consumers for "the very best" in quality products and service. This is the hallmark upon which Knudsen Corporation aggressively builds to an even greater future.

Lawry's Foods, Inc.

Products with a "perceivable difference" led to well-seasoned success

When Lawry's The Prime Rib restaurant opened in Beverly Hills, California in 1938, there were three shakers on every table — one salt, one pepper and one "seasoned salt." The seasoned salt, which had been blended to secret perfection by the restaurant's co-owner, Lawrence Frank, disappeared frequently. So Frank and his partner, Walter Van de Kamp, set up a small manufacturing company and offered the seasoned salt for sale to their customers. It was just a little sideline, because everyone knew that the spice business was so small you couldn't make much of a mark in it.

Everyone, that is, except Frank's son, Richard. He became convinced that seasoned salt had excellent marketing possibilities. His cousin, Ralph Frank, shared his enthusiasm and even took small bottles of the seasoning along on his World War II duty. "We figured that if seasoned salt could make Navy food more palatable, just think of what it could do in the average American kitchen," Richard said.

In 1950 Richard became general manager of Lawry's Products, Inc. (now Lawry's Foods, Inc.) and Ralph became national sales manager. They built on the idea of manufacturing and marketing quality products with a "perceivable difference." They would leave the pure spices to other companies, concentrating their efforts on specially formulated seasoning blends and related products.

The concept worked. During the next 30 years annual sales grew from $400,000 to more than $70 million.

But back in 1950 the young entrepreneurs' emphasis was on finding markets. By 1953, they had outgrown a small plant and office in downtown Los Angeles and moved to an expandable site a few miles east, where the Golden State and Pasadena Freeways meet.

At the same time, the company was introducing another innovative product — Lawry's Spaghetti Sauce Mix with Imported Mushrooms. As the first dehydrated sauce mix, it created an entirely new product category in the grocery industry. Brokers and consumers were skeptical at first, but today this early product outsells all competitors. Such foresight and innovation have not been uncommon at Lawry's. In the mid-'60s, the introduction of Lawry's Taco Seasoning Mix anticipated the growing popularity of Mexican foods and led to a line of south-of-the border seasoning products.

Today, Lawry's Seasoned Salt, the 40-year old secret blend of 17 herbs and spices, is the world's largest-selling seasoning blend. The company has capitalized on the idea of blending spices and herbs — there are 85 consumer products now — to enhance the flavor of foods, making it easy for the cook at home to achieve quality results, conveniently and consistently. The company also sells to the institutional market through its Foodservice Division.

Just as Lawry's products fit a special category, so does its corporate headquarters, Lawry's California Center. The complex, grown since 1953 from one acre to 14, combines offices, manufacturing plant, gardens, shops and restaurants. It is designed to recapture the style and spirit of Los Angeles' Mexican heritage.

Lawry's co-workers share this "oasis" — now a major visitor attraction — in industrial Los Angeles with more than 350,000 guests every year. Guided tours are offered at no charge. Luncheon alfresco is served year-round. During California's balmy summer evenings, the gardens are the setting for romantic under-the-stars dining at Steak Fiesta. Two very different retail operations, the Gift & Patio Shop and the Wine & Gourmet Shop, present another facet of California's relaxed and enjoyable lifestyle to visitors.

In the late 1970s Lawry's Foods reached a stage in its development where President Richard Frank felt the need for the resources of a larger company to continue the growth. The merger with Thomas J. Lipton, Inc. in 1979 was long and carefully considered. "Lipton's standards, ethics and business philosophy are so close as to be nearly identical to our own," said Frank. "Both companies were founded on the principle that high quality foods, well presented and advertised, are the keys to success."

The original downtown manufacturing plant (inset). Richard N. Frank, President and CEO of Lawry's Foods, Inc.

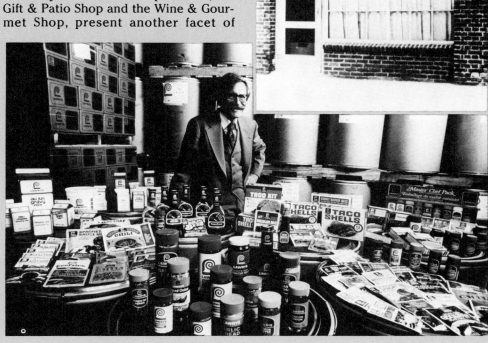

Lear Siegler, Inc.

A company with diversity and momentum

The year was 1954. Dwight D. Eisenhower was president of the United States. Television was the focal point of family life. You could send a letter for three cents, and you could still buy a Nash, Willys, Studebaker, Packard, Hudson or DeSoto.

Rocky Marciano was heavyweight boxing champion. Englishman Roger Bannister broke the four-minute barrier in the mile run. And the New York Giants, led by a new baseball sensation named Willie Mays, won the World Series.

In the small rural community of Centralia, Illinois, 10 investors purchased the Siegler Heater Company — a firm with one plant, one product line and annual sales of $6.5 million. It was the beginning of Lear Siegler, Inc., now headquartered in Santa Monica.

The next 25 years were exciting and eventful. The company established a strong base of operations and diversified wisely. It established strong employee, customer and supplier relationships and developed and refined workable management strategies and techniques. As a result, annual sales grew from $6.5 million to $1.3 billion, and annual earnings increased from $775,000 to $63.3 million. Every year was profitable, and Lear Siegler shareholders received dividends every quarter after the first year of operations.

Internal growth was supplemented by mergers and acquisitions which complemented existing operations or established the company in important new markets.

For example, the merger with Lear, Incorporated in 1962 provided the base for LSI's technological accomplishments in aerospace and electronics. Few corporate mergers have produced such an excellent blend of people, products, capabilities and facilities. Benefits included a strengthened position in government markets and a greatly increased potential for internal growth.

It was at this time that the name of the company was changed from The Siegler Corporation to Lear Siegler, Inc. to capitalize on the outstanding reputation that Lear had attained during 32 years as a designer and developer of aerospace electronics.

The company diversified further in 1966 when it acquired American Metal

Headquarters for Lear Siegler are in Santa Monica. The company was known as The Siegler Corporation from 1954 until 1962, when it merged with Lear Incorporated. The name was changed to Lear Siegler, Inc. at that time.

Products Company. This transaction was particularly significant because it provided entry into two important markets — automotive and furniture. LSI became the nation's largest independent manufacturer of automobile seat assemblies and the second largest supplier of truck axle housings.

In 1968 Lear Siegler entered the machine and cutting tool market by acquiring two outstanding firms in this industry — National Broach & Machine Company of Detroit and National Twist Drill & Tool Company of Rochester, Michigan.

Top management of the company was realigned in 1971 following the death of John G. Brooks, who had been chairman and chief executive officer since the company was founded in 1954. The board of directors elected Robert T. Campion president and chief executive officer, Robert L. Purcell chairman of the board and K. Robert Hahn executive vice president. Purcell had been executive vice president and Campion and Hahn had served as senior vice presidents.

Campion assumed the additional duties of chairman in 1974.

Lear Siegler grew substantially in sales, earnings, personnel, facilities, products and markets served with the addition of Royal Industries, Inc. in 1977. Sales surpassed $1 billion on an annualized basis, and LSI became an important factor in the automotive replacement market. Its participation in the agricultural industry also increased significantly.

Royal had annual sales of $280 million, 15 divisions and 6,500 employees.

The second largest acquisition in company history — only Royal was larger — occurred in January 1980. LSI acquired Rapistan Incorporated, one of the nation's largest manufacturers of conveyor equipment, systems and services. The firm, headquartered in Grand Rapids, Michigan, had annual sales of approximately $140 million.

Lear Siegler has always recognized the contributions of its employees, who have a widely diversified range of professional skills and disciplines. LSI's 25-year success story is due in large part to their loyalty, dedication and productivity. The future is expected to be equally rewarding.

Los Angeles Dodgers

Team's new home began new baseball era

Since their arrival in 1958, leaving Brooklyn behind, the Dodgers have become as much a part of the Los Angeles landscape as palm trees and beaches, Hollywood and its stars and starlets.

After 22 years, Los Angeles and the Dodgers are as inseparable as New York and the Yankees, Green Bay and the Packers, Boston and the Celtics.

This was the vision of Walter O'Malley when he boldly, controversially, uprooted his franchise from Flatbush following the 1957 season.

The city officially welcomed major league baseball on April 18, 1958. Thousands lined Broadway in downtown Los Angeles as the players, manager Walter Alston, and the coaching staff paraded by in convertibles.

A love affair between a city and its baseball team had only just begun.

The following season, the Dodgers made one of the most dramatic comebacks. in baseball history. Never before had a team risen from seventh place to a pennant, but the Dodgers did, winning a two-game National League playoff from Milwaukee. Capping a dream season, they dispatched the Chicago White Sox in six games to win the World Series.

The '59 Dodgers were a blend of great names from the Brooklyn past (Duke Snider, Carl Furillo, Jim Gilliam, Johnny Podres) and budding stars of the future (Don Drysdale, Sandy Koufax, Maury Wills, Ron Fairly). There was a vital trade acquisition, Wally Moon, and a shooting star named Larry Sherry, who was to be the World Series hero, winning two games and saving the other two victories.

It was Walter Alston's second world championship, and there would be two more, in 1963 and 1965, when they conquered New York and Minnesota, respectively.

The '60s ushered in a new era of Dodgers baseball. The names of the past gave way to glittering new stars. Koufax and Drysdale formed a pitching tandem perhaps unmatched in baseball annals. Koufax was to fashion four no-hitters and a perfect game and Drysdale was to set an all-time record of 58-2/3 consecutive scoreless innings. At their best in the big games, they accounted for three of the four wins in the memorable sweep of the Yankees in the '63 Series, Koufax taking

Sandy Koufax

the first and fourth games.

There was much more to the exciting Dodgers of the early '60s than Koufax and Drysdale, however, There was the brilliant base-stealing of Maury Wills, who broke Ty Cobb's record with 104 thefts in 1962. That same year, Tommy Davis won his first of two successive batting crowns with a .346 average, leading the league with 230 hits and 153 runs batted in. Still, the Dodgers finished that season bitterly disappointed, losers in a pennant playoff to the dreaded rivals from the north, the Giants.

The '62 season marked the unveiling of O'Malley's sparkling new Dodger Stadium, which would be the model for future baseball parks. The Dodgers set an all-time attendance record of 2,755,184 in the first season of the first privately-financed ballpark built since Jake Ruppert constructed the original Yankee Stadium in 1923. In 1978 they would become the first team in history to surpass three million at the gate, drawing 3,347,845.

Dodger Stadium

Koufax, Drysdale, Wills, Gilliam, Ron Perranoski, the Davises, Willie and Tommy, Frank Howard...these were some of the stars who made the Dodgers the preeminent team in the National League from 1963-66. Three pennants and two world championships were produced in those four years, with only St. Louis in 1964 getting in the way of total league dominance by these great Dodger teams.

After falling on hard times in the late '60s, following the retirements of Koufax and Drysdale and the trade of Wills to Pittsburgh, a new Dodger era began to take shape.

This one featured the "Babes of Summer," a takeoff on Roger Kahn's "Boys of Summer" bestseller chronicling the lives of the Brooklyn Dodger greats.

They emerged in 1973 — Ron Cey, Steve Garvey, Bill Buckner, Joe Ferguson, Bill Russell, Davey Lopes; and only a great second half surge by Cincinnati prevented the "Babes of Summer" from winning the National League West.

This they accomplished the following season but fell to Oakland, in the midst of a dynasty of its own, in the '74 World Series.

The Dodgers chased the Reds again the following two seasons, finishing second. Alston retired following the '76 campaign, and in their 20th season in Los Angeles the Dodgers welcomed colorful Tommy Lasorda, the former third base coach, as manager.

Behind the pitching of Don Sutton, Tommy John and Burt Hooton, and the hitting of the likes of Garvey, Cey, Reggie

Smith, Lopes, Russell and Dusty Baker, the Dodgers won back-to-back National League pennants in Lasorda's first two seasons at the helm. The script was identical in '77 and '78: Victory in four games over Philadelphia in the League Champ-ionship Series and defeat in six games at the hands of the Yankees in the World Series.

The names change, but the beat goes on. As they bid to regain National League supremacy in 1980, their wounds from a painful (physically and emotionally) 1979 season mended, the Dodgers can be sure of one thing.

Their love affair with the city of Los Angeles has never been on more solid ground.

Occidental Life Insurance Company of California

Pioneering spirit spurred growth of a "star in the west"

By 1906, agricultural Los Angeles was emerging as a hub of business activity. Much of the business, however, was generated by East Coast firms. Of the 35 life insurance companies operating in California, for example, only one was headquartered there.

An imaginative young entrepreneur with a penchant for the name Occidental — Karl K. Kennedy — convinced 14 prominent Los Angeles citizens to finance a local life insurance company. And, on June 30, 1906, the new Occidental Life Insurance Co. began operations in the Grosse Building at Sixth and Spring streets. In those early days, the few company employees had to climb a ladder to their second floor offices with only packing crates for desks!

In the first year, the company sold 130 policies for $602,000 of life insurance; in the following year, health and accident coverage were added.

The early years saw rapid development. From 1908 to 1930, Occidental Life expanded into 16 states and territories, including Alaska and Hawaii, and also into Canada. By 1925, the company had achieved "medium size" with $100 million of insurance in force.

1930 was an especially significant year. Transamerica Corporation, created by Bank of America founder A. P. Giannini to hold and control the stock of the bank and other properties he assembled, purchased 100 percent ownership of Occidental Life. (Transamerica divested itself of Bank of America stock in 1952.)

Despite the Depression, the 1930s were years of growth for Occidental Life. The company entered the group insurance field, expanded into 13 more states and

Occidental Life Insurance Company's first headquarters was the Grosse Building.

The old Chamber of Commerce building became Occidental's home office in 1947 and remained so until the early '60s. Located on 12th and Broadway, the building was constructed in 1923. The photo was taken about 1948.

the Philippines, and became the first West Coast insurance company to use radio advertising from coast to coast.

In these years the company pioneered the development of term insurance, created to cover terminating needs, such as mortgage protection, income during the growing family years and education funds. The widespread acceptance of Occidental's innovative term concepts was to set a dynamic pattern of growth for the future.

After World War II, Occidental purchased the Los Angeles Chamber of Commerce building at 12th and Broadway and spent the next decade expanding nationally.

In 1956, the company ended its first half century 12th in size among the 1,100 North American life insurance companies. To celebrate its 50th year, Occidental Life entered the 1956 Pasadena Tournament of Roses Parade and won Grand Prize. The event was the start of a tradition which, for 25 years, has featured a previous year's Rose Queen on an Occidental float.

The 1960s were years of unparalleled development for the company. In 1961, plans were announced for construction of Occidental Center, the present home office. The company rounded out the decade by expanding into Puerto Rico, the Netherlands, England, Australia and Newfoundland.

With the guidance of Earl Clark, presi-dent and chief executive officer during this era, Occidental Life jumped from $13.6 billion of life insurance in force in 1963 to $30.9 billion of life insurance in force one decade later.

As the 1970s opened, so did the newest addition to Occidental Center — the 10-story Broadway unit built on the site of the old 12th and Broadway structure.

On the home front, the company created *comprehensive medical rehabilitation,* a program to assist the catastrophically injured who are covered under its group plan — one of the few major health carriers to offer this service.

Since the company's growth in the pension field mushroomed, Occidental Life moved this business to Transamerica Life Insurance and Annuity Co. in 1977, establishing one of the first all-pension companies.

Today, Occidental Life is a major employer in Los Angeles with more than 3,000 employees working in Occidental Center.

Under the direction of Meno T. Lake, president and chief executive officer, Occidental Life is now the ninth largest insurance company in North America in terms of its more than $60 billion of insurance in force.

The Olga Company

Garter belt and $10 investment became $43 million enterprise

The year was 1941. Newlyweds Olga and Jan Erteszek had just arrived in Los Angeles from war-torn Poland and, to make ends meet, Olga turned her hand to fashion design. Riding the old trolley, she had been dismayed at women stepping up into the car exposing unsightly stocking tops rolled over heavy elastic bands. So she created a pretty lacy garter belt and took it to the buyer at Bullock's Wilshire. An investment of $10 produced two dozen garments to fill the first order and The Olga Company was born...another testimony to America, the land of opportunity.

While Olga developed innovative design concepts for the intimate apparel industry, Jan Erteszek concentrated on innovations in the quality of corporate life.

Guided by the principle that those who produce results should also participate in them, in 1954 the company pioneered an intensive Employee Profit Sharing Plan for which all are eligible. In 1973, an additional Employee Stock Bonus Plan was initiated through which each can become a shareholder.

Additionally, participation through creativity is encouraged at every level of activity. Through the instrument of creative meetings, employees in all areas contribute. The result is not only improved performance but a more meaningful working environment as well.

Steadily, conservatively, the company expanded through controlled diversification into all segments of intimate ap-

"Behind every OLGA there really is an Olga" — Olga Erteszek, co-founder and vice president — Design.

parel — girdles, bras, lingerie, at-home wear — and, from a modest beginning, grew into a $43 million-plus international corporation.

The company was owned by the Erteszeks until 1967 when it went public. In 1978, a minority interest was purchased by Wacoal Corporation, a multi-national intimate apparel company based in Japan.

Olga's successful growth has been attributed to unique designs and a trend-setting style of corporate life.

A spirit of "corporate family" has prevailed since the company's first Christ-

Olga's stretch-top gown collection introduced a contemporary new fashion freedom for sleeping and lounging in the 1980s.

mas get-together when the "entire" staff of seven dined at the Erteszeks' home. This tradition never lapsed and is now held in a grand ballroom. At the 1979 event, when "associates" were invited to say "season's greetings" in their native tongues, there were 27 nationalities represented.

Olga "associates" have strived to contribute to the various communities in which they live and work. One of the most popular projects is the annual Christmas Doll Program: on their own time, with supplies provided by the company, employees design and sew original doll outfits. Each year, hundreds of the elaborately costumed dolls are donated to local children's hospitals.

Jan Erteszek serves on the boards of various institutions including Ticor, The

Los Angeles Area and California State Chambers of Commerce, California State University and Colleges Foundation, Whittier College, Hollywood Presbyterian Medical Center, Merchants and Manufacturers Association.

Olga Erteszek is the only member of the intimate apparel industry appointed to the prestigious Council of Fashion Designers of America created by President Johnson. She is also on the Los Angeles Area Council of The Boy Scouts of America and the board of directors of Muses, an auxiliary to the Los Angeles Museum of Science and Industry.

As of 1979, The Olga Company employed 1700 "associates" and conducted its manufacturing operations in 13 facilities located in Southern California and Mexicali, Mexico. It is the fourth

largest private employer in Van Nuys and ranks 13th among manufacturers in Ventura County. More than 2000 department and specialty stores throughout the world are served by the company.

Net sales in 1979 were the highest in Olga history. Jan Erteszek is chairman of the board and president — chief executive officer. Olga Erteszek — Design — is one of nine vice presidents. A distinguished board of directors includes high-ranking officers from the fields of finance, education and industry.

Recognizing that modern business is not only a way to make a living but a way of life, The Olga Company aspires to provide for all of its "associates" not only economic rewards but a sense of meaning that adds to the total adventure of life.

Pacific Mutual Life Insurance Company

The company and Los Angeles: an enduring partnership

Just as the pueblo structures of Los Angeles are synonymous with early history of the city, the Pacific Mutual Building on West Sixth Street parallels the phenomenal growth of the City of the Angels. History of the building and the company equates with the mobius development of Los Angeles. Today Pacific Mutual is one of the largest financial institutions based in the West.

There have been numerous architectural and design changes of the PM Building, but the abiding principle of the company itself — concern for its policyowners — has remained unchanged.

Pacific Mutual started in Sacramento. Initial subscribers included Leland Stanford, Mark Hopkins, and Charles Crocker. From the beginning, management resourcefulness, and choosing the right person for leadership at the right time, became Pacific Mutual's hallmarks. Dr. George A. Moore, president from 1880 to 1905, early exemplified the combination of circumstance and citizen that would help Pacific Mutual prosper.

Moore moved the company to San Francisco in 1881, where proof of PM''s strength was evident with the completion of a new seven-story edifice. In the 1906 earthquake, the walls did not tumble, but subsequent fire and dynamite ravaged the interior.

Incredibly, Pacific Mutual had recently

merged with Conservative Life in Los Angeles. Meeting on the rubble of the earthquake aftermath, the directors ordered the company's move to Los Angeles.

George I. Cochran steered Pacific Mutual from 1906 to 1935. In 1908, the first PM Building — a six-story structure — was completed. Growth under Cochran's leadership necessitated enlargement in 1918, and in 1920, construction of the pre-

A 1920 rendering of the original Pacific Mutual building, prepared by the architect to show Pacific Mutual exactly how the new building would appear. The rendering, stored away and almost forgotten for over fifty years, was re-discovered during renovation in 1973.

sent and additional 12-story structure was completed.

The country as a whole was booming, and PM was fortuitously located in a land that would rapidly become famous throughout the world. The celluloid exports of 1920s Hollywood were bringing thousands of people to Southern California's golden promise.

Then came the Depression. President Cochran had instituted a "Non-Cancellable Disability Income Policy" in 1918. When the Depression hit full force, many "Non-Can" policyowners started a trickle of claims that soon became a floodtide. Though a modernization of the six-story building was completed in 1936, a "modernization" that basically encased the old building in cement, the company could not cover up its Non-Can woes.

Rising to meet the challenge was Asa V. Call, who guided the company through a reorganization blueprint initiated by California Insurance Commissioner, Samuel L. Carpenter. In 1936, a national actuarial expert testified that the company would not be able to restore all Non-Can payments before 1973. The expert was wrong. With the leadership of Call, and the continued population growth in the West, Pacific Mutual achieved full restoration by 1957. The accomplishment had taken 21 years and $31 million, but the abiding company

Asa V. Call was Pacific Mutual's chief executive for seventeen years, 1942-1959, and a director from 1932-1978.

principle of concern for the policyowners had been upheld.

After World War II, T. S. Burnett anticipated the development of suburban shopping centers and guided PM into a post-war investment program in their construction and ownership. In 1959, Burnett oversaw the mutualization of PM. In its August 8, 1959 issue, *Business Week* proclaimed the recovery at Pacific Mutual "the end of a reorganization saga

that may well become a classic in American business."

In 1948, Pacific Mutual energetically moved into the group insurance and pensions market, in which it is today a nationwide leader.

The company itself knew a good product, becoming the first private enterprise west of the Mississippi to install and utilize a UNIVAC I computer.

Growth was so strong that PM even outgrew the many-times renovated building at Sixth and Olive, and moved its home office to Newport Beach. However, Pacific Mutual by no means pulled up its Los Angeles stakes.

After still another redesign in 1973, tenant occupancy reached 100 percent, testifying to the utility of the renovations with the maintenance of the charm of PM's link to Los Angeles history.

Pacific Mutual in Los Angeles is the story of a building, one that has housed not only management people, but the financial well-being of hundreds of thousands of Americans. The attractive qualities of Los Angeles, and Pacific Mutual's concerns for its policyowners — both long established — endure in partnership into Los Angeles' third century.

Paramount Pictures Corporation

Its first feature length film produced in a rented barn

The Paramount studio, as we know it today, is the legacy of film pioneers Adolph Zukor, Jesse Lasky, Cecil B. DeMille and Samuel Goldwyn, and traces its origin to 1912.

Adolph Zukor, a Hungarian immigrant who managed a successful fur business in Chicago, came to New York in 1903 to investigate his investment in a penny arcade. Enthusiastic over the future of "flickers," Zukor abandoned his fur trade and concentrated on movie exhibition. Convinced that the movie audience was hungry for better entertainment, he joined forces with theatrical producer Daniel Frohman and presented a film version of Sarah Bernhardt's QUEEN ELIZABETH as a Broadway attraction on July 12, 1912. The showmen, incorporated as Famous Players in Famous Plays, contracted stage stars to interpret their famous roles before the camera — James K. Hackett with THE PRISONER OF ZENDA, James (father of Eugene) O'Neill

The Bronson Street entrance to the Paramount Studio, Hollywood's most enduring landmark through whose portals have walked the legendary figures of the film industry.

as THE COUNT OF MONTE CRISTO, Minnie Maddern Fiske in TESS OF THE D'URBERVILLES, and Mary Pickford in A GOOD LITTLE DEVIL (Zukor created the first movie star with Pickford in 1913).

Jesse Lasky, an ex-vaudevillian who had lost a bundle in a restaurant/theater venture, was encouraged by his brother-in-law Sam Goldfish to make a film of THE SQUAW MAN, a hit play with Dustin Farnum, and shoot it in an authentic western locale with director Oscar Apfel and actor/playwright Cecil B. DeMille. With capital of $20,000, the Jesse Lasky Feature Play Company, DeMille, Farnum, and Apfel journeyed to Arizona, but found the terrain forbidding and re-boarded the train to the last stop — Hollywood. DeMille rented an abandoned barn on the corner of Selma and Vine Streets for $25 a month, and happily cabled Goldfish who replied, "Fine, but don't make any long term commitments." Production began Christmas week in 1913 on what became the first feature length Hollywood film, and its success led to continued productions based on established literary and theatrical properties, complementing the quality of Zukor's eastern productions.

Both Zukor and Lasky were distributing their films through a production company named Paramount. The name was taken from an apartment complex, and the emblem of a mountain haloed by stars was a doodle scribbled during a business conference by Paramount head William Hodkinson. In 1916, Zukor and Lasky merged as Famous Players-Lasky, and by the following year they had purchased control of their distributor — which included films from Morosco, Pallas, Bosworth, Realart, Cosmopolitan, and Artcraft. These companies employed such names as William S. Hart, Marion

Davies, D. W. Griffith, the Gish Sisters, and Douglas Fairbanks — the romance of Pickford and Fairbanks began in the shade of the Vine Street barn. Sam Goldfish severed connections with Zukor/Lasky, changed his name to Goldwyn and entered independent production.

In 1919, Paramount expanded production by building an east coast studio in Astoria to accommodate the shooting of motion pictures with a New York locale

The first Hollywood studio — formerly a barn at Selma and Vine Streets — which housed the Jesse Lasky Feature Play Company where Cecil B. DeMille assisted director Oscar Apfel in the shooting of THE SQUAW MAN. The barn was transported to the Paramount lot thirteen years later in 1926 and was awarded landmark status in 1956.

as well as easing the pressures of west coast activity. Superstar Gloria Swanson loved the excitement of Manhattan and shot most of her films there, as did Rudolph Valentino, Ed Wynn, W. C. Fields, and D. W. Griffith in the '20s. When sound arrived and the movies found a voice, many Broadway stars made their film debuts in the Long Island City structure — Jeanne Eagels, the Marx Brothers, Walter Huston, Gertrude Lawrence, Claudette Colbert, Ethel Merman, and Ginger Rogers. The depression years curtailed east coast production and the studio closed in the late '30s.

By 1926, Zukor and Lasky had purchased as much land (nine acres) surrounding the barn as possible and still were curtailed by lack of space. They acquired the United Studio between Melrose and Bronson on Marathon Street encompassing 26 acres and physically transferred all buildings and shooting stages to accommodate their 70 contract players, 20 directors and hundreds of technicians. As part of the improvement construction, the Bronson gate was erected. The gate is possibly Hollywood's most identifiable landmark and through its portals have passed the movie capital's aristrocracy — Marlene Dietrich, Mae West, Bing Crosby, Clark Gable, Bob Hope, Dorothy Lamour, Gary Cooper, Alan Ladd, John Ford, George Stevens, Barbara Stanwyck, Carole Lombard, Jack Benny, Ernst Lubitsch, Gloria Swanson, Billy Wilder — the list is endless.

The pioneers are gone, but the barn was moved to the Paramount lot and awarded landmark status in 1956, 43 years after production began on THE SQUAW MAN. In October 1979, the barn was transported to 1737 North Vine Street where it will be the focal point of a Hollywood Museum.

Peat, Marwick, Mitchell & Co.

"Serving Los Angeles' audit, tax and consulting needs since 1920"

Peat, Marwick, Mitchell & Co. (the "Co." stands for copartnership, not company) traces its history to the early days of the accounting profession in both the United Kingdom and the United States. Two Scotsmen, James Marwick and Simpson Robert Mitchell, formed a partnership in New York City in 1897.

Marwick and Mitchell established offices in Europe prior to World War I, the first American public accounting firm to do so. While overseas, Marwick met Sir William Peat, senior partner of W. B. Peat & Co., a distinguished British firm. After the war, the U.S. and British firms merged, producing the present firm.

As the demand for accounting services spread across the U.S.A. and Canada, the firm rapidly multiplied its number of offices. When PMM&Co. opened its Los Angeles office in 1920, the firm had 16 offices in the U.S. and 11 abroad. Today, there are 100 offices in the U.S. and almost 300 worldwide — providing audit, tax and consulting services to more than 50,000 clients in 80 countries. These clients range in size from Fortune 500 corporations to local owner-operated companies.

In addition to serving the Los Angeles business community, the office also functions as regional headquarters for the firm's western region. Larry D. Horner, vice chairman and regional partner, heads this 14-office region.

In the '50s, PMM&Co.'s Los Angeles practice had six partners and employed approximately 80 people; today, there is a staff of well over 650, with some 60 partners.

During this 30-year growth period, the Los Angeles office had six managing partners: Vernon Burgett, James W. Leisner, Walter S. Sutton (all retired), the late Seymour M. Bohrer, followed by Horner in 1977. William D. Schulte became managing partner of the office in 1980.

In 1971, the Los Angeles office moved into the ARCO Towers, occupying four floors. Former locations were all on South Spring Street. The Century City and Orange County offices opened in the '60s.

From its earliest days, PMM&Co. has had a diversified client base that closely paralleled the Los Angeles business environment. Archives show audits of Mary Pickford Productions, and today, 20th Century-Fox is one of many clients from the area's famed entertainment industry. Longtime Los Angeles clients include Western Air Lines, Inc., since 1927; Continental Airlines, since 1940; City Investing Company in 1904 and served by Los Angeles since 1970; and Western Gear, a major manufacturer, since 1953.

Savings and loan associations played a vital role in California's phenomenal construction record, and they also added to PMM&Co.'s growth in Los Angeles; Home Savings and Loan Association, California Federal Savings and Loan, and Glendale Federal Savings and Loan are among these clients.

The twenty-seven year span of PMM's Los Angeles managing partnership is documented at the 1974 alumni reunion. From left, Vernon Burgett, MP from '50 to '59 retirement; the late Seymour M. Bohrer, MP from '74 to '77; James W. Leisner, from '59 to '72; and Walter S. Sutton, who served as MP from '72 through June '74.

The view from the managing partners' office includes the familiar Los Angeles City Hall tower. William D. Schulte, managing partner, on the right, is pictured with Larry D. Horner, vice-chairman — regional partner for PMM's Western Region.

In the late '60s, when California banks began having audits by public accountants, Security Pacific, Union Bank and Wells Fargo became clients. Today, PMM&Co. continues to serve a large number of banking clients — from the large multinationals to smaller banks and foreign banking agencies.

Foreign investment in the U.S. was a phenomenon of the '70s and continues in the '80s. PMM&Co's Los Angeles office helps foreign-based clients, many from the Pacific Basin, establish and conduct business in the U.S. with the same attention given American clients when they expand abroad; international tax plays a major part in these services. Multilingual accountants and partners are involved in the Japanese and Korean segment of this practice.

Through the years, PMM&Co. has offered the Los Angeles business community a wide range of skills. In addition to providing audit and tax services, the office has highly qualified professionals who provide diversified services such as: planning and financially related consulting, EDP and systems, industrial engineering, employee benefits, and executive compensation and search.

PMM&Co. looks forward to the expansion and growth of Los Angeles and is dedicated to participating in that growth by providing the skills of its professional accountants, tax advisors and business consultants in the challenging years ahead. The firm has been an active participant in civic, professional, educational and charitable activities and is committed to continuing its tradition of community involvement.

SAFECO Title Insurance Company

From cows to computers, innovation marked underwriter's history

In 1908 in Riverside, 50 miles east of downtown Los Angeles, a land abstract company was founded with less than $1,500 capital. The little maverick firm soon became a leader in its market — setting a pattern of growth which would become characteristic of its successor, SAFECO Title Insurance Company.

When Union Title and Abstract Com-

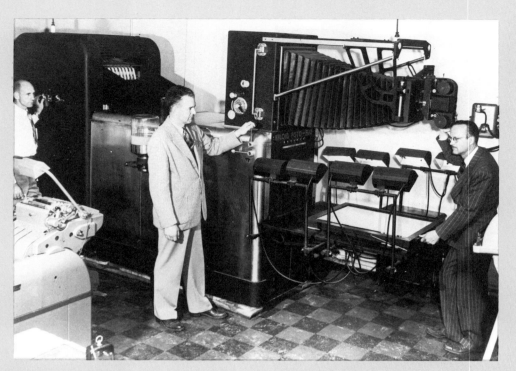

pany began in Riverside, the towns surrounding Los Angeles depended largely on unguaranteed certificates of title as evidence of land rights. Union's business from these certificates grew rapidly under its first manager, Glenn A. Schaefer.

California's booming real estate market soon brought a new challenge to Union: investors demanded greater protection than the new company's certificates provided. The business of insuring land ownership rights was concentrated in Los Angeles and San Francisco. Schaefer saw a need for expanded use of this financial protection in California's rural areas. He organized the Title Insurance Company of Riverside to accomplish this goal.

William S. Porter, president of Santa Barbara Abstract and Guaranty Company, was enthused by the new venture and, in 1921, consolidated his firm with the Riverside company. In 1922 the name was changed to Security Title Insurance and Guarantee Company and an aggressive acquisition program began.

Headquarters were moved to the San Joaquin Valley with the purchase of the Fresno Abstract Company in 1922. By 1925, when Schaefer was elected president, Security Title operated in 13 counties and had brought widespread use of title insurance to California's heartland. It had also established one of the first in-plant printing operations in Southern California.

Security's image as "the cow county title company" began to fade with its 1925 decision to start writing title insurance in Los Angeles. Headquarters were

Foto-Flo camera/printer was the most efficient microfilm system of its day. SAFECO and the Haloid Company built this Santa Ana installation in 1948.

The Security Title Building at Sixth and Grand was completed in 1927. It remained the company's headquarters until a move to the Wilshire district in the mid-1950s.

moved to the city the following year, and construction began on a height-limit Security Title building.

In 1928 the chain entered Orange County by purchasing a substantial interest in Reliance Title Company. The Santa Ana firm had been established in

1924 with the objective of dramatically cutting title search time in the county through improved methods. It continued this fresh approach to the business by introducing microfilm in the late 1930s.

The Depression forced Security to abandon its Los Angeles County title records plant, built at a cost of $1.5 million. Strength in the surrounding counties nevertheless helped the company to survive those difficult years in good health and the real estate boom which followed World War II brought better times. By 1948, Porter (who had succeeded Schaefer as president) could report that the insurer ranked fourth nationally in both assets and gross revenues.

Acquisitions continued under Porter's successor, William Breliant. It was a bare-knuckles period which included dramatic take-over bids and a brief rate war. By 1959, eleven more firms had been merged into the Security Title system, including Reliance Title and a Los Angeles underwriter, Land Title Insurance Company.

Land Title was the crowning achievement of Security's acquisitions under Breliant. Its plant of Los Angeles County land records more than adequately replaced the Security plant abandoned during the Depression. Begun in 1947, these records employed the most advanced method of that day — IBM punch cards.

SAFECO Corporation, then known as General America, acquired the Security Title organization in 1964. This Seattle insurance family also had a forty-year history of independence, innovation and emphasis on efficient work methods. SAFECO was a pioneer in computer applications, and the machine-readable Los Angeles land records immediately suggested automation. By 1967 Security Title had developed the nation's first online computer title plant.

Headquarters were moved to a one-block SAFECO complex in the San Fernando Valley in 1970. The new quarters were impressive, but it was clear that size and stature alone would no longer assure growth. The rapidly expanding market began to favor truly national title service organizations.

An expansion program was launched in 1973, and the name SAFECO Title Insurance Company was adopted. Within five years SAFECO Title had achieved the objective of a national system of offices and agents. The speed, convenience and protection which SAFECO brought to Los Angeles land transfers had become available to real estate markets from coast to coast.

The Salvation Army

Fighting the good fight in Los Angeles for nearly a century

The Salvation Army was founded in London, England in 1865 by William Booth. A Methodist minister, Booth saw the need to fight a holy war against the sin and degradation, prostitution, drug usage and white slavery running rampant in the streets of London.

The early days in England brought suffering, abuse and the threat of death to the dedicated members of The Salvation Army. But, in spite of these initial difficulties, the work of The Army flourished. Booth, recognizing the misery of poverty in his day, initiated The Salvation Army's social service departments based on his philosophy of "soup, soap and salvation." His soldiers fed and clothed the poor, then brought them Christian guidance and instruction, helping the converts to find a new mode of existence and a brighter life because of Booth's care and concern for their souls.

In 1880, George Scott Railton, a follower of William Booth, brought seven "Hallelujah Lassies" from England to New York City officially to begin the work of The Army in America. Seven years later, on May 8, 1887, The Salvation Army was established in Los Angeles with a tent meeting held on a vacant lot at the corner of Temple Street and Broadway.

The Salvation Army's work expanded in Los Angeles with the opening of Corps (churches) and facilities for social welfare services. During World War I, The Army offered rest and recreation services to the military overseas. Front Line canteens were opened and staffed by officers and volunteers, and the "Doughnut Girl" became the nationally familiar symbol of the organization's war effort.

The Salvation Army mobilized its personnel and resources once again to meet another national crisis during the Great Depression of the '30s. Emergency food stations and shelters were set up to help the hundreds of thousands affected by the disastrous economic situation.

In World War II, at the initiation of The Salvation Army, six other organizations joined to establish the U.S.O., providing needed services to American men and women in the armed forces at home and abroad.

Today in Los Angeles The Salvation Army continues to offer a wide range of services to people in need. In the inner

A Salvation Army band marches through downtown Los Angeles in front of the "Pico House" preparing to conduct an open air meeting, circa 1897.

Salvation Army's second Corps building in Los Angeles offered Christian meetings every night and lodging and work for men around the turn of the century.

A plaque on the corner of Temple Street and Broadway marks the spot of the first Salvation Army meeting in Los Angeles.

city a year 'round child care program is operated. Located near the downtown business district, the Evangeline Residence offers a safe and comfortable environment for single working women and students away from home. In addition, The Salvation Army offers housing and meals to local senior citizens.

The desperate needs of men and women with drug or alcohol related problems are met by the organization's Adult Rehabilitation Center program which provides them with a place to live, food, work and a cash allowance — the opportunity to make a new start. The Army operates a full alcoholic recovery program in the "skid row" section of Los Angeles in addition to these rehabilitation centers.

Assistance offered to needy families and individuals by The Salvation Army's Family Service Bureau takes the form of counseling, limited short-term financial aid, food, clothing and household goods. Similar assistance is available to families of prison inmates and the Army's Correctional Services Program follows through in dealing with the offender and his family during and after incarceration.

Booth Memorial Center is a 24-hour residential home for unwed mothers providing its residents with a full complement of services geared to their particular needs including medical care, counseling and schooling.

In addition to a recreational center for inner-city youth, The Salvation Army provides the opportunity for thousands of southern Californians, young and old, to enjoy an outdoor experience at two camps operated in the Malibu mountains.

The Service Extension program provides the scope for a variety of volunteer services and is the vehicle for supplying social and welfare services to communities where there is no Salvation Army center. Mobile canteens, often operated by volunteers, are ready to respond swiftly to calls from police, fire departments, civil defense agencies and other organizations in times of emergency and disaster.

The Corps Community Centers are the heart of The Salvation Army. These centers serve the spiritual, social and recreational needs of the whole neighborhood with their programs for pre-school children, singles, family groups and senior citizens.

The Salvation Army has been fighting the good fight in Los Angeles since 1887 and continues to do so today with the same dedication as its founder.

Security Pacific National Bank

Historic growth results in statewide banking services for Californians

The history and growth of Security Pacific National Bank is linked inseparably with the progress of southern California from the late rancho period of 1870s — a time when population was sparse and settlements were few and removed from each other. Connecting routes were wagon tracks on the landscape.

Many offices of the bank had their beginning as independent banks in communities founded during the migrations of people to the West in the mid- and late 1800s. Today's Security Pacific Corporation and its subsidiary bank, with more than 1,180 combined offices throughout the world, is the result of mergers and consolidation by many of these early day banks and the opening of new offices. Its historical roots go back to April 10, 1871, when The Farmers and Merchants Bank in Los Angeles (pop. 5,700) opened for business as the first incorporated bank in the city.

Shortly after, in 1889, another important ingredient in Security Pacific's history was born — Security Trust & Savings Bank, a name closely associated with the career of Joseph F. Sartori, founder of Security Pacific National Bank, which evolved into today's SPNB.

Several important mergers were finalized in the 1920s and many new banking offices opened for business. On March 30, 1929, the Los Angeles-First National Trust and Savings Bank (dating back to 1875) and Security Trust & Savings Bank consolidated to form Security-First National Bank of Los Angeles, with Sartori as chief executive officer.

The bank favorably weathered the

Farmers & Merchants banking office, oldest branch in the Security Pacific Bank, when it opened its fourth location in 1905 at Main and 4th Street in Los Angeles. Founded in 1871 as first incorporated bank in Los Angeles, Farmers and Merchants Bank merged with Security Bank in 1956.

storms of depression and World War II, and experienced economic recovery nurtured by the postwar period of internal and international expansion.

In 1956 The Farmers and Merchants Bank merged into the Security system, becoming the oldest predecessor bank. In 1957, Citizens National Trust and Savings Bank of Riverside and Security Trust and Savings of San Diego added Riverside, San Bernardino and San Diego counties to the bank's service area.

The Security system continued to widen its service network in ensuing years through mergers with other banking institutions — a group of San Joaquin Valley banks in 1959, Pacific National Bank of San Francisco (1968), Bank of Sacramento and Mother Lode Bank in historic "Gold Rush" country (1970), Humboldt National Bank (1978) and Inyo-Monro Bank on the eastern slopes of the Sierra Nevada mountains (1979).

From 1956 to 1979 Security Pacific Bank's locations increased from 146 to

In Weil Building on Main Street in Los Angeles, Security Trust and Savings Bank opened its first banking office in 1889, giving Security name to the Security Pacific Bank and Corporation.

575 community banking offices in California and to 37 foreign offices. In addition, there are 524 domestic and 44 foreign offices of subsidiaries related to its banking. Total assets grew from $2.1 billion in 1956 to $25 billion at the end of 1979 and its staff from 5,300 to nearly 25,000. Today Security Pacific Bank is one of the 10 largest banks in the country and is the second largest bank in California.

From 1968 to 1978, under the leadership of Frederick G. Larkin Jr., Security Pacific Bank extended its international banking capability. At first it helped establish Western American Bank (Europe) Ltd., a London-based merchant bank. Then, in 1969, it opened its first overseas representative office in Tokyo and now has offices in all major financial capitals of the world.

In 1972 Security Pacific Bank became a subsidiary of the newly formed one-bank holding company, Security Pacific Corporation. While the bank remains by far the largest subsidiary, Security Pacific Corporation now operates subsidiaries which engage in leasing, mortgage banking, investment management, venture capital and financial services — in many states and some foreign countries.

Security Pacific Corporation and the bank are managed by a team of executives under the leadership of the president of the bank and of the corporation, Chief Executive Officer Richard J. Flamson III. World headquarters of the organization are located on historic Bunker Hill in downtown Los Angeles, in 55-story Security Pacific Plaza.

The growth of SPB parallels the development of California. New vistas on the horizon promise a continuation of Security Pacific's achievements and contributions to the communities it serves.

See's Candy Shops, Inc.

Quality and grandmotherly image helped to build successful enterprise

While Los Angeles commemorates the bicentennial of a city still in the on-going process of being born, See's Candy also observes an anniversary — its 60th anniversary of the opening of its first shop in Los Angeles, on Western Avenue.

In 1971, on See's 50th, the trade publication *Candy Industry* wrote:

"The image of See's is compounded of fact and folklore, a conglomerate of family heritage and corporate entity, of large modern candy making facilities and quaint retail stores, along with persistent evidence of expansion in an era when other industry voices are saying that the retail store as we have known it is dead."

Mary See is part of the fact as well as the folklore. She was already 71 years of age in 1921 when her son Charles A. See founded the company in her image. It was an era for such grandmotherly images in the candy industry; Charles See created one so thoroughly that he himself is often not remembered as the founder. Yet Mary See was a very real person, proud of the company, and articulate about her role in an interview shortly before she died, at age 85.

The See family had emigrated from Canada to Los Angeles in 1919. Charles A. See had been a pharmacist in a small Ontario mining town; after a fire destroyed his two drugstores, he started over in Canada as a chocolate salesman.

During the rationing years of World War II, Charles See would not use substitute ingredients and so could sometimes keep his shops open only a few hours a week.

217

This is the way See's candy was delivered in the late 1920s.

When he died in 1949 at age 67 in his Beverly Hills home, the Los Angeles *Times* described him as "a man who had built a three-man candy company into a chain of 78 establishments employing more than 2,000." The article added — "His only employees in his first store besides himself were a candymaker and a salesman."

His small enterprise was — like other candy companies started in the U.S. at that time — inspired by the Laura Secord candy company in Canada.

During the Depression of the early 1930s, Charles See cut his price from 80 cents to 50 cents a pound and told his landlords — Lower rent is better than no rent; reduce the rent to See's and we'll survive together. Hugh Fry, who then started with See's delivering candy around Los Angeles by motorcycle, was general manager when he retired more than 40 years later.

Charles See was tenaciously devoted to quality. His suppliers added a new phrase to their sales jargon. They sold "top quality," and then above that, "See's quality." Small suppliers who learned this lesson well became millionaires.

During the rationing of World War II, Charles See often opened his stores only a few hours a week, rather than use substitute ingredients. Those long lines waiting for a See's shop to open helped create the See's image.

After Charles See's death, his son Laurance made the decision that tied See's to California's shopping center growth: Wherever possible, future See's shops would be in major shopping centers. After Laurance See's death in 1969, Charles B. "Harry" See gave the company the forward momentum lost during his brother's illness. He also named Charles N. Huggins, who had come to top management under Edward G. Peck in the South San Francisco-based division of the company, as next president of See's. A short time later, Harry See negotiated the sale of the family company to Blue Chip Stamps.

Under Charles Huggins, See's since 1972 has enjoyed its greatest period of growth and development of inner-company communications, combining tradition and the skills of the individual candymaker with all the quality controls, technological advances, management techniques and human and product resources available to a company like See's.

See's candies are made today in its kitchens on La Cienega Boulevard in Los Angeles and El Camino Real in South San Francisco. They are sold by the company's own employees through some 190 See's Candy Shops from the Mississippi River to Hawaii, and around the world through See's rapidly expanding Quantity Order Division, for company gift giving, employee group purchasing and fund raising by non-profit organizations.

Smith International, Inc.

Progress and success were never a coincidence

H. C. Smith began serving southern California drillers by sharpening fish tail bits in his Whittier blacksmith shop in the early 1900s. With his knowledge of metals, he used his equipment to modify and improve oil tools and eventually to design and construct new tools.

To keep pace with the rapidly changing needs of the growing petroleum industry of the 1920s, Smith bought a secondhand engine lathe, opened the H. C. Smith Manufacturing Company, and installed the first welding outfit in the Whittier area. Aware of his inventiveness and use of modern technology, drillers in the area began relying on him to provide bits and other tools for their rigs. The company prospered during the 1920s, but in 1929, just before the stock market crash, Smith decided to retire. The growing company was sold to Globe Oil Tools.

Smith ended his self-imposed retirement after seven years. The oil industry had been in a recession due to the De-pression, the price of oil had dropped to ten cents a barrel and, as a result, many oil tool manufacturers were going into receivership. Smith, however, knew the industry, had a thorough knowledge of oil tools and felt he could operate profitably. In May 1936, he acquired Allen Brothers Oil Tools in Compton, California, hired fifteen employees and by 1937 was once again open for business.

The new firm was called the H. C. Smith Oil Tool Company. It designed and de-

Smith International's world headquarters, Newport Beach, California.

veloped new equipment and added new products to the Smith line, prospering under Smith's leadership. In the early 1940s, however, the firm phased out its production of oil tools for a time and began working seven days a week to produce supplies to help America mobilize for war.

The company advanced rapidly during the postwar period. Smith hired additional engineers, invested in new and modern equipment and purchased land adjacent to the Compton plant for expansion purposes. The company branched out in other ways and before the 1940s were over, sales offices were opened throughout California and in the mid-continent fields.

The 1950s brought many advancements, one of which was the building of the forge shop. Smith began designing and manufacturing three-cone rock bits for the petroleum market and also produced bits for use in the mining industry. As the decade came to a close, the company had sales locations throughout the United States and in South America, Mexico and Canada, as well.

The year 1959 was a turning point for the firm. The company's continuing policy of expansion coupled with a desire to diversify were factors in its decision to make Smith a public corporation that year. The corporation was called Smith Industries International, Inc. (later changed to Smith International, Inc. in

1969) and the name of the H. C. Smith Oil Tool Company was changed to Smith Tool Company (and later to Smith Tool). The corporation began a program of internal expansion and selective external diversification.

Smith International's petroleum drill bits were originally the backbone of the business. The strength of this product group continues to be important to the success of the company's plans for the future. In the late 1960s two key acquisitions were made — Drilco and Servco. These three core businesses, all related to drilling activity, provided the basis for internally generated growth in the decade of the '70s. The Dyna-Drill downhole mud motor, Smith-Gruner mining and industrial drill bit product lines, and most recently, the Tungsten Carbide Manufacturing operation were all outgrowths of the original Smith Tool petroleum drill bit company.

Drilco has since evolved into three separate operations: the original oilfield tubular products business, plus the mining and industrial tubular product line at Drilco Industrial and a full service Canadian manufacturing operation. Servco provided directional drilling services in the international market and various remedial and well abandonment products and services in the domestic and international markets. These operations led to the acquisition of Emco, a domestic directional drilling company, to provide

worldwide directional drilling capabilities. Servco is currently developing a wide range of downhole instrumentation for the directional market.

Externally, in 1979, Smith made two acquisitions in the flow control and expendable mining tools areas, and started what is expected to be a substantial well stimulation business within a few years.

Smith International, Inc. was ranked among the Fortune 500 largest U.S. industrial corporations in 1979, and its common stock is listed on the New York and Pacific Stock Exchanges where its trading symbol is SII.

Of the huge and successful corporation which he founded, H. C. Smith made the following comment just before his death in 1967:

"Progress has not been a coincidence at Smith. I had a goal and a plan when I started the company and I was fortunate enough to find capable and dedicated people to achieve these goals over the years."

Today, Smith International, Inc. — headquartered in Newport Beach — is one of the world's leading manufacturers and suppliers of a broad range of drilling tools, equipment and related services to the energy industries. The company is also a leader in the technical development of oil and gas well drilling and mining tools and equipment. It serves the oil, gas, geothermal, water well drilling, mining and construction industries.

Standard Oil Company of California

From Pico 4 to global force: A century of creativity

In California in the 1870s, men prospected for oil as their forefathers prospected for gold. With a grubstake and a seat-of-the-pants knowledge of geology, you could find your fortune — or lose your shirt.

Frederick Taylor had the gambler's temperament. He drilled Pico Canyon, north of Los Angeles, and struck oil. Taylor's bearded crews were able to boast the most productive well in California — Pico No. 4.

But Taylor's abundance became a marketing nightmare. And he joined a group of oil merchants and investors to form Pacific Coast Oil Company on September 10, 1879 — a firm which would later evolve into Standard Oil Company of California.

Pacific Coast grew, but so did others. The business then was so cutthroat that little Pacific might have gone under but for its union with Standard Oil Company, which bought the oil-rich firm in 1900 and provided funds to build the largest refinery in the state at Richmond.

With Standard's backing and Pacific's wildcat heritage, the California company thrived — often against the odds. With "new-fangled" rotary drills and slim geologic prospects it probed rattlesnake-infested Kern County. Despite the industry's jeering at mighty Standard's "scratching gravel like any other chicken," the wildcatters' Midway Field blew in, in January 1910.

New York headquarters sent record sums to search for more and to expand production. Richmond grew, and a second great refinery — El Segundo — was built in Southern California.

But this picture quickly clouded. On May 16, 1911, the Supreme Court mandated the Standard subsidiaries' absolute separation. Fortunately, Standard Oil (California) — headquartered in San Francisco — was fitted for survival. It had oil fields, refineries, pipelines, tankers and a tradition of exploring — with technology *and* intuition.

The emphasis on exploration and production brought spectacular gushers — Montebello, Elk Hills, Huntington Beach — and sobering dry holes. It set the pattern, too, that ultimately carried the corporation throughout the United States

Frederick Taylor's Pico Canyon strike in the 1870s made him owner of the most productive well in California and set the stage for the founding, in 1879, of Pacific Coast Oil — grandfather of Standard Oil of California.

From modest origins as a small California company selling kerosene and fuel oil, Standard Oil of California has become a major supplier of petroleum products worldwide. Its tanker fleet today is the third largest oil company fleet in the world.

and the world.

During the Great Depression the original strikes in Bahrain and Saudi Arabia were Socal's. With the discoveries came a familiar problem — finding markets for crude in a time of surplus. Socal teamed with Texaco, which had outlets in

Europe, Africa and Asia but no accessible production, to form the California Texas Oil Company (Caltex).

Caltex and Socal played a vital role in World War II. Running wide open to meet Allied needs, Caltex refineries were strategic targets; facilities were bombed, employees captured. Socal answered Pacific Theater needs with prodigious quantities of fuels; chemicals; lubricants. With the Asian rubber plantations in enemy hands, Socal built a plant at El Segundo to supply butadiene for synthetics.

After the war, exploration resumed and a new push was given to research. Chevron Chemical was formed. Chevron Oil Field Research was founded at La Habra in 1948. Here were developed the techniques for drilling in increasingly difficult environments: offshore, in northernmost Alaska, as well as in the blazing deserts of Africa and Asia.

Research, too, is now delineating probable power sources for the future — geothermal (at Heber), solar, oil shale and tar sands. Socal's primary focus, though, remains oil and gas. A century from its founding Socal nurtures the wildcatter's enduring dream: the next massive discovery — perhaps in California, where it all began.

Ralph C. Sutro Co.

Pioneer mortgage bankers in homelike setting

Photograph of etching done by San Francisco artist Alec Stern of Ralph C. Sutro Co. present headquarters, opened Armistice Day 1955.

In 1910 Ralph C. Sutro, young cashier/manager of a small country bank in Nebraska, heeded the advice of Horace Greeley — "Go west, young man, go west and grow up with the country." Sutro settled first in Spokane, Washington, where he originated, sold and serviced small first mortgages on farm, home and commercial properties. A decade later he moved to Los Angeles and established the mortgage loan investment and construction finance department of a stock and bond firm, since dissolved. Then, in 1927, Sutro as sole proprietor founded the mortgage banking firm which still bears his name.

The company's first office consisted of two rooms on the fifth floor of the then brand new Lincoln Building at 8th and Hill Streets. It was staffed with one secretary/bookkeeper and one part-time outside salesman and was capitalized with $11,000 of borrowed funds.

In the Depression year of 1935 the company moved to the E. Clem Wilson (now Mutual of Omaha) Building in the new Miracle Mile at the northeast corner of Wilshire Boulevard and LaBrea Avenue. Twenty years later — on Armistice Day (Veterans Day), 1955 — the Ralph C. Sutro Co. moved a short four blocks east to its new building on a 1-1/2 acre site at 4900 Wilshire Boulevard near Highland

This was the view from the first Ralph C. Sutro Co. office at 8th and Hill Streets, in 1924.

Avenue. The new facility was designed by Clifford Burlew, R.B.D. and Ralph Sutro's second son, Paul, a builder-developer who supervised the construction and furnishing.

The low profile 2-story glass and stucco structure with adjoining parking area is landscaped with tree ferns, pines and junipers and overlooks a spring-fed stream. The complex serves as headquarters and trademark of a mortgage banking enterprise long known for its professionalism and community interest. It has been twice recognized by Los Angeles Beautiful awards.

Initially the new quarters also housed Sutro School of Music, Dance, Drama, founded in 1922 by Ellabelle Sutro (Mrs. Ralph) with composer/pianist Julius V. Seyler. The youthful talents of many prominent present day performers were nurtured there.

During the mid-'30s the founder's elder son, Robert, a certified public accountant and a reserve officer in the United States Army, joined the firm. He was followed a few years later by Paul Sutro, and soon after by Edwin S. Bingham, Jr. At the time of the bombing of Pearl Harbor, Robert Sutro was called

to active military duty and, upon discharge five years later, returned to the mortgage banking business.

Ralph C. Sutro Co.'s expansion since World War II has continued steadily for more than 30 years. From serving a clientele of private investors it moved on in its role as California mortgage correspondent to represent more than 100 major financial institutions, including numerous employee benefit funds.

The company's physical expansion and increased volume of business were accompanied by geographical expansion to 16 branches — 10 in California and six in Arizona.

Paralleling geographical and physical expansion was financial growth. When the Wilshire Boulevard home office opened in 1955, the principal amount of mortgages under service with the company approximated $24 million. By 1979 it exceeded $1 billion. When in 1979 the company passed from private ownership by family and close associates to affiliates of Greenwich Savings Bank of New York, the merged portfolios exceeded $2 billion.

Today Ralph C. Sutro Co. is a full-service mortgage banking company. Its institutional investors, located nationwide and in Canada, include life insurance companies, mutual savings banks, savings and loan associations, retirement and personal benefit funds, as well as agencies of the federal and state governments.

Thrifty Corporation

Serving Los Angeles for half a century

In 1919 two brothers, Harry Borun and Robert Borun, and their brother-in-law, Norman Levin, created a new Los Angeles wholesale drug and sundry enterprise under the name of Borun Brothers. Ten years later, the small wholesaler decided to create its own outlets and opened the first Thrifty "Cut Rate" drug store in downtown Los Angeles.

By the end of 1934, 17 Thrifty Cut Rate Drug Stores were in operation. In 1935, the present company was incorporated under the name Thrifty Drug Stores Co. Inc.

In the summer of 1942, the company opened one of the first self service drug stores in the United States. That same year sales reached $17 million and 58 drug stores were in operation.

During the first 50 years of operation, 1929-1979, Thrifty altered its corporate direction five times, virtually always on the upward trend. Each of the periods has been given a name to identify its character and to reflect the company's performance.

The "adolescent period" of 1929-52 signified Thrifty's development with tiny "cut rate" drug stores featuring rough pine counters for merchandise and displaying a limited number of items with highly advertised loss leaders.

Starting in 1953, Thrifty emerged into the "super" drug store field. In 1957, Harry Borun became chairman of the board, Robert Borun, vice chairman, and Leonard H. Straus became president of Thrifty Drug Stores Co. Inc. Dramatic changes in the direction of growth were instituted. Larger stores were introduced; merchandise lines were broadened and grocery items eliminated; promotional items were emphasized; new stores were opened in premature growth areas to secure strategic real estate locations at low occupancy costs. A new sensitized human relations program was instituted, entitled Thrifty's Code of Personnel Administration, and it received a commendation from the State of California for advanced practice in the field of human relations. Company stock was listed on the New York Stock Exchange in 1965. The period 1952 through 1966 saw a 20 percent compound growth rate in net income, and expansion from 96 to 272 stores. This truly represented a "golden period" in

1934 version of a Thrifty "cut rate" drug store.

1937 version of Thrifty's fleet which in 1980 numbers more than 300 units.

the company's history.

The years 1967 to 1973 have been designated the "bronze period" of Thrifty's development. The explosion of the discount store industry required Thrifty to adopt a more aggressive but still limited discount merchandising approach. Although profits rose at a compound rate of growth of 7 percent, a labor dispute and the adoption of the LIFO method of costing merchandise inventory resulted in a profit slump in 1974. During this era Thrifty acquired United Merchandising Corp., sporting goods chain, The Newman Importing Co., encompassing worldwide import capability, and Wonder World Company of Nevada, discount department stores.

"Total discount," — elimination of low-end promotional items, massive display of brand name consumable merchandise and revitalized store operations and advertising — were the keynotes of Thrifty's "renaissance" period from 1974 through 1976. Prescription de-

partment pricing policies were restructured, grocery type merchandising leaders were reinstituted, and the previous emphasis on new store openings was shifted to the renovation of existing stores. The results were rewarding: personnel were exhilarated, consumer acceptance high, and same store sales increases were double the rate of the last 20 years.

These new concepts were implemented with such rewarding results that the period starting in 1977 was named the "metamorphosis period" signifying a complete and dramatic change in Thrifty's operation. In January 1977, Thrifty Drug Stores Co. Inc. was renamed THRIFTY CORPORATION to reflect the broadened scope of the company and its subsidiaries. In 1979, Leonard H. Straus was named chairman of the board and chief executive officer and Richard G. Eils became the president and chief operating officer.

The remodeling of existing stores continued to gain momentum and by February 1980 the company was operating 523 retail drug and discount stores in nine western states, 55 Big 5 sporting goods stores, 33 food service units, four discount department stores and an importing business.

Thrifty now employs more than 13,000 persons, a large portion of whom are in Southern California, and sales in calendar 1980 will approximate $1 billion.

Thrifty is proud of its first 50 years of growth and development and looks forward with optimism to sharing the next half century with Los Angeles and the West.

Times Mirror

A little newspaper becomes a great media company

In a dusty, adobe-brick printing shop on Temple Street, the first copy of the *Los Angeles Daily Times* clattered off a small press on December 4, 1881.

A four-page ink-spattered paper with fewer than 1,000 readers, *The Times* seemed fated for failure. Within a month, its financial backers fled. But at the little shop on Temple Street, called the Mirror Printing Office and Book Bindery, the printers continued to publish the paper.

A few months later an adventurous Civil War veteran, Harrison Gray Otis, appeared in the doorway. He went to work first as a $15-a-week employee but he swiftly became the editor, publisher and owner.

Convinced that Los Angeles was destined to become a great metropolis, General Otis dedicated himself to making *The Times* match the city's growth. In 1884 the newspaper and printing shop were incorporated as The Times Mirror Company and in 1887 moved to the corner of First and Broadway.

General Otis built the company into a position of strength. He was succeeded by his son-in-law and longtime employee, Harry Chandler, a visionary who promoted the Los Angeles and Metropolitan aqueducts and backed the development of the San Fernando Valley, the California Institute of Technology and the Memorial Coliseum. The Los Angeles Civic Center and Union Railroad Station originated in the restless imagination of Harry Chandler.

Chandler's son Norman carried on the tradition, bringing enormous dedication to the job when he became publisher of *The Times* in 1944. Under Norman Chandler's thoughtful and soft-spoken guidance, the newspaper gained a solidity it had never known before. He brought *The Times* into a leadership position among the area's most important business institutions, and he set an example by campaigning for the economic and cultural development of Los Angeles. Along the way the newspaper won its first two Pulitzer prizes.

Until the late 1940s Times Mirror consisted primarily of *The Times* and the original printing company, renamed Times Mirror Press, which was well on its way to its present position as the West's largest printer of telephone directories.

The Mirror Printing Office and Book Bindery, where the Los Angeles Times *was printed until 1887.*

First edition of The Times, *published Sunday, December 4, 1881.*

This eagle, symbol of The Times *and Times Mirror, perched atop successive headquarters buildings for many years.*

In 1948, Times Mirror began acquiring Publishers Paper Co. in Oregon, which today is a major wholly owned newsprint and forest products operation.

More expansion loomed on the horizon. Naming his son, Otis, publisher of

The Times in 1960, Norman Chandler set the stage for a remarkable two decades of diversification. Times Mirror acquired six newspapers including three metropolitan dailies: *Newsday* on Long Island, the *Dallas Times Herald* and, in Connecticut, *The Hartford Courant.* The company also acquired seven book publishing companies, including the New American Library, which publishes Signet and Mentor paperbacks, and Harry N. Abrams, Inc., the world's foremost publisher of art books. Magazines published by Times Mirror now include *The Sporting News, Popular Science, Outdoor Life, Golf, Ski* and *How To*.

Times Mirror also became a major force in cable television systems, serving nearly 500,000 subscribers in 13 states. The company owns television stations in Dallas and Austin, Texas; St. Louis, Missouri; Harrisburg, Pennsylvania; Birmingham, Alabama; and Syracuse and Elmira, New York. Other subsidiaries produce charts, maps and supplies for artists and draftsmen.

Centerpiece of all the company's activities is the flagship *Los Angeles Times*. Under the guidance of Otis Chandler, who served as publisher until early 1980 when he became editor-in-chief of all Times Mirror media, *The Times* climbed spectacularly from a successful local newspaper to one of international re-

nown. Circulation topped the one million mark. Nearly 30 foreign and domestic news bureaus were added. *The Times* won eight more Pulitzer prizes along with countless other awards. Most journalists rank it among the nation's top three newspapers.

Born in the 1880s, *The Times* and Times Mirror entered the 1980s with a remarkable record of growth, a record which parallels the dramatic growth of Los Angeles itself.

Tosco Corporation

Pioneer in alternative energy technologies

A quarter of a century ago, few people foresaw the worldwide shortage of conventional crude oil supplies that became dramatically obvious in the early 1970s. Fewer still began the arduous effort to develop new technology systems to produce high quality fuels from plentiful alternate domestic resources such as the enormous U.S. oil shale deposits.

Tosco had that foresight, along with the realization that rising imports could destroy the economies of many developing countries, which would need to use their own oil shale deposits in order to survive. These compelling reasons underlay the formation of The Oil Shale Corporation in the mid-'50s.

The Oil Shale Corporation, whose name was later shortened to its acronym, Tosco Corporation, has since become the leading worldwide pioneer in the development of oil shale production systems, and a major owner of domestic reserves. Moreover, as a result of a bold diversification plan in the 1970s, Tosco today is also the nation's second largest independent refiner of gasoline.

Tosco was organized in 1955 and acquired certain patents for a rudimentary process for extracting oil from shale, originally conceived in Sweden. Beginning solely as a research and development company, Tosco focused its first efforts on perfecting a viable retorting process. By the mid-1960s, the TOSCO II oil shale retorting system, a highly modified and expanded version of the Swedish beginning, was developed and tested in the laboratories, pilot plants and at field-demonstration scale.

A 1,000-ton-per-day semi-works plant and associated mine and other facilities were completed in 1965 by Tosco's newly-formed Colony joint venture at Parachute, Colorado, on the western

First bench test of TOSCO retort at Denver Research Institute, 1956. TOSCO is the nation's leading pioneer in the development of oil shale technology.

slope of the Rockies. Building on that work, in 1969, a second-phase semi-works demonstration program was launched that successfully confirmed the commercial feasibility of every aspect of Tosco's oil shale production system.

Throughout the 1960s, Tosco acquired oil shale properties in the West for eventual commercial development.

As the decade came to a close, however, the nucleus of the company's present management team — now headed by Morton M. Winston, president and chief executive officer — realized the need for Tosco to generate a much larger cash-flow in order to continue funding its bold development activities and its growing expansion opportunities.

In 1970, Tosco took the first step and acquired a 24,000-barrel-per-day refinery at Bakersfield, California, today one of the most sophisticated, heavy-sour crude refineries in the world. The opera-

The Coker complex at TOSCO's Avon Refinery in Martinez, California, outside of San Francisco.

ting and financial success of the Bakersfield facility led to the purchase in 1972 of the entire former Lion Oil Company system, including its 37,000-barrel-per-day refinery at El Dorado, Arkansas, which has since been expanded.

Tosco became the nation's second largest independent refiner of gasoline in April 1976 with its purchase and expan-

sion of a 110,000-barrel-per-day refinery at Avon, California, from Phillips Petroleum Company.

In a more modest way, Tosco added coal reserves, mining and marketing to its energy-related activities by purchasing three Pennsylvania operations in 1975. A further acquisition, two years later, of properties in Pennsylvania and Maryland brought recoverable coal tonnage to approximately one million tons annually.

Tosco continues to build on the technological tradition which has been its cornerstone for the past 25 years. Current activities are focused on research in innovative techniques for the economic production of clean oil and gas fuel from a broad range of difficult hydrocarbon materials that are in ample supply, such as coal, petroleum coke and heavy oils, and on the continuous improvement of its proprietary shale oil production system.

Touche Ross & Co.

And then there were eight

In 1947, the merger of three distinctively different accounting partnerships created a new, national entity. The diverse character of their individual practices and the geographic dispersion of their offices and clients made them, upon consummation of the merger, a major force in the accounting profession in the United States. Thus, the Big Seven became the Big Eight by the stroke of a pen. The entry of the new firm — Touche, Niven, Bailey & Smart, now Touche Ross & Co. — into this professional grouping is testimony to a commitment to providing quality service, teamwork, and vision.

The three parts of the new whole were Touche, Niven & Co., Allen R. Smart & Co., and George Bailey & Company. Both Touche, Niven and Allen R. Smart traced their professional roots to 19th century England and Scotland. East coast-based Touche, Niven was the largest of the trio, having a solid reputation in retailing and manufacturing with such clients as R. H. Macy and Pillsbury. Equally strong in similar industries in the midwest and on the west coast was Allen R. Smart & Co., which added Sears Roebuck & Co., Boeing Airplane and the National Supply Company as clients of the new firm.

George Bailey & Company became a legal entity only a month before the

The 33 partners of the new firm met for the first time at the Moraine Hotel, Highland Park, Illinois, September, 1947.

Touche, Niven, Bailey & Smart merger was official on August 20, 1947. Bailey had been a senior partner with Ernst & Ernst in Detroit and had left to form his own firm there. His group of 12 former Ernst & Ernst associates was immediately busy with such impressive

clients as Chrysler, American Motors, and Fruehauf Trailer. George Bailey recognized the inevitability of the growth of the business and financial community in that postwar economy and realized, too, that his newer, smaller firm would need additional resources to be part of that wave. He was the driving force behind the merger; his vision, perseverence and energy made the merger successful.

Touche Ross' presence in Los Angeles

dates back to the 1923 opening of a small Touche, Niven office in the Consolidated Building. An early client was the Los Angeles Transit Railway, the famous "Yellow Cars." The office began to emerge as a significant force in the Los Angeles financial community in the 1950s, under the leadership of Partner in Charge, Ralph Hunt. Hunt had been with Ernst & Ernst, and later was a Douglas Aircraft executive, before he joined Touche Ross. His familiarity with and presence in the local business community brought American Savings (First Charter Financial Co.) into the fold of Touche, Niven clients. When that S&L decided to go public, Hunt and other Touche, Niven professionals assisted them in the complex process. As other S&L's followed their lead, Touche was called upon to help. Today, Touche Ross continues to provide services to a large number of savings and loan associations, and is proud of its commitment to that important California industry.

Within that same growth period, Ralph

TOUCHE, NIVEN & CO.
ALLEN R. SMART & CO.
GEORGE BAILEY & COMPANY
announce the formation of a partnership to merge their practices as
— CERTIFIED PUBLIC ACCOUNTANTS —
on September 1, 1947 under the name of
TOUCHE, NIVEN, BAILEY & SMART
NEW YORK • CHICAGO • DETROIT • ST. LOUIS • PITTSBURGH
CLEVELAND • MINNEAPOLIS • LOS ANGELES • SEATTLE • DAYTON
DETROIT
1380 National Bank Building • *Telephone:* Cadillac 8813
AUGUST 20, 1947

The official announcement of the formation of the new firm as it appeared August 20, 1947, in newspapers around the country.

Hunt worked closely with two gentlemen, Tex Thornton and Roy Ash, who needed assistance in the purchase of a small northern California firm, Litton Electronics. It grew to become Litton Industries, one of Los Angeles' largest companies and one of Touche Ross' largest multi-national clients.

The Los Angeles office continued to

expand professionally by internal growth and merger. Under the direction of Ralph Hunt's successor, Dick Stratford, the local partnership Pritkin, Finkel & Company merged with Touche Ross & Co. in 1967. Other smaller local partnerships joined the office over the years. In 1975, the firm merged nationally with J. K. Lasser & Company, further broadening its scope of services and resources. Locally, the office grew from two partners and eight staff persons in 1947 to its current 32 partners and 300 professionals.

All of the founding partners believed in building a practice through quality before anything else; quality in product and in service, quality in people and quality in social contribution. Both Western Regional Partner, Robert Dodson, and Partner in Charge, James Seitz, continue to uphold this tradition in the Los Angeles office. Together with all 700 U.S. Touche Ross partners, the firm continues its commitment to growth, teamwork and dedication to service begun by the original 33 partners 33 years ago.

United States Borax & Chemical Corporation

Pioneers in borate mining, chemistry and production since 1872

The roots of the borax story are as American as apple pie, as Californian as the sun, the sand and the sea and as much a part of the soul of the West as any of the romance that threads through its history.

The early history of U.S. Borax is perhaps better known than that of any corporate entity in North America. Millions of people have heard the song — the clarion call of "Death Valley Days" — and associate with it the Twenty Mule Team that is the company's living corporate trademark.

The corporate history began when Francis Marion ("Borax") Smith discovered a new and rich source of cottonball borax at Teel's Marsh, Nevada in 1872. Total annual consumption of borax in the U.S.A. in 1872 was only 600 tons. Borax was not a household word and industrial use of borates was limited.

"Borax" Smith, the subsequent founder of Pacific Coast Borax Company (the predecessor of U.S. Borax), took a visionary's approach to the marketing of his product. He headed East, set up a

The famous 20 MULE TEAM® at Harmony Borax Works, about 1888.

small office in New York and launched a one-man advertising blitz on the innocent Easteners. He produced posters, folders, cards, giveaway games, and puzzles extolling the virtues of borax. Fabulous claims were made for the miracle product, borax.

"It could, when used in washing water,

226

prevent diphtheria, lung fever and kidney trouble, and borax shampoos would postpone the decay of mental faculties" — all this, on top of perfectly legitimate claims as a sanitizer, preservative, cleanser and water conditioner. Through such aggressive promotion he created a new consumer market for his miracle product. The demand for borax increased and the company prospered.

In 1882 borax was discovered in Death Valley, California. In order to solve the problem of transporting borax from the Harmony Borax Works in the Valley to the town of Mojave over 165 miles of desert, the famous twenty mule teams were conceived. These teams which hauled borax from 1883 to 1889 became a world famous symbol, and today that symbol is the trademark of the products made by U.S. Borax.

In 1888, F. M. Smith purchased Harmony Borax and combined it with his other holdings to form the Pacific Coast Borax Company.

During the next half century, the demand for borax grew and the center of Pacific Coast Borax's operations was constantly shifting. The company mined numerous areas within Death Valley and ultimately moved operations outside the Valley.

In 1925 a large deposit of a new sodium borate ore was found in the Kramer District of Kern County in the Mojave Desert. This deposit proved to be the richest, largest, and most accessible

1905 Pacific Coast Borax Company advertisement.

store of borax ever. Underground mining operations began in 1927, and in 1957 the entire complex was converted to open pit mining. Today, this open pit is one of the world's most economical and advanced mining and ore processing operations. The largest single expansion of the plant in recent years took place when a new $75 million Boric Acid plant was built in 1979 adjacent to the open pit.

In 1956, Pacific Coast Borax Company merged with the United States Potash Company to form United States Borax & Chemical Corporation. Headquartered in Los Angeles, U.S. Borax is today the world's largest producer of borax and borate chemicals.

U.S. Borax was also a pioneer in recognizing the potential of Los Angeles Harbor as a deep water port and major center for world marketing. In 1915, the company acquired land on the Wilmington waterfront where a massive borax refinery and bulk shipping operation was constructed. This facility has been in continuous operation ever since.

One hundred years ago, the uses of borax were very limited. Francis "Borax" Smith did much to create new markets. Today, research is the key to continued corporate growth and profitability in an increasingly competitive marketplace. Many of the world's industries depend on borates. There are more than 100 industrial processes in which boric acid, borax and other borate compounds are used. Some of the most important uses are in insulation and textile fiber glass, glassware, lenses, porcelain enamel, ceramics, cosmetics, medicines, fire retardants, shields for nuclear reactors and in countless other products. And in the home, 20 Mule Team BORAX®, BORATEEM®, and BORAXO® Hand Cleaners are commonplace. "Borax" Smith was right — this is truly a miracle product.

Van de Kamp's Holland Dutch Bakers, Inc.

With ingenuity and $200, brothers-in-law built successful bakery

In 1915, two brothers-in-law from Milwaukee, Lawrence L. Frank, a furniture salesman, and Theodore J. Van de Kamp, an insurance investigative reporter, took a chance on potato chips. The recently introduced product, known at that time as Saratoga Chips, were first sold through an aperture in the front door of the young entrepreneurs' rented store at 236-1/2 South Spring Street in busy downtown Los Angeles, a facility only 8-1/2 feet wide. The new enterprise was underwritten by $100 invested by each partner.

Curious customers queued up on the sidewalk for their taste of the new Saratoga Chip and, within hours, the

supply was exhausted. Mrs. Frank, sister of Van de Kamp, and her sister, Marion, were the salesladies — the first of thousands who would follow as the multiple-unit retail bakery grew into a system of 1,000 outlets known as Van de Kamp's Holland Dutch Bakers, Inc. Mrs. Frank designed the famous Van de Kamp's Dutch uniform.

Van de Kamp's first Windmill store was opened in 1921, on Western Avenue just south of Beverly Boulevard, Los Angeles. The Windmill was "portable," consisting of a base, tower and vanes. The height of the tower was such as to pass beneath then existing trolley lines.

Beneath the window of that first store was the sign — "Made Clean, Kept Clean, Sold Clean." At a time when merchants did not always adhere to cleanliness, the expression and demonstration of this principle drew much attention. Business prospered, new stores opened and macaroons and pretzels were added.

A 1916 display sign showed a Dutch Boy and caption "Ya, I luf dos pretzels." In the background was a Dutch windmill and thus a trademark was born. It was destined to be a symbol of good things to eat for many years to come. That year the young partners acquired a bakery production shop at the rear of the Saratoga Chips store, and in 1917 the first exclusively retail bakery opened.

Business the first two years was plentiful but not profitable. In 1919, however, six retail stores and a wholesale operation accounted for $331,511 in sales and $5,144 profit.

The bakery "spread out" in 1921, as a store between downtown and Hollywood was opened. It was built in the shape of a large windmill and it performed the dual function of a retail outlet as well as a spectacular outdoor advertising display. Eight more followed that year.

The blue neonized vanes of the windmills revolved, becoming landmarks in the neighborhoods they served and to aircraft overhead. During the '20s windmills dominated the scene as other innovative entrepreneurs burst forth with stores built in the shapes and colors of oranges, doughnuts, hot dogs, chili bowls and derby hats.

By 1928, Van de Kamp's achieved widespread public acceptance through its 63 stores and sales exceeded $2 million.

New baking kitchens were completed in 1931, just south of Glendale, a location Van de Kamp chose as ideal for expansion. He visualized eventual construction of a north-south super highway paralleling the Southern Pacific Railroad,

First store was opened January 6, 1915, at 236-1/2 South Spring Street in busy downtown Los Angeles. First two salesladies were Van de Kamp sisters, Mrs. Henrietta Frank, left, who was wife of co-founder Lawrence L. Frank, and Miss Marion Van de Kamp. Co-founder Theodore J. Van de Kamp is in background.

which bounded the kitchens. His prediction came true when the Golden State Freeway was built. Van de Kamp's keen real estate judgment in selecting store locations was confirmed by the many banks which now occupy former Windmill store sites.

Frank believed in the concept of supermarkets providing complete shopping convenience under one roof so the company gradually replaced free-standing stores with supermarket outlets. With self-service it became necessary to pre-package more than 100 varieties of bread, rolls, coffee cake, cake, pies, doughnuts and cookies. Frank's career was one of the most

romantic and spectacular in the food industry and his achievements involved many different aspects of food service. Both co-founders attached the utmost significance to the human element in business and demonstrated well their belief in cleanliness and service.

In 1956, Van de Kamp's was purchased by General Host Corporation and continued its growth in California, Arizona, and Nevada. In February 1979, the bakery, with annual sales of $50 million and 1,000 outlets was acquired by local company executives Jack W. Leeney, president, and Odell C. "Ole" Nordberg, executive vice president, and other investors. Under their direction Van de Kamp's aggressively pursues the principles and ideals practiced by the co-founders. Research and development may be emphasized more today, but like the sign said back in 1915, Van de Kamp's is the place for good quality bakery foods *"Made Clean, Kept Clean, Sold Clean."*

Western Airlines

Pioneering airline born out of Southern California civic pride

Fired with civic pride and determination, Los Angeles business and civic leaders joined in 1925 to put together what is today the nation's senior airline.

Western Air Express was incorporated in July 1925, and launched its first flight on April 17, 1926, using Southern California-built Douglas M-2 biplanes (the first commercial "airliner" built by the famous aircraft manufacturer).

Today that Los Angeles born and nurtured company is called Western Airlines.

The story of Western's formation actually goes back to early 1925 when Congress gave the U.S. Post Office authority to contract with private companies for the carriage of air mail. This important development gave rise to a number of budding air carriers. For several years, the federal government had been operating a transcontinental air mail route with San Francisco as the western terminus. Consequently, the Southern Californians were forced to watch their air mail shipments moved to and from the Northern California area via train.

The move by Congress provided an opportunity for Southern Californians to have air mail service which would tie in directly to the government's transcontinental service at Salt Lake City, and Los Angeles business leaders were not about to let this advantage slip away. Hence, Western was formed.

Having captured the air mail contract for Route No. 4 — Los Angeles to Salt Lake City via Las Vegas — and chosen the wood-and-fabric M-2's, Western was off and flying.

The first pilot hired was University of Southern California track star Fred W. Kelly, who had picked up a gold medal in the 1912 Olympics and who had become a pilot in the aviation section of the U.S. Army Signal Corps.

Western carried its first passengers just a month after it began mail service,

Southern Californians gathered at Vail Field, Los Angeles, on April 17, 1926, to view the launching of Western Air Express' first flight over Contract Air Mail Route 4 — Los Angeles to Salt Lake City via Las Vegas.

Western Air Express, today's Western Air Lines, Inc., encouraged the use of air mail in this early advertising brochure. While other fledgling airlines failed and faded into history, Western met with early success reflecting Southern Californians' ready acceptance of air transportation.

but for many years mail would be the bread-and-butter of the airline business, and Southern California was by all measurements ready for air mail service. At the end of 1926, Western reported a net profit of $28,674.19, and by October 1927, it became the first airline in history to pay a cash dividend to its stockholders.

During the ensuing years, the Los Angeles airline grew and became known as a leader among airlines, truly an industry giant (by standards of the era). The Guggenheim Foundation recognized Western and the West for leadership in 1928 when it chose the airline to set up a "model airway" between Los Angeles and San Francisco. The "model" would determine whether or not an airline could survive on passengers alone (no mail contracts). The latest in technical perfections and passenger safety and comfort were incorporated.

Under the guidance of Herbert Hoover Jr., son of the president, Western developed the first air-to-ground radio, in cooperation with Thorpe Hiscock of Boeing. Western pioneered the use of the directional radio compass for air navigation and was the first to successfully attempt inflight television (in cooperation with Los Angeles' Don Lee Broadcasting, forerunner of today's KHJ-TV and radio).

All has not been smooth flying, however, for Southern California's airline. While its route system has grown from a contract mail route of 650 miles in 1926 to an international network of approximately 40,000 route miles today, it has faced and survived its share of political and financial challenges.

Having grown into the nation's largest airline in 1930 and just having opened a magnificent $1 million airport at Alhambra, Western was forced by the Postmaster General into a consolidation of most of its route system with Transcontinental Air Transport. The consolidated company, which was first known as Transcontinental and Western Air Express, went on to become TWA. All that remained of Western Air Express was the historic Los Angeles-to-Salt Lake City route (to which had been added San Diego) and another contract route between Cheyenne, Wyoming and Pueblo, Colorado, via Denver.

The rebuilding of Western itself had just gotten back on track when in 1934 all air mail contracts were cancelled due to alleged misconduct of the Postmaster General and the airline chiefs. Many airlines of the era simply disappeared, but Western was among the survivors.

For more than half a century now, Western Air Lines has proudly plied the airways, reflecting its California heritage with such service innovations as Champagne Flights and Fiesta Flights and maintaining a tradition of excellence and leadership among the world's airlines.

As Los Angeles passes its bicentennial milestone in 1980, its senior airline will reach a milestone of its own, producing annual revenues of $1 billion for the first time in providing service to 45 cities in 15 states, the District of Columbia, Canada and Mexico.

Western Gear Corporation

Move to dynamic Los Angeles area spurs worldwide growth

In the 1920s and '30s, Los Angeles was the scene of a tremendous oil boom. Oil fields dotted the landscape all the way from Hollywood to Long Beach.

Gear drives to operate the oil field pumping units in Southern California were supplied from the San Francisco and Seattle plants of a company which would later become known as Western Gear Corporation.

To be nearer this activity, the company set up shop at 38th Street and Alameda in Vernon, just east of Los Angeles, in the mid '30s. Business at the small plant was good and hundreds of oil field pumping units were built and shipped to serve the prospering Los Angeles petroleum industry.

By 1941, manufacturers in the Los Angeles area were preparing for defense. Western Gear was no exception. But the plant at 38th and Alameda, although almost entirely converted to war work, principally in the field of aviation, was too small for the forthcoming requirements of military business.

In Lynwood, in the southeastern section of the Los Angeles area, a 30-acre site was selected and purchased at the corner of Alameda and Imperial Highway. Ground was broken for this new complex on December 1, 1941, just six days before Pearl Harbor.

With the outbreak of hostilities throughout the world, completion of the Lynwood facility and a swing into full production became a matter of urgent priority. Construction materials virtually flew together to form the future worldwide headquarters of Western Gear Corporation. On Tuesday morning of March 2, 1942, just 92 days following groundbreaking and 85 days after Pearl Harbor, this new plant started production.

Nine days later, on March 10, 1942, the first delivery was made to the United States Navy: main azimuth drives for new five-inch antiaircraft guns. While this type of work along with activity in aerospace continued throughout the war, it was secondary to servicing of propulsion drive units for submarines and production of an ever-broadening range of products in support of military programs.

Meanwhile, the plant in Vernon was on

The 1906 San Francisco earthquake completely destroyed the facilities of the company which would become known as Western Gear Corporation.

a war footing, too. This facility began to develop its capability to produce precision gears for aircraft applications long before the war, with work for such companies as the Boeing Airplane Company, Consolidated Vultee Aircraft Corporation, Douglas Aircraft Company and the Lockheed Corporation. The crisis of war brought full-scale production of critical equipment for thousands of military combat aircraft.

The years since World War II have become years of change and growth. Military aerospace experience led to development and manufacture of systems for commercial aviation. This work was facilitated by the purchase of Mission Electric Company of Pasadena. Ultimately, this acquisition was consolidated with other aerospace-oriented manufacturing in a modern, large plant now located in the City of Industry, about a half hour's drive east of downtown Los Angeles, and renamed the Applied Technology Division.

With executive offices located at the plant in Lynwood, Western Gear has grown into an international manufacturer involved in the energy, transporta-

The production floor of the Lynwood facility as it looked in 1942 when it opened. Today, Western Gear plants feature modern, computer controlled machine tools.

tion, metals, construction and communications industries. The corporation currently consists of eight factories in the United States and five overseas.

From manufacturer of gears and gear components to advanced systems for high performance aerospace applications, the evolution of Western Gear continues. Today, Western Gear - designed, manufactured and tested products are flying in virtually every commercial and military aircraft currently in operation in the free world.

As for tomorrow, Western Gear, approaching its centennial year, looks forward to the future and the ever-present challenge of moving beyond current technology.

Western Gear is driven by the same dynamic force which has made Los Angeles what it is today: dedicated people, expert in their craft, who are enthusiastic in their work and genuine in their quest for involvement.

The company states its business philosophy, the rule that guides its decisions, in this way:

"Keeping in mind always the Dignity of Man and the rights of all, we wish to perform a needed service in such a manner as to reflect credit on the company and make a good investment for the stockholders while opportunities for advancement and satisfaction are being created for deserving employees who contribute in its progress."

Wyle Laboratories

Working at the frontiers of advanced technology

In 1949, a 30-year old engineer named Frank S. Wyle had an idea that turned out to be right for the times; and from his original concept, a diversified, high-technology services and manufacturing company has been developed, whose revenues in the last year of the '70s approached one quarter billion dollars.

What Board Chairman Wyle saw was a Southern California aircraft industry in transition, making the enormous leap from propeller-driven to jet-powered aircraft. He saw that the traditional way of checking out components by flight tests had limited applicability to the new jet era, and reasoned that more of these components would have to be qualified in the laboratory.

And so, with $5,000 to invest, he started the first company exclusively dedicated to serving the jet-oriented aircraft industry with professional independent testing services. It made good business sense, he believed, for the hundreds of component and sub-system suppliers in the area to draw upon centralized testing facilities for product qualification, and he was right. Wyle Laboratories got underway with a few employees in a small building located in El Segundo, California, still the headquarters city, near the Los Angeles International Airport.

Business prospered, and the company applied its resources to testing components for such well-known military and commercial aircraft as the F-86, the Boeing 707 and the Douglas DC-8. By the fiscal year ended January 31, 1956, Wyle Laboratories had sales of $2.4 million.

Not long afterwards, Americans were startled by the beeping of the first "Sputnik" from space, and the response was a tremendous marshalling of resources to meet the Soviet challenge. This massive effort, first in rocketry for defense, and later in the space exploration program, meant new opportunities for Wyle Laboratories.

The company busily expanded both internally and by acquisition to build on its testing base with allied products and services. With growth, Wyle Laboratories became publicly held in March 1961, reporting annual sales of $7 million for that year. At about this time, the company first entered the electronics dis-

This Wyle solar simulator assures the evaluation of solar equipment in a controlled indoor environment independent of weather conditions.

A portion of Saturn V including the Apollo Space Capsule undergoing vibration testing during the late '60s.

tribution field. By the end of 1979, that business alone had burgeoned to $160 million in sales, and Wyle was distributing more than 60,000 different items.

Meantime, President Kennedy's commitment to place a man on the moon before the decade's end launched Wyle's technical efforts to solve some of technology's most difficult problems. It was not known, for example, whether sections of the Saturn vehicle could withstand the tremendous noise and vibration of blast-off, but Wyle engineers designed and built the largest vibration system then known. The company's financial progress continued to keep pace with its technical gains, and by fiscal 1968 sales approached $50 million.

After the success of the Apollo program, the '70s meant new vistas of opportunity, and again Wyle was ready. In 1970, Stanley A. Wainer, who had long played a key role in the company's growth, assumed its presidency. Progress in the '70s was rapid. Sales topped the $100 million mark in 1974 and surpassed $200 million five years later, a total which rose to nearly $250 million in the following year. Today, the New York Stock Exchange listed company employs some 2,500 people at 35 operating locations throughout the United States.

Changing times have also meant new technical frontiers. Wyle is still involved in space through its support of NASA's Space Shuttle Program, but contemporary society has other urgent needs — energy, for one. Wyle's solar simulator is one of the nation's most advanced and places the company in the front ranks of the effort to develop this attractive, renewable resource. Nuclear safety is imperative for the nation and the world, and Wyle's sophisticated test facilities and expertise are helping meet the need for safe nuclear power. The company's Scientific Services and Systems Group is involved in these areas, as well as many others — from acoustic research to solving noise-abatement problems for the coal industry. And through its six manufacturing divisions, Wyle also produces a wide range of high quality industrial products.

Stanley A. Wainer, President and Chief Executive officer, comments: "Wyle Laboratories is a company born of a vision, and developed by a commitment to excellence. Those qualities should continue to serve us well in the '80s at the advanced edge of technology."

Historical/cultural monuments in the city of Los Angeles, declared as such by the Los Angeles Cultural Heritage Board

1. *Leonis Adobe*, 23537 Calabasas Road, Calabasas (8/6/62).
2. *Bolton Hall*, 10116 Commerce Avenue, Tujunga (8/6/62).
3. *Plaza Church*, 100 Sunset Boulevard. (8/6/62).
4. *Angel's Flight*, 3rd and Hill Streets (awaiting reconstruction in Bunker Hill; 8/6/62).
5. *"Salt Box" (Victorian house)*, Heritage Square (destroyed by fire; 8/6/62).
6. *Bradbury Building*, 304 South Broadway (9/21/62).
7. *Andres Pico Adobe*, 10940 Sepulveda Boulevard, Mission Hills (9/21/62).
8. *The Foy House*, 633 South Witmer Street (9/21/62).
9. *Shadow Ranch House*, 22633 Vanowen Street, Canoga Park (11/2/62).
10. *The Eagle Rock*, northern terminus of Figueroa Street (11/16/62).

11. *Site of the Rochester (West Temple Apartments)*, 1012 West Temple Street. (temporarily located at Bruno and Alameda Streets; 1/4/63).
12. *Hollyhock House*, Barnsdall Park, 4800 Hollywood Boulevard. (1/4/63).
13. *Rocha House*, 2400 Shenandoah Street (1/28/63).
14. *Chatsworth Community Church*, Oakwood Memorial Park, 22601 Lassen Street, Chatsworth (2/15/63).
15. *The Towers of Simor Rodia (Watts Towers)*, 1765 East 107th Street. (3/1/63).
16. *St. Joseph's Church*, 218 East 12th Street (5/10/63).
17. *St. Vibiana's Cathedral*, 114 East 2nd Street (5/10/63).
18. *Site of Hyde Park Congregational Church*, 6501 Crenshaw Boulevard (building demolished; 5/10/63).

19. *Moreton Bay Fig Tree*, 11000 National Boulevard (5/10/63).
20. *Two stone gates*, at the intersection of Beachwood, Westshire and Belden drives (5/24/63).
21. *Drum Barracks*, 1053 and 1055 Cary Avenue, Wilmington (6/7/63).
22. *The Palms*, Southern Pacific Railroad Depot, Heritage Square, 3800 Homer Street (formerly at National Boulevard and Vinton Avenue; 8/9/63).
23. *San Fernando Mission*, 15151 San Fernando Mission Boulevard (8/9-63).
24. *Oak tree*, Louise Avenue, 210 feet south of Ventura Boulevard, Encino (9/6/63).
25. *General Phineas Banning residence*, Banning Park, 401 East M

Spring Street looking north from Fourth, circa 1905.

Street, Wilmington (10/11/63).

26. *Site of the first cemetery of the city of Los Angeles,* 521 North Main Street (3/20/64).

27. *The Castle,* Heritage Square (destroyed by fire; formerly residence, 325 S. Bunker Hill Avenue (5/8/64).

28. *William Andrews Clark Memorial Library,* 2520 Cimarron Street (10/9/64).

29. *Campo de Cahuenga,* 3919 Lankershim Boulevard, North Hollywood (11/13/64).

30. *Doheny Mansion,* 8 Chester Place (1/8/65).

31. *Rancho Sombra del Roble,* 23555 Justice Street, Canoga Park (1/22/65).

32. *St. Saviour's Chapel,* Harvard School, 3700 Coldwater Canyon Avenue, North Hollywood (2/5/65).

33. *Arts and crafts building,* Barnsdall Park, 4800 Hollywood Boulevard (2/26/65).

34. *Barnsdall Park* (2/26/65).

35. *Site of the birthplace of Adlai E. Stevenson III,* 2639 Monmouth Avenue (8/20/65).

36. *The Watts Station,* 1686 East 103rd Street (12/3/65).

37. *Fire Station No. 23,* 225 East 5th Street (2/18/66).

38. *Site of Founder's Oak and Founder's Oak Island,* Haverford Avenue between Sunset Boulevard and Antioch Street, Pacific Palisades (3/25/66).

39. *Residence,* 1425 Miramar Street (6/15/66).

40. *Hale House,* Heritage Square, 3800 Homer Street (6/15/66).

41. *144 deodar trees,* White Oak Avenue, Granada Hills (8/3/66).

42. *San Antonio Winery,* 737 Lamar Street (9/14/66).

43. *California Club Building,* 538 South Flower Street (11/2/66).

44. *Hangar No. 1 Building,* 5701 West Imperial Highway (11/16/66).

45. *Residence,* 818 S. Bonnie Brae Street (2/8/67).

46. *Central Library building and grounds,* 630 West 5th Street (3/1/67).

47. *St. John's Episcopal Church,* 1537 Neptune Avenue, Wilmington (3/15/67).

48. *Chavez Ravine Arboretum,* Elysian Park (4/26/67).

49. *76 mature olive trees* lining both sides of Lassen Street between Topanga Canyon Boulevard and Farralone Avenue, Chatsworth (5/10/67).

50. *Area of Mission Wells and the Settling Basin,* Havana and Bleeker Streets, Sylmar (5/10/67).

51-52 *Residences* at 1300 and 1330 Carroll Avenue (5/24/67).

53. *Old St. Peter's Episcopal Church,* Harbor View Memorial Park, 24th Street and Grand Avenue, San Pedro (12/6/67).

54. *Site of Old 6th Street Wooden Bridge,* across Hollenbeck Park Lake (5/22/68).

55. *Grauman's (now Mann's) Chinese Theater,* 6925 Hollywood Boulevard (6/5/68).

56. *Bullock's Wilshire,* 3050 Wilshire Boulevard (6/5/68).

57. *Second Church of Christ Scientist of Los Angeles,* 948 W. Adams Boulevard (7/17/68).

58. *A & M Records Studio,* 1416 North La Brea Avenue (formerly Charlie Chaplin Studio (2/5/69).

59. *Eagle Rock City Hall,* 2035 Colorado Boulevard (2/26/69).

60. *Biltmore Hotel,* 515 So. Olive Street (7/2/69).

61. *Philharmonic Auditorium,* 427 West 5th Street (7/2/69).

62. *Judson Studios,* 200 South Avenue 66 (8/13/69).

63. *McGroarty home and grounds,* 7570 McGroarty Terrace, Tujunga (2/4/70).

64. *Plaza Park,* bordered by Sunset Boulevard and Plaza, Main and Los Angeles Streets (4/1/70).

65. *Valley Knudsen garden and residence,* Heritage Square, 3802 Homer Street (4/15/70).

66. *Site of St. Paul's Cathedral,* 615 South Figueroa Street (demolished 1980; 5/6/70).

67. *Cedar trees* lining both sides of Los Feliz Boulevard between Riverside Drive and Western Avenue (5/20/70).

68. *Charles Lummis residence and surrounding gardens,* 200 East Avenue 43 (9/2/70).

69. *Los Angeles Athletic Club,* 431 West 7th Street (9/16/70).

70. *Widney Hall,* University Park, USC Campus (12/16/70).

71. *Site of First African Methodist Episcopal Church,* 801 South Towne Avenue (destroyed by fire; 1/6/71).

72. *Automobile Club of Southern California,* 2601 South Figueroa Street (2/3/71).

73-79 *Residences* at 1316, 1320, 1324, 1329, 1344, 1345, 1355 Carroll Avenue (2/3/71).

80. *Palm Court,* Alexandria Hotel, 5th and Spring streets (3/3/71).

81. *Memorial Library,* 4625 West Olympic Boulevard (4/7/71).

82. *River Station area / Southern Pacific Railroad* (6/16/71).

83-88. *Residences* at 1317, 1325, 1333, 1345, 1353, 1401 Alvarado Terrace (7/7/71).

89. *People's Temple Christian Church,* 1366 South Alvarado Street (formerly First Church of Christ Scientist; 7/7/71).

90. *St. Vincent de Paul Church,* 621 West Adams Boulevard (7/21/71).

91. *Korean Royal Church,* 407 South New Hampshire Avenue (formerly Temple Sinai East; 11/17/71).

92. *Old stagecoach trail,* Chatsworth (1/5/72).

93. *Pepper trees,* Canoga Avenue, Woodland Hills (1/5/72).

94. *Palm trees,* Highland Avenue (1/26/72).

95. *Rindge House,* 2263 South Harvard Boulevard (2/23/72).

96. *Residence, 8161 Hollywood Boulevard (2/23/72).*

97. *Residence,* 1620 Pleasant Avenue (building demolished; 2/23/72).

98. *Mount Pleasant House,* Heritage Square, 3800 Homer Street (3/15/72).

99. *Residence,* 1036-38 South Bonnie Brae Street (4/5/72).

100. *General Douglas MacArthur/Westlake Park* (5/1/72).

101. *Union Station and grounds,* 800 North Alameda Street (8/2/72).

102. *Residence,* 1030 Macy Street (10/4/72).

103. *Residence,* 629 West 18th Street (10/4/72).

104. *Coles P.E. Buffet,* 118 East 6th Street (10/18/72).

105. *Hiner House,* 4757 North Figueroa Street (11/15/72).

106. *San Encino Abbey,* 6211 Arroyo Glen (11/15/72).

107. *Residence,* 432 North Avenue 66 (11/15/72).

108. *Residence,* Heritage Square (1/3/73).

109. *Residence,* 1325 Carroll Avenue (1/3/73).

110. *Los Angeles Police Academy rock garden,* Elysian Park (1/17/73).

111. *"Hollywood" sign,* Mount Lee (2/7/73).

112. *Gabrielino Indian settlement site,* Griffith Park (2/21/73).

113. *1610 W. 7th St. (formerly Young's Market* (3/7/73).

114. *Wilshire United Methodist Church,* 4350 Wilshire Boulevard (3/7/73).

115. *Evans residence,* 419 South Lorranine Boulevard (3/21/73).

116. *Wilshire Boulevard Temple,* 3663 Wilshire Boulevard (3/21/73).

117. *Residence,* 2218 South Harvard Boulevard (4/4/73).

118. *Pellissier Building (also known as the Franklin Life Building).* Wilshire Boulevard and Western Avenue (5/16/73).

119. *Cohn-Goldwater Building,* 525 East 12th Street (5/16/73).

120. *St. Sophia Cathedral,* 1324 South Normandie Avenue (6/6/73).

121. *Garfield Building lobby,* 403 West 8th Street (8/22/73).

122. *Buck House,* 805 South Genesee Avenue (3/20/74).

123. *Lovell House,* 4616 Dundee Drive (3/20/74).

124. *Tierman House,* 2323 Micheltorena Street (4/3/74).

125. *Global Marine House,* 811 West 7th Street (4/17/74).

126. *Franklin Avenue Bridge (also known as the Shakespeare Bridge),* between St. George Street and Myra Avenue (4/17/74).

127. *Exposition Club House,* 3990 Menlo Avenue (5/1/74).

128. *Hancock Memorial Museum,* University Park, USC campus (5/15/74).

129. *Residence,* 767 Garland Avenue (6/19/74).

130. *Novarro House,* 5609 Valley Oak Drive (7/17/74).

131. *Dunbar Hotel,* 4225 South Central Avenue (9/4/74).

132. *Stoney Point,* North Chatsworth (11/20/74).

133. *Minnie Hill Palmer residence,* Chatsworth Park South (11/20/74).

134. *Crossroads of the World,* 6671 Sunset Boulevard (12/4/74).

135. *Canoga Mission Gallery,* 23130 Sherman Way, Canoga Park (12/4/74).

136. *St. Mary of the Angels,* 4510 Finley Avenue (12/4/74).

137. *Finney's Cafeteria,* 217 West 6th Street (1/15/75).

138. *Coca-Cola Building,* 1334 South Central Avenue (2/5/75).

139. *Shrine Auditorium,* 665 West Jefferson Boulevard (3/5/75).

140. *Cast Iron Commercial Building,* 740-748 South San Pedro Street (3/19/75).

141. *Chatsworth Reservoir kiln site,* southeast of Woolsey Canyon Road and Valley Circle Boulevard, Chatsworth (4/2/75).

142. *Residence,* 5905 El Mio Drive (4/16/75).

143. *Residence,* 6028 Hayes Avenue (4/16/75).

144-145. *Residences* at 2054 and 3537 Griffin Avenue (5/21/75).

146. *Municipal Ferry Building,* Main Channel, San Pedro Harbor (9/17/75).

147. *Dodson residence,* 859 West 13th Street, San Pedro (9/17/75).

148. *Coral trees,* San Vicente Boulevard between 26th Street and Bringham Avenue (1/7/76).

149. *Ennis House,* 2607 Glendower Avenue (3/3/76).

150. *Los Angeles City Hall,* 200 N. Spring Street (3/24/76).

151. *Chauteau Marmont,* 8221 Sunset Boulevard (3/24/76).

152. *Faith Bible Church,* 18531 Gresham Street, Northridge (4/7/76).

153. *Site of Lincoln Park Carousel,* Mission Road and Valley Boulevard (4/21/76).

154. *Fireboat No. 2 and Firehouse No. 112.* Berth 227 at the foot of Old Dock Street, San Pedro (5/5/76).

155. *Memory Chapel,* Calvary Presbyterian Church, 1160 North Marine Avenue, Wilmington (5/5/76).

156. *Fire Station No. 1.* 2230 Pasadena Avenue (7/7/76).

157. *Residence,* 3110 North Broadway (7/7/76).

158. *The Mary Andrews Clark residence of the YWCA,* 306 Loma Drive (7/7/76).

159. *Ralph J. Bunche Home,* 1221 East 40th Place (7/27/76).

160. *Camp Manzanar,* Inyo County (9/15/76).

161. *Wolfer Printing Company Building,* 416 Wall Street (9/15/76).

162. *William Mulholland Memorial Fountain,* Los Feliz Boulevard and Riverside Drive (10/6/76).

163. *Site of the first Walt Disney Studio,* 2725 Hyperion Avenue (10/6/76).

164. *Glendale-Hyperion Bridge,* Los Angeles River and Golden State Freeway, Ettrick Street and Glenfeliz Boulevard (10/20/76).

165. *Fire Station No. 27,* 1355 North Cahuenga Boulevard (10/20/76).

166. *Carriage House,* 1417 Kellam Avenue (11/3/76).

167. *Residence,* 633 West 15th Street (11/17/76).

168. *Griffith Observatory,* 2500 East Observatory Road, Griffith Park (11/17/76).

169. *Residence of William Grant Still,* 1262 Victoria Avenue (12/1/76).

170. *Paul R. Williams residence* 1690 Victoria Avenue (12/1/76).

171. *Timm's Landing,* Northwest end of fish slip, landscaped park in front of Fishermen's Co-op Building, San Pedro (2/16/77).

172. *Stonehurst Recreation Center Building, 9901 Dronfield Street, Sun Valley (3/9/77).*

173. *Welsh Presbyterian Church,* 1153 South Valencia Street (4/20/77).

174. *5112-5595 Village Green* (5/4/77).

175. *YWCA Hollywood Studio Club,* 1215 Lodi Place, (5/4/77).

176. *Residence,* 1321 Carroll Avenue (7/13/77).

177. *Subway Terminal Building,* 417 South Hill Street (7/27/77).

178. *Herald Examiner Building,* 1111 South Broadway (8/17/77).

179. *Site of residence,* 919 West 20th Street (8/17/77).

180. *Site of the filming of the first talking film,* 5800 Sunset Boulevard (9/21/77).

181. *Site of the burial place of J. B. Lankershim,* north end of Nichols Canyon Road (1/18/78).

182. *Ivy Substation,* 9015 Venice Boulevard (2/1/78).

183. *West facade of the Pan Pacific Auditorium,* 7600 Beverly Boulevard (3/1/78).

184. *Tower of Wooden Pallets,* 15357 Magnolia Boulevard, Van Nuys (4/19/78).

185. *President's House, the Carriage House and Formal Gardens,* Los Angeles Campus, Pepperdine University, 7851 Budlong Avenue (4/19/78).

186. *Morgan House,* Harbor Area YWCA, 437 West 9th Street, San Pedro (5/3/78).

187. *Korean Bell and Belfry of Friendship,* Angel's Gate Park, Gaffey and 37th Streets, San Pedro (5/3/78).

188. *U.S.S. Los Angeles Naval Monument,* John S. Gibson Jr. Park, San Pedro (5/3/78).

189-191. *Residences* at 1407, 1411, 1441-1443-1/2 Carroll Avenue (5/3/78).

192. *Site of Franklin Garden Apartments,* 6915-6933 Franklin Avenue (6/7/78).

193. *Pantages Theater,* 6233 Hollywood Boulevard (7/5/78).

194. *Hollywood Walk of Fame,* Hollywood Boulevard between Gower Street and Sycamore Avenue and Vine Street between Yucca Street and Sunset Boulevard (7/5/78).

195. *Oviatt Building,* 617 South Olive Street (7/19/78).

196. *Variety Arts Center Building,* 940 South Figueroa Street (8/9/78).

197. *Residence,* 2141 West Adams Boulevard (8/23/78).

198. *KCET Studios,* 4401 Sunset Boulevard (9/20/78).

199. *David Familian Chapel of Temple Adat Ari El,* 5540 Laurel Canyon Boulevard, North Hollywood (9/20/78).

200. *Second Baptist Church,* 2412 Griffith Avenue (10/18/78).

201. *Van Nuys Woman's Club Building,* 14836 Sylvan St., Van Nuys (10/18/78).

202. *Valley Municipal Building* (Van Nuys City Hall), 14410 Sylvan Street, Van Nuys (10/18/78).

203. *Baird House* (Volunteer League Community Center), 14603 Hamlin Street, Van Nuys (10/18/78).

204. *Lederer Residence and immediate environs,* 23134 Sherman Way, Canoga Park, (11/15/78).

205. *Los Angeles Stock Exchange Building,* 618 South Spring Street, Los Angeles (1/3/79).

206. *Residence,* 724 East Edgeware Road, Los Angeles (1/3/79).

207. *Residence,* 1334 Kellam Avenue, Los Angeles (1/17/79).

208. *Residence and carriage house,* 845 South Lake Street, Los Angeles, (1/17/79).

209. *Wilshire Christian Church Building,* 634 South Normandie Ave., Los Angeles (1/17/79).

210. *Terrace Park and Powers Place,* Powers Place and 14th Street, Los Angeles, (2/21/71).

211. *Granite-block paving,* Bruno Street, between Alameda and North Main Streets (3/7/79).

212. *Stimson residence,* 2421 South Figueroa Street, Los Angeles (5/16/79).

213. *S. S. Catalina* (5/16/79).

214. *Mount Carmel High School,* 7011 South Hoover St., Los Angeles (6/6/79).

215. *Bob's Market,* 1234 Bellevue Avenue, Los Angeles (6/6/79).

216. *Residence,* 917 Douglas Street, Los Angeles (6/6/79).

217. *Residence,* 1101 Douglas Street, Los Angeles (6/6/79).

218. *Residence,* 945 East Edgeware Rd., Los Angeles (6/6/79).

219. *Residence,* 1239 Boston Street, Los Angeles (6/6/79).

220. *Residence,* 1343 Kellam Avenue, Los Angeles (6/6/79).

221. *Residence and Carriage House,* 1347 Kellam Avenue, Los Angeles (6/6/79).

222. *Residence,* 1405 Kellam Avenue, Los Angeles (6/6/79).

223. *Residence,* 824 East Kensington Road, Los Angeles (6/20/79).

224. *Macy St. Viaduct,* crossing the Los Angeles River between Mission Rd. and Vignes St., Los Angeles (8/1/79).

225. *Los Angeles Theatre,* 615 South Broadway, Los Angeles (8/15/79).

226. *The Masquers Club Building,* 1765 North Sycamore Avenue, Hollywood (8/29/79).

227. *Janes House,* 6541 Hollywood Boulevard, Hollywood (4/3/80).

Index

*C. Prudhomme standing on the spot where gold was first discovered in
California in 1842, Placerita Canyon. Photo circa 1931.*

Hacienda of Juan Francisco Reyes, one of the first land grants in the San Fernando Valley. Seated on the horse is his great-grandson, Juan Chavez.

Index

Hoover Dam under construction.

The Curtis Airplane No. 1, which won the Scientific American Cup, at Dominguez Field.

Index

See, Charles A.: 217-18.
See, Charles B. "Harry": 218.
See, Mary: 217.
See's Candy Shops, Inc.: 217-18.
Seitz, James: 226.
Selig, William: 87.
Señán, Father José: 26-27.
Serra, Padre Junipero: *19*-20.
Serrano, Jacinta: *26.*
Settlers, list of original: 22.
Seventh Regiment, the: *60.*
Simon Museum, Norton: *156.*
Simon's Drive-in: *101.*
Sinclair, Harry F.: 182.
Sinclair, Upton: 103.
Six, Robert F.: 194.
*Sixty Years in Southern
    California:* 88.
Slauson Tower, The: *170.*
Smart, Allen R.: 225.
Smith, Francis Marion "Borax":
    226-27.
Smith, H.C.: 218-19.
Smith International, Inc.: 218-19.
Smith, Jedediah: 31, *31.*
Somerville, John Alexander: 146.
Sontag Drug Store: *79.*
South Coast Air Quality
    Management District: 131-32.
Southern Pacific Railroad: 47, 49,
    56, 61, 75.
Southwest Museum: *54.*
S.S. Rex, the: *104.*
Standard Metropolitan Statistical
    Area: 122, 126.
Standard Oil Company of
    California: 220.
Standford, Leland: 210.
State Normal School: *42.*
Stearns, Abel: 30-31, 47.
Steffens, Lincoln: 78.
Sterling, Christine (Mrs.): *120.*
Stuart, Dwight L.: 190.
Stuart, E.A.: 190.
Summers, Gene A.: 186.
Supplee, Henderson, Jr.: 181.
Sutro, Ellabelle (Mrs. Ralph): 221.
Sutro, Paul: 221.
Sutro, Ralph C.: 220.
Sutro Co.,, Ralph C.: 221.

T

Tanner, Charles: 197.
Taper Forum, Mark: 134.
Taylor, Frederick: 220.
Temple, F.P.J.: 49.
Temple, Jonathan: *33.*
Temple, John: 46.
Terminal Railroad: 61.
Thalberg, Irving: 88.
Thrifty Corporation: 222.

Thornton, Tex: 226.
Throop, Amos G.: *123.*
Throop Polytechnic Institute: 53.
Times Mirror: 223.
Tollenaere, Lawrence R.: 179.
Tosco Corporation (The Oil Shale
    Corporation): 224-25.
Touche Ross & Co.: 225-26.
Tournament of Roses: 58-*59.*
Townsend, Dr. Francis: 103.
Two Years Before the Mast: 33.

U

Un-American Activities
    Committees: 143.
Union Passenger Terminl: 104.
United Air Terminal, the: *101.*
United States Borax & Chemical
    Corporation: 226-27.
Universal Studios: *164.*
University of California at Irvine:
    124, 126.
University of California at Los
    Angeles: 99, 125.
University of Southern California:
    124.
Union Pacific Railroad: 57.
Union Station: *99.*
Ute Indians: 31.

Los Angeles Coliseum, the site of 1932 Olympics.

V

Van de Kamp, Theodore J.: 227.
Van de Kamp, Walter: 205.
Van de Kamp's Holland Dutch
    Bakers, Inc.: 227-28.
Vanderlip, Frank: *70.*
Van Dyke, J.W.: 181.
Van Guysling, George: 87.
Vasquez, Tiburcio: *43*-44.
Verdugo, Casa: *45.*
Verdugo, José María: 27.
Vizcaino, Sebastian: *18,* 18.

W

Wainer, Stanley A.: 231.
"Walnut Elephant," the: *175.*
Warner Brothers studios: *119.*
Waters, Ethel: 146.
Watterson, Mark: 66.
Watterson, Wilfred: 66.
Watts district: *145.*
Watts Towers, the: *147.*
Wayfarer's Chapel, the: *161.*
Weisman, Walter L.: 178.
Western Airlines: 228-29.
Western Gear Corporation: 230.
Whinney Murray Ernst & Ernst:
    197.

Whinney, Smith, and Whinney:
    197.
White, Stephen (Sen.): 61, 63.
Whittier College: *123.*
Whittington, Ed: 77.
Wilcox, Mr. and Mrs. Horace: *86.*
Widney, Robert M. (Judge): 57.
Williams, Paul: 146.
Wilshire, H. Gaylord: *78*-79.
Winnett, P.G.: *78.*
Winston, Morton M.: 225.
Wolfskill, William: 31, 49.
Wood, Sam: *116.*
Workman, William (W.W.): 31, *31,*
    49, *92.*
Wright, Frank Lloyd: *161.*
Wrigley, William Jr.: 60.
Wyle, Frank S.: 231.
Wyle Laboratories: 231.

Y

Yorty, Sam: 147, 155.
Yoshizawa, K.: 177.
Young, William: *66.*
Yuma Indians: 20, 23.

Z

Zoetrope Studios: *164.*
Zukor, Adolph: 211-12.

Acknowledgements

The editors and publishers of *Los Angeles: Two Hundred* are indebted to a number of people and organizations, who over the many months of preparation and production, believed as we did that Los Angeles area citizens and visitors should have an entertaining and pictorially-interesting history.

Our special thanks, of course, to author David Lavender, whose cooperation and dedication helped create the book.

In addition, we wish to thank the volunteer and staff leadership of the Los Angeles Chamber of Commerce, for their support and assistance.

Others who contributed to the success of *Los Angeles: Two Hundred,* include Sherry Suffens, without whom we might never have gotten started; Christine Newport; Harriott Moore; Diane Phillips; Don and Jane Hoyt, Dr. Doyce Nunis and Betty Jane Hoyt.

For assistance, authentication of manuscript and his continuing interest in the American Portrait Series, a special thanks to Jim Moss, director, California Historical Society.

And for superb contributions far beyond her area of responsibility, to Dr. Carolyn Wagner, assistant to director, California Historical Society.

Others who contributed to the book's success are: Richard Lillard, Marie Flagg, Paula Sullivan, Caroline Johnson, Karres, Lisa, Erich, Bob, Ger, Victoria and, of course, Leigh Flowe and the CHP staff including: Pat Briggs, Barbara Jameson, Linda Logdson, Nancy Coats, Lin Mullis, Suzie Hicks, Nina LeMaire, Wally King, Tim Colwell, Sharon Rue.

Credits

Construction of the Los Angeles Aqueduct.

Concept and design by Continental Heritage Press, Inc., Tulsa.
Printed and bound by Walsworth Publishing, Marceline, Missouri.
Type set in Cheltenham.
Text sheets are Warrenflo by S. D. Warren Company.
Endleaves are Multicolor Antique.
Cover is Kingston by Holliston Mills.

240